ARAB REACH

ARAB REACH

THE SECRET WAR AGAINST ISRAEL

Hoag Levins

DOUBLEDAY & COMPANY, INC.
Garden City, New York 1983

Library of Congress Cataloging in Publication Data
Levins, Hoag.
Arab reach.
Bibliography: p. 293
Includes index.
1. Jewish-Arab relations—1973–
2. Arab countries—Foreign relations.
1. Title.
DS119.7.L475   1983   956'.048   AACR2
ISBN: 0-385-18057-8
Library of Congress Catalog Card Number 82–45255
Copyright © 1983 by Hoag Levins

To Sandy Levins,

whose support
and assistance
made it possible

ACKNOWLEDGMENTS

Several people made it possible for me to successfully complete this project.

My wife, Sandy, has been a workhorse attending to myriad details throughout all phases of this undertaking.

My agent, Steve Axelrod of the Sterling Lord Agency, and my editor, Hugh O'Neill of Doubleday, have been of inestimable assistance.

I am also particularly grateful to Alan Halpern, father of America's metropolitan magazines and literary consultant extraordinaire.

And I am greatly indebted to Vilma Lieberman, Bernie Pasquilini and Evelyn Leatherberry, who are the brains behind the Philadelphia Free Library's Computer Based Information Center. The Center—one of Philadelphia's most valuable but least appreciated resources in this new age of electro-research—has been an extraordinary asset for me.

Hayes Hibberd and the staff at Sessler's Book Shop in Philadelphia scoured the world to obtain the often elusive reference books required for this work. I greatly appreciated their efforts.

Jimmy Nicholson of the Philadelphia *Daily News* was a bulwark of support and editorial advice throughout the project.

And it was Sheryl Nathans, a reporter for WKBS-TV in Philadelphia and former magazine editor, who originally suggested that I explore, and write about, the Middle East crisis.

All mistakes in this work are my own.

CONTENTS

ARAB REACH

1

VICTORY ON THE HILL

Just before 6 P.M. on October 28, 1981, even as the packed galleries above the U. S. Senate chamber were rumbling their reaction to the AWACS vote, and even as the camera crews were bulldozing their way through the crowded Capitol halls, recording the pandemonium and cries of disbelief, the Arabs and their friends were slipping away through the side doors to the refuge of their waiting limousines. In ones and twos they pulled away, ultimately headed in the same direction and soon forming caravans of sleek, somber-colored vehicles moving down the twist of road which follows Rock Creek and its tributaries toward the Maryland line. It had been a particularly beautiful fall day, crisp and dry with an invigorating chill, and the creek's woods were wild with color: swaths of yellows tumbling down the inclines, splashes of crimson and rust running along the ravines and riverbeds.

Beyond the final curve on Broad Branch Road loomed the residence of the Tunisian ambassador. Physically, the building was on the northwestern edge of Washington. But visually, it was from another world. Sprawling across the crest of the highest hill, it resembled nothing so much as a Moorish castle perched above the Mediterranean. Its pillars were tightly twisted, like licorice sticks executed in concrete. Its arches were lobed, like those of a Córdoba mosque. Many of its portals were done in grids rather than glass, like the stone screens of a harem wall. Balconies were curlicues of wrought iron, and red clay roof tiles were carpeted with bursts of creeping ivy and vine. The windows and the patios and the front turret—like a drawbridge tower—were all fringed with intricate stucco reliefs, like drapes of white lace gone solid.

The ethereal quality of the distant mansion was further heightened by the setting sun, which continued to bathe the structure in a warm glow even as the line of limousines in the valley below switched on their headlights to continue their climb. Up they came, turning onto the private road which makes the final ascent, into the horseshoe of hedgerows at the final drive and to a halt before the massive mahogany doors held open by servants in bow ties and silk lapels.

And out they came, streams of Asian and African diplomats led by Saudi Arabian Ambassador Faisal Alhegelan. Still more limousines disgorged U. S. State Department officials, European diplomats and two of the most powerful senators in Washington: John Tower of Texas and Charles Percy of Illinois.

Inside the foyer, crisscrossed by servants toting silver trays of hors d'oeuvres and bottles of champagne, the laughing crowd was greeted by Tunisian Ambassador Ali Hedda, who moved from guest to guest, switching effortlessly from English to French to Arabic. With great fanfare, Ali Hedda made sure each guest was provided with a small box of jelly beans—a cause for outbursts of surprised delight.

By matching the color of the jelly beans in the individual boxes to the different-colored jelly beans strewn across the banquet tables in the adjoining rooms, each guest found his assigned seat for dinner—a feast highlighted by cornish hen stuffed with cous-cous. This use of Ronald Reagan's favorite candy treat as a playful conversation item was just one of the jovial touches which helped make the night a high-spirited celebration of what one of the guests described as "a triumvirate of triumphant forces—Ronald Reagan, the U. S. Senate and the Saudis."

Originally, this banquet at Hedda's palatial residence had been planned as a small, quiet farewell gathering. After seven years as Tunisian representative in the United States, the fifty-two-year-old diplomat was moving on to a new post. But during the latter part of October 1981 the date of the scheduled banquet and the highly controversial Senate vote on the AWACS issue came to coincide and Hedda's affair quickly evolved as site of a victory party for the Arabs and their supporters.

Earlier, even as the servants had been preparing the ice buckets, news of the Senate roll call had flashed across the TV and radio. After months of vicious debate and brutal political infighting, the Senate had cast a momentous 52–48 vote in favor of the Arabs and against Israel. And throughout the night, the halls at Hedda's resounded with the glee of a crowd whose members told and retold the story, and toasted and retoasted the defeat of Israel.

Some of the loudest toasts were from John Tower, chairman of the Senate Armed Services Committee, and Charles Percy, chairman of the Senate Foreign Relations Committee. Each had played a crucial role in undercutting the Israel lobby's campaign in Congress during the bruising months of struggle.

Tower and Percy threw their arms around each other as the Arab banquet crowd cheered.

"Here was the great guy," said Percy, hefting his champagne goblet to Tower.

Tower hoisted his own goblet to Percy. "Here was our leader," he said, beaming.

The event so robustly celebrated at Ali Hedda's that night had to do with more than a single Senate vote. That AWACS vote represented nothing less than a revolution within the capital's established order. Things were not likely ever to be the same again. The Arab lobby had established itself as a major force in American politics and was continuing to consolidate and strengthen its position.

Meanwhile, the Israel lobby had suffered a second crushing defeat and was continuing its decline.

Up until 1978 the Israel and Arab lobbies in Washington existed at either extreme of the scale: the Israel lobby being noted for its invincibility and clout, the Arab lobby for its invisibility and impotence.

Since 1947 this solid Israeli grip on America's internal political processes has been one of the three most important pillars upon which Israel's existence has depended. The other two pillars have been its exclusive access to the high-technology weapons systems of the American arsenal and its own secret weapons systems, which are detailed later in this work.

In 1978, suddenly, two of those Israeli pillars—exclusive access to America's state-of-the-art weapons systems and monopolistic hold on the Washington political machinery which directly controlled U.S. foreign policy in the Middle East—were challenged by an emerging Arab lobby.

In its first public contest against the most powerful lobbying group in Washington, the Arabs worked in tandem with newly organized Arab-American political organizations and cooperative American corporations which had multimillion-dollar stakes in projects throughout the Muslim Middle East.

That 1978 battle in the Senate is really the story of an airplane, an amazing airplane named for a predatory bird, but physically resembling nothing so much as a sheet-metal killer wasp.

The $30 million F-15 Eagle does what every other military plane in the world does—only faster, more accurately and from farther away. Built by McDonnell Douglas for the United States Air Force, the craft was designed as the world's most advanced attack jet. No other nation—not even the Soviet Union—has produced a plane which can match this one's performance. It is a record setter for altitude and speed levels; its radar is the most sophisticated; its ability to execute intricate maneuvers, including straight-up climbs, unprecedented.

In an all-out battle between half a dozen of any other kinds of jets and one Eagle, the Eagle is the sure winner. Grouped in squadrons, the planes' unusual capabilities allow for the seizure of huge swaths of sky. If any popular movie were cited to suggest to the layman the sort of battle techniques the F-15 development represents for aerial warfare, it would not be *Fighter Aces* but *Star Wars*.

In the beginning of aerial warfare, planes battled each other one-on-one with guns crudely bolted to their fuselages. Dueling pilots came close enough to see each other's faces as their propeller crafts jabbed this way and that, seeking advantage. This method of fighting changed as rapidly as the shape of the airplanes themselves. Planes became faster and guns became heavier and more powerful, able to hit other planes from increasing distances. This distance—the "lethal reaction area" commanded by any plane—is the single most important factor in the outcome of most aerial conflicts. Think of it as something similar to the advantage a long-armed boxer enjoys over a shorter-armed opponent—a plane which can begin ripping holes in another plane before that other plane can effectively rip back usually wins.

By the late 1960s planes no longer relied on either human eyesight or bullets in such battles. Radar and computer-assisted sensing systems scanned not only across clouds but around the curve of the earth beyond. Weapons were no longer guns but small jet planes packed with high explosives—missiles—launched from the belly racks of a larger manned plane and guided electronically toward the enemy plane, which could be no more than an infinitesimal speck on the horizon.

Total electro-mechanical war—battles fought between pieces of self-guiding, self-adjusting, self-actuating machinery rather than individual human beings—became a reality with the advent and widespread use of the Phantom F-4 jet. That plane had been fitted with the most extensive systems of computer-assisted flight-control and weapons-guidance systems ever installed in an aircraft. The Phantom era of aerial supremacy ended in 1976 with the arrival of the F-15.

The F-15 is a quantum leap over the Phantom. It is not a jet fighter into which computer equipment has been installed but, rather, a space-age computer system of extraordinary complexity to which wings, wheels and two incredibly powerful jet engines have been attached. The Phantom and similar aircraft were vehicles flown and operated by men assisted by computers. The F-15 is a vehicle flown and operated by computers assisted, when necessary, by men.

Its cockpit lacks the traditional bristle of levers, dials, toggles and handles and has, instead, a few digital panels. It is the first fully digital-controlled warplane. In operation, its central IBM brain takes into account the information provided by its various sensing, analyzing and data-storage systems and provides commands for the pilot to follow. In some cases these commands are translated into simple dot patterns to be followed on a screen—so as not to risk confusing the human at a time when split-second reactions are required to avoid destruction or to destroy another piece of machinery moving at supersonic speeds.

One of the most important features of the F-15 is the enormous "lethal reaction area" commanded by its computer sensors and weapons systems across any given stretch of territory. For a better visual feel of this phenomenon, imagine that a dim aura of colored light emanates from the plane, illuminating the craft's absolute killing range as it passes over your home in the night sky.

That illumination would reach out in all directions, ultimately forming a ball of light more than two hundred miles in diameter. Nothing moves inside that space without the F-15's central computer detecting it, analyzing it with radar beacons as "friend or foe" and, if required, locking it on target and destroying it with a guided missile, all of this occurring in a period of time shorter than that required to read this paragraph.

And the F-15, for all its awesome powers, is only an individual smaller part of a larger weapons system and battle technique unfamiliar to most Americans, who still think of air war in terms of the highly popularized World War II air battles.

During the Vietnam War, the United States military began linking individual warplanes into a computer system which then used the planes as moving "parts" of a larger flock pattern of aircraft being controlled and coordinated from a single command post. By the 1970s this technology became the basis for the development of AWACS—Airborne Warning and Control Systems.

This is the basic principle: The AWACS's electronic systems provide a picture of the entire region, like a gigantic eye in the sky able to see everything moving everywhere in any given battle region. The AWACS—whose screens and scans and computer consoles look something like the inside of a NASA control center—can track six hundred different targets in the air, on land or across water simultaneously. It can identify and target for destruction 240 targets simultaneously.

The AWACS command crews then use the F-15s to respond to the entire battleground below, moving the individual planes much like blips across the screen of a large video game to intercept and destroy approaching planes here, bomb a tank corps there or missile a patrol cruiser farther on down the field.

This development—aerial electronic systems warfare—was perfected and deployed as the new standard practice of the United States Air Force in the late 1970s. It represents a complete revolution of battle tactics and defense systems. Think of it as a sort of electro-assembly of dozens of airplanes—an octopus-like apparatus able to descend and seize the entire sky along a thousand-mile battlefront. At the end of each of its invisible electronic tentacles is an F-15 fighter jet functioning as a direct extension of the mother ship's computer. This aerial constellation of linked airplanes is capable of performing mind-boggling feats of warfare.

At the same time, such individual constellations are only parts of a larger system of space-age battle machinery connected by the invisible control matrix emanating from AWACS mother ships. This "electronic womb" or "electronic atmosphere" is spun across an entire war zone, monitoring and directing armies, artillery brigades and missile-launching armored corps on the ground; flotillas of missile-launching ships at sea; and constellations of missile-launching jets in the sky. This electro-apparatus functions as a single, enormous machine moving whichever of its parts are needed for defense or attack.

War in the 1980s has largely become a contest between rival computers seeking to establish "electronic dominance" over a battlefield. This was graphically illustrated during the Falkland Islands War of 1982, when the Argentine military used a handful of new "thinking" weapons to ravage the previously invincible British fleet. The British had failed to provide their South Atlantic flotilla with the AWACS-like equipment needed to envelope the war zone in a defensive electronic cocoon which could have thwarted the high-tech Argentine ship killers.

During that same summer of 1982, the Israeli military launched its stunning blitzkrieg into Lebanon and provided yet further proof of the importance and potency of the new electro-war techniques. Deploying a vast arsenal of American "wizard weapons" along electronic grids thrown across southern Lebanon, the Israelis decimated defensive missile batteries, obliterated portions of the Syrian Air Force and laid waste to major cities and towns south of Beirut. Coordinating the attacks was a fleet of American "Hawkeye" radar command planes—tiny, early versions of the AWACS.

However, such electro-war is not without its problems, even for those who win. The high-tech weapons and the inordinately complex systems required to support and maintain them are expensive beyond anything the military or individual governments have known before. And this has been of increasing concern to Israel, a country isolated from the international economy, whose domestic fiscal condition is routinely described as "a nightmare."

Since the early 1970s, when the first generations of the new electro-weaponry became available, as Muslim nations started amassing large surpluses from oil revenues, they began acquiring massive amounts of military equipment. By the end of the 1970s, the Muslim oil powers of the Middle East had become the world's largest purchasers of sophisticated, space-age American and European weapons systems. Cost was never an obstacle. On occasion, Muslim rulers have ordered entire navies and air forces as single purchases. At the same time, Muslim states have begun several programs which are establishing indigenous electro-weapons industries capable of designing and mass-producing the new weapons at various sites in the Middle East. One of the largest of these is to be the Al Assard Missile City, which has been laid out in the interior of Saudi Arabia.

Since 1973, when Israel confronted an Egyptian army equipped with state-of-the-art Soviet electronic weapons—and just barely escaped defeat—that country's leaders have quickened their attempts to retain a technological edge over neighboring Muslim forces. But the long-term prospect for this is not good. Given the limitless financial resources and the increasing technological sophistication in all areas of the Muslim oil world, the Israeli intelligence services have reported that their nation "must face the prospect that by the end of the 1980s the military balance in quality as well as quantity could swing in favor of the Arabs."

It was with an eye to this latter prospect that the Israeli Government in the early 1970s exercised its traditional option and took an active part in the development of the Pentagon's top-secret F-15 project. Since its creation in 1948, Israel has enjoyed direct access to the innermost circles of the United States' military agencies and planning offices.

This direct access—through which Israel's government has often functioned within the Pentagon in a manner similar to an unofficial department of that agency—has been one of the central pillars of the special relationship which has existed between America and Israel since the late 1940s.

The tenets of that tradition have never been written down or ratified by Congress, but have been scrupulously observed by every administration since Truman's. The United States Government has routinely provided Israel with the most advanced weapons produced by the Pentagon as soon as those weapons were available. It has not been uncommon for Israeli units to receive such state-of-the-art weaponry from America even before America's own troops and installations have been fully equipped with the new items.

It is this edge—of sophisticated military tools capable of decimating the lesser-equipped Muslim armies of the Middle East—which has been the primary factor in Israel's sweeping battlefield triumphs.

In 1973, as the Muslim states achieved a level of military technological sophistication nearing that of Israel, Israel's armies no longer enjoyed their freedom of movement or invincibility. It was only with massive supports and the direct involvement of the United States military that Israel was able to hold back the Muslim attacks seeking to regain Jerusalem and the other territories seized with the air cover of Israeli Phantom squadrons in 1967.

That same year the United States Government was entering the final stages of the development program aimed at producing a new generation of aircraft which would make the Phantom F-4 class obsolete. Israel eventually was allowed to step into this program. The Phantom, when it was the state-of-the-art leader of its field, had been the main component of aerial superiority of the Israeli Air Force. With the coming of the F-15, the United States had begun to supply large numbers of the obsolete Phantoms to such Muslim states as Saudi Arabia, which were greatly expanding their air forces with huge petro-dollar purchases of planes, weapons and support networks.

While the new F-15 was designed for American needs as an air-to-air long-distance fighter, in Israel it would be used in a somewhat different manner in the frequent border skirmishes. Israeli test pilots in 1974 took part in the testing and engineering refinements of the F-15 prototypes, pioneering the maneuvers which allowed the plane to turn the tight, slow loops which provided absolute superiority over the older Phantoms in situations of close-in dogfights.[1]

These developments set the scene in which the Israeli Government expected to maintain its overwhelming control of the skies in the Middle East throughout the 1980s. Along with its intimate involvement in the F-15 design, the Israeli Government also maintained di-

rect involvement in the subsequent stages of the project's development—particularly production planning. The plane's landing gear,
for instance, is not manufactured in the United States but under special contracts in Israel by the Israeli Aircraft Industries—the national weapons conglomerate which makes everything from patrol
boats to missile systems for export.

In 1975, going through normal formalities, Israel officially requested to be equipped with the F-15 by the United States when the
plane went into production.

In January 1976 the first F-15s rolled off the assembly lines and
were shipped to some of America's primary tactical air squadrons.
The second batch coming off the assembly lines was shipped to Israel.

But, shortly after taking office, President Jimmy Carter announced
that Saudi Arabia was "interested" in F-15s, and by February 1978
the Carter administration proposed that Congress grant permission
for the sale of more than five dozen F-15s—or a flock of planes
twice the size being given to Israel—to Saudi Arabia.

Carter's action was not just a move raising a controversial question about airplanes. The legislation he proposed represented an
epochal change in the relationship between the United States and Israel and a profound change in the long-term balance of power in the
Middle East.

The proposed legislation would close the door on the thirty-year-
old tradition through which the Israeli military functioned as a direct technological extension of the Pentagon. It would also set the
precedent of linking all further shipments of advanced equipment to
Israel with shipments of the same advanced equipment to Muslim
states.

The vote that came before the Senate for final resolution in May
of 1978 was not a vote about computerized jets. Instead, it was a
vote about the future direction of American policy in the Middle
East, and resulted in the first full-scale showdown between the old,
entrenched Israel lobby in Washington and the new, untested Arab
lobby backed by the Arab industrial complex centered in Houston.

A top congressional aide of the era explained, "The Arabs just
suddenly appeared in Washington in 1978. It was that quick. Boom!
One day you didn't see them. The next day, there they were. The
progress they made was incredible. Four years before, the Arab

lobby was a joke. You had maybe two people here who knew what they were doing. The others were all very polite and basically nice guys, but basically dumb as shit about the system. They were tiptoeing around like nuns in a whorehouse, afraid of offending anybody. They didn't know what they were doing or even how to find out. They didn't even understand the theory of the system, let alone how it works here on the Hill on a day-to-day basis. And then, wham! Arabs are everywhere; know exactly what they are doing; are very slick about doing it It was amazing."

While the Israeli Government supplemented its Washington political apparatus with twenty-one paid foreign agents to lobby in Congress against the F-15 measure, the governments of Saudi Arabia, Iraq, Algeria, Libya and the United Arab Emirates had a total of twenty-five paid foreign agents lobbying in Congress.

And, at the same time, the Saudi Arabian Government launched a top-secret project setting up a private intelligence network capable of reaching into the highest levels of government. The details of this group—called the Group for International Study and Evaluation—were laid out in an exclusive investigative report in *8 Days*, an independent Arab journal published in London and covering the Middle East.[2]

The Group for International Study and Evaluation—GISE—was totally funded by Saudi Arabia, but set up as a subsidiary of the Insurance Company of North America. Its internal documents indicated that its chief purpose was to gather intelligence and pass that information directly to such top Saudi officials as Finance Minister Mohammed Abalkhail. The Insurance Company of North America later severed its ties with the organization. The Saudi-paid organizer and manager of this private intelligence group was Minos Zombanakis, chairman of the financial firm of Blyth Eastman Dillon International. Two of the group's paid operatives in Washington were Robert Ellsworth, former congressman, former Deputy Secretary of Defense and former Ambassador to NATO, and Lowell Pumphrey, a former top official with the United States Treasury Department.

These were only a few of the former Washington heavies the Muslim governments retained, often at six-figure fees, to assist in the new offensive inside the American political arena, which had previously been dominated by the Israel lobby.

Frederick Dutton was retained as a consultant and lobbyist by Algeria and Saudi Arabia. Dutton, an attorney, formerly was a special assistant to President John F. Kennedy for legislative affairs and later an assistant secretary of the State Department charged with guiding administrative foreign policy legislation through Congress.

Clark Clifford was retained as a consultant and lobbyist by Algeria. Clifford, who began his political career as the adviser to Harry Truman, who designed Truman's winning strategy of appealing to liberal urban ethnic groups, was also a member of the Foreign Intelligence Advisory Board during the Kennedy administration and the Secretary of Defense during the Johnson administration. Originally one of the architects of the Vietnam War, Clifford later became a leading antiwar figure in the Administration, and was the person who convinced Johnson to give the speech in which he declared he would not seek re-election.

Senator J. William Fulbright was hired as a consultant and lobbyist by both Saudi Arabia and the United Arab Emirates. Fulbright spent thirty years in the Senate and was formerly chairman of the Senate Foreign Relations Committee. He became one of the leading antiwar figures in Congress and was instrumental in orchestrating the political pressures which overturned America's thirty-year commitment to the government of South Vietnam.

Complementing such expert advisers were the services of Cook, Rueff, Spann and Weiser, a Columbia, South Carolina, firm which was previously unknown in Washington, but which suddenly became a force with its $1 million contract from Saudi Arabia. The firm coordinated and planned such programs as that in which members of the Saudi ruling family came to the capital to personally discuss the F-15 vote with senators in direct competition with similar visits being made by such Israeli officials as Menachem Begin and Moshe Dayan. There were also massive national mail campaigns and advertising and letter-writing programs aimed at publications in every state in the Union.

The top congressional aide who was directly involved in the events surrounding that 1978 Senate vote on the F-15 recalled, "It was the most intense lobbying I'd ever seen in ten years on the Hill. There were literally days when you could not walk in the halls because of people and groups clamoring for one side or the other on the F-15 thing. I mean, it was all-out war. We had every Jewish organization you can imagine, and bigwigs from Israel, coming in regularly. There was arm-twisting like you can't believe—on both sides. Everything but the kitchen sink came floating down the halls on that one. And to tell you the truth, I didn't expect it to go the way it did. I mean, the outcome of the vote really stunned a lot of people around here."

On the same day in May 1978 that Israel celebrated its thirtieth anniversary as a state, the U. S. Senate voted 54–44 in favor of the Arab lobby and F-15s for Saudi Arabia. And even as the headlines were detailing that unprecedented defeat of the Israel lobby by the new Arab lobby, limousines were delivering Arab officials at the Fairfax Hotel off Dupont Circle in Washington. There, led by Saudi officials, the Arab lobby began laying out plans for the next political offensive: AWACS mother ships.

The sheer cost—billions per AWACS and required support systems—prevented Israel from acquiring the system when the Pentagon first rolled its production models off the assembly lines in 1978. Possession of such a system by a Muslim nation has awesome implications for the balance of power in the Middle East conflict, which has, for more than three decades, pitted the high-tech weapons superpower, Israel, against Muslim armies with more men but grossly inferior equipment.

But in 1981, shortly after coming into office, Ronald Reagan announced that he was about to cross yet another threshold in Middle East relations: providing Arab nations with state-of-the-art American weapons systems which had *not* been given to Israel. For the first time the White House was proposing to arm the Arabs with space-age weapons systems superior to those it provided to Israel.

By early summer of 1981, even before the Reagan administration had officially informed Congress of its proposal to supply AWACS to Saudi Arabia, the Israel and Arab lobbies were mobilizing the most extensive, intensive and expensive lobbying efforts in the postwar history of the American capital.

For Israel two things were at stake. One was the actual transfer of the AWACS and the precedent—favoring further Arab purchases of superior American weapons systems—it represented. The second was the reputation—and, hence, the continuing power—of Israel's Washington lobby. Punctured and severely damaged by the 1978 de-

feat on the F-15s, the lobby could not lose another major battle on
the AWACS without suffering permanent harm to the aura of its political clout.

Even as the Reagan White House staff was still preparing the document with which it would announce its AWACS sale plans to the
Congress, the American Israel Public Affairs Committee (AIPAC)
—leader of the national task force of Jewish lobbying organizations
—was flooding congressional offices with five detailed memoranda
condemning the proposed sale. AIPAC, which has a $1.3 million
annual budget and thirty full-time staff members, operates in close
cooperation with the Israeli Government and has been the guiding,
organizing force of the Israel lobby for thirty-five years. From the
beginning the Israeli Government made it clear that it was totally
opposed to any transfer of weapons to the Saudis. The cabinet of Israeli Prime Minister Menachem Begin voted unanimously against
the sale and announced it wanted the Congress to halt the planned
White House actions.

Time magazine wrote, "Israel has been interfering skillfully and
successfully in U.S. politics for decades and will be doing so again
with a vengeance in the weeks to come over the Saudi AWACS
sale."

Senator Charles McC. Mathias, Jr., of Maryland, writing in *Foreign Affairs* magazine as the Israel lobby was cranking up its anti-
AWACS campaign, wrote, "When an issue of importance to Israel
comes before the Congress, AIPAC promptly and unfailingly provides all members with data and documentation, supplemented as
circumstances dictate, with telephone calls and personal visits. Beyond that, signs of hesitation or opposition on the part of a Senator
or Representative can usually be relied on to call forth large numbers of letters and telegrams, or visits and phone calls from influential constituents."[3]

Political columnists Jack Germond and Jules Witcover explained,
"Jews pay close attention to the issues. They follow campaigns and
candidates. They vote in disproportionate numbers; although they
make up less than 3 percent of the population, they cast 4 percent of
the vote and are often decisive in close contests in such important
states as New York, California, Pennsylvania, Illinois and Florida.
Plus, they know how to use their money in politics."

The Philadelphia *Inquirer* reported, "The pro-Israel lobby has been buttonholing senators, providing background information, organizing seminars on AWACS, and arranging for influential Jews to contact their senators."

The New York *Times* reported that in their contacts with senators, Israel lobby leaders "have their own powerful, if unmentioned, weapon: campaign contributions from Jewish donors. With campaign costs skyrocketing, almost every senator is forced to raise money from out of state, and Democrats, in particular, rely heavily on Jewish sources in such states as New York and California."

The Economist of London reported, "One third of Democratic party funds came from Jews. Jewish organizations now have war chests for supporting pro-Israeli candidates and defeating anti-Israeli ones in local and national contests. This broadens the impact of Jewish attitudes well beyond those districts where Jewish voters are concentrated."

In an unusually candid lament to reporters during the opening stages of the lobbying campaign, Illinois Democratic Representative Dan Rostenkowski said that he favored the sale of AWACS to Saudi Arabia but had pledged to vote against it because "I didn't want Jewish groups coming down on me."

In September, Menachem Begin came to the United States to personally direct the overall lobbying efforts against the President. Taking over four floors of the ultraposh Waldorf Towers in New York, and assisted by the largest entourage of aides and agents ever brought to the United States by an Israeli Premier, Begin fine-tuned the national anti-AWACS campaign to full blast.

The ad campaigns, which began as he arrived, even included some full-page newspaper displays which raised the anti-AWACS crusade to the level of a celestial command.

The International Rabbinic Committee of New York ads declared that "The proposed sale of AWACS and other weaponry to Saudi Arabia must be halted" and asked for donations for further lobbying. As they quoted Talmudic law, the ads appealed to "all individuals and organizations to spare no effort in protesting this disastrous mistake. It is imperative that every voice be heard; it is forbidden to remain silent."

At the same time, the computer banks of AIPAC were disgorging mammoth national mailings, seeking to raise money for the anti-AWACS lobbying effort against the White House.

In one of its mailings the organization explained that "already, AIPAC has devoted countless hours in a monumental lobbying effort to head off this sale."

Another mailing explained, "AIPAC urgently needs your assistance to increase its lobbying efforts at this critical time. For while we are an organization called by the New York *Times* 'the most powerful, best-run and effective foreign policy interest group in Washington,' we are up against unusually formidable competition on this one."

In a personal letter mass-mailed throughout the country, AIPAC Executive Director Thomas A. Dine explained, "Congressional offices are paying special attention to mail on this issue. That is why I have enclosed, for your signature, a memorandum protesting the sale of AWACS and other sophisticated arms to Saudi Arabia. That's right—AIPAC wants to deluge each and every congressional office with protests of concerned Americans."[4]

Another AIPAC national mailing asked for $1,000 donations and promised that, in return, the donor would receive a year's subscription to AIPAC's newsletter, an autographed copy of *Israel's Defense Line,* by the founder of AIPAC, quarterly legislative updates from AIPAC, "PLUS private briefings by the director or a member of AIPAC's senior legislative staff whenever you visit Washington, D.C."

Maynard Wishner, president of the American Jewish Committee, said, "I don't remember any issue in which the Jewish community was better organized, more responsive, more united, more coordinated in its thinking and its processes."

Meanwhile, two miles northwest of the Senate chambers, at Twenty-first and Massachusetts Avenue in Washington, D.C., similar efforts were under way at the "Saudi Bunker"—the suite of six rooms on the sixth floor of the Fairfax Hotel serving as headquarters for the Arab lobbying campaign.

It was from here that Prince Bandar bin Sultan ran the Arab counteroffensive against the Israel lobby. Educated in American schools and trained for his position as a Saudi Air Force major by the United States Air Force, the prince is both dapper and demure, an epitome of the Saudi approach, which, according to *Middle East* magazine, "prefers the scalpel to the bludgeon." Chief lobbyist in the U.S. for the Saudis on the AWACS issue, Bandar is the son of the Kingdom's Defense Minister. The late Kings Faisal and Khalid were his uncles, as is the current King Fahd.

Traveling in a chauffeured BMW on his daily rounds, Bandar unobtrusively moved from his town house in the exclusive capital section overlooking Kalorama Park to the Saudi Embassy nearby where Saudi Ambassador Faisal Alhegelan had seventeen military attachés assigned full-time on AWACS lobbying duty. It was from the embassy that Bandar and Alhegelan ran their corps of high-priced American public relations firms and political consultants. One of them—Fred Dutton, the fifty-eight-year-old former White House assistant to the President and executive director of the Democratic Party Platform Committee, who is now a $270,000-a-year agent of the Saudi Government, was a frequent companion of Bandar during this period.

From the embassy, Bandar would make frequent visits to the offices of congressional leaders, such as Senate Majority Leader Howard Baker. Often he used Baker's facilities to coordinate the day-to-day Arab action on Capitol Hill. At the height of the AWACS controversy, Bandar traveled to Huntsville, Tennessee, staying in Howard Baker's guest house as the two held strategy sessions aimed at turning key senators in favor of the Arab position. Back at the Fairfax—home base—the prince and his extensive staff held daily sessions with friends from other Arab embassies and organizations.

Throughout the summer, as the boyishly young official circulated about Washington's offices and suites, he kept a photograph in his pocket which he used to answer questions about his status within the House of Saud or about the stability of the U.S.-Saudi ties.

The photograph showed the late King Abdul-Aziz ibn Saud with President Franklin D. Roosevelt. In 1945, while visiting the crucial Eastern war zone for conferences with Allied leaders, Roosevelt requested a meeting with the Arab monarch aboard the U.S. cruiser *Quincy*. The two dined on rice and lamb stew and grapefruit and opened the official relationship which has connected the two governments since that time. Three years later Ibn Saud watched U.S. oil construction crews complete their new cities in his deserts as he cradled a new grandson in his arms. Now thirty-three years old and a member of the innermost circle of Ibn Saud's heirs, Bandar, son of Sultan, son of the founder of the kingdom, is one of the most powerful men in the world. And from his sixth-floor "bunker" the young Muslim flier—who may yet come to command the weapons systems he is procuring—flexed every facet of the oil, financial and political clout his family now enjoys as he transformed the Fairfax Hotel into a new landmark on the Washington power map.

The Fairfax—its front facade columned in granite and bedecked with flags, its doormen stiff and proper, like parade Marines, its driveway not of concrete but inlaid mosaics of red brick and cob- blestones—is one of the ultraswank hotels serving the capital's Em- bassy Row and Georgetown district. The lobby is white marble and polished brass, the flower vases cut crystal. There is a diamond shop directly across from the Jockey Club entrance. Liveried luggage at- tendants snap to as clusters of somber-looking young men wearing three-piece suits and speaking Arabic bustle back and forth. In the lounge are the traditional decorations of the Virginia horsey set: chairs of dark oak and red leather, portraits of horses and hounds. Prints of the hunt. But now the walls have also been lined with shrimp-colored couches. And each is plumped high with luxurious tiers of pillows—like the divans of an oriental potentate.

Directly out the back door of the Fairfax is the Casba restaurant and just a short distance farther is Arabian Nights—two of the sev- eral new establishments serving this posh neighborhood's growing demand for the cuisine of Islamic Asia and North Africa. Up the street—both sides of which are clustered with the embassies of Muslim nations—is the United States Islamic Center. Its single, cen- tral minaret towering cathedral-like over the valley of Rock Creek Park, the institution is both a mosque and a meeting ground for the capital's rapidly growing community of Muslims.

A few minutes walk west from the Fairfax is the campus of Georgetown University, whose Center for Contemporary Arab Stud- ies has become a hub of Arab cultural and political activity in Wash- ington. It is there, for instance, that Hisham Shirabi, professor of history and founder of the new Association of Arab University Graduates, coordinates the national organizing activities of that group of young Arab professionals. The AAUG is just one of the many new Arab-American activist groups formed in the late 1970s in an attempt to create the same sort of grass roots political influ- ence wielded by Israel via American Jewish organizations.

The Arab counterpart to the American Israel Public Affairs Committee is the National Association of Arab-Americans. Like AIPAC, which is a domestic political lobbying organization closely coordinating its actions with a foreign embassy—Israel—the NAAA is a domestic political lobbying organization closely coordinating its actions with a foreign embassy—Saudi Arabia. Also like AIPAC, NAAA functions as an umbrella group—orchestrating the overall lobbying activities of more than a half dozen other groups of Americans of Arab ancestry from New York to California.

In May 1981 the annual NAAA convention in San Francisco served as the forum from which a national pro-Arab lobbying effort on the AWACS issue was organized and launched. From the beginning, the group's spokesmen moved into the Washington face-off in high spirits. David Sadd, executive director of NAAA, explained that the "AWACS [controversy] is the best thing that could possibly happen to us, because for two months there is going to be nothing but debate over Saudi Arabia, Israel and the Middle East and a lot of people are going to get a hell of an education."

During those two months Sadd's group directed the national letter-writing and telephone and telegram campaigns aimed at pressing the Arab cause home to various senators via their home-state constituencies. NAAA contacted several hundred American corporations that have multimillion-dollar stakes in Middle Eastern contracts for goods and services and suggested that they take an active, corporate part in the congressional struggle. The inference of the polite request was clear. E. H. Boullioun, senior vice-president of the Boeing Corporation, made a personal written plea to 1,600 subcontractors, suppliers and vendors of Boeing to assist in the Arab lobbying effort by applying pressure on their senators. Boullioun wrote, "A negative decision on this issue may affect Saudi Arabia's attitude toward other U.S. products."

The full potential of this approach can be appreciated by considering that in 1981 more than seven hundred of America's largest corporations in forty-two states held contracts for approximately $35 billion worth of business with Saudi Arabia. And each of those corporations, like Boeing, had hundreds of subcontractors and vendors equally dependent on maintaining the good graces of Muslim leaders whose countries now collectively represent the single richest market in the world.

And, as always, oil played a pivotal, although not very public, role in the AWACS lobbying effort.

In September 1981, even as many American newspapers were reporting on their front pages that the Senate was leaning overwhelmingly in favor of the Israel lobby on the AWACS issue, editorial writers were heralding the decline of the Arab oil powers because of the "oil glut."

For the previous year, there had seemed to be a surplus of oil around the world. So much oil, in fact, that the storage depots across the United States were filled to overflowing.

But the newspaper accounts largely failed to take the mechanics of the oil glut into serious consideration. The entire world's oil-supply situation was still ultimately controlled by a single nation whose oil output is so prodigious that it can cause a global glut or shortage at will: Saudi Arabia. For a year the Saudis had greatly increased their production to create an oversupply and the political leverage needed to back their call for pricing unity among OPEC members.

And even as substantial sections of the American press were openly gloating at the "decline" of Arab oil power, the New York *Times* was reporting to its business readers that "The loss of Saudi Arabia's oil production throughout war, revolution or catastrophe would throw the world into what would likely be one of the most painful economic tailspins in history."[5]

A reduction of only two million barrels a day in Saudi Arabia's oil-pumping networks could spell the difference between a global oil glut and a global oil shortage. The world's petroleum supply grids are that precariously balanced.

At the same time, in September, as the AWACS battle reached fever pitch, the oil majors of the United States announced that because of the "high costs of maintaining inventories" they were greatly reducing oil stocks in their various depots. Normally, the same companies start *building* inventories during this period to prepare for heavy demands for winter heating oil.

And, simultaneously, the White House and offices of Congress received the draft of the new U. S. General Accounting Office report which said, "The U. S. Government is almost totally unprepared to deal with disruptions of oil imports. Oil import disruptions—such as the 1973 oil embargo and the 1979 Iranian shortfall—pose a significant threat to national security, and the lack of effective contingency planning and program development to date is serious and requires immediate action."[6]

In the final week before the Senate cast its historic vote on AWACS, the American Petroleum Institute reported that the incoming flow of oil to the United States dropped by 25 percent—the largest weekly drop in oil imports since 1973. The Petroleum Institute reported this to be "a one-week aberration" due to the failure of scheduled tanker shipments to arrive.

On the day of the vote, a contingent of twenty-three of America's top corporate executives from such firms as IBM, TWA, American Airlines, Proctor and Gamble, Owens-Illinois and others sent what has become known as the "Riyadh Telex." The twenty-three were on a fact-finding mission to the Middle East sponsored by Time Incorporated and, while visiting Riyadh, sent the telex to senators preparing to vote on the AWACS issue in Washington. Fresh from meetings with Saudi officials, the American executives warned the senators that a victory by the Israel lobby blocking the AWACS sale would "substantially impair U.S. ability to protect its legitimate interests in the Middle East."

As the pro-AWACS and anti-AWACS factions maneuvered for dominance within the capital's political machinery that summer, the country witnessed some of the most dramatic political and diplomatic events of our times.

Never had the courtship of the goodwill of such Muslim nations as Saudi Arabia assumed such high priority in the White House.

President Reagan, who had campaigned for office on a pledge of revitalizing American industry and solving the energy crisis, announced the newly expanded relationship with Saudi Arabia as "a cornerstone" of American policy. He described Saudi Arabia as one of America's "closest friends." And in a televised address defending the AWACS weapons package, Reagan indicated that the United States was adjusting to Saudi desires because that Arab country and its neighbors "provide the bulk of the energy needed to turn the wheels of industry in the Western world."

Never had the White House moved so resolutely against Israel in actions and words.

In a nationally broadcast, precedent-setting attack on Israel's lobbying apparatus in Washington, President Reagan warned the Begin government that "It is not the business of other nations to make

American foreign policy." Under the direct sponsorship of Reagan, former Presidents Gerald Ford and Jimmy Carter began campaigning in favor of Saudi Arabia and against the Israel lobby. Former President Richard Nixon blasted the "intense opposition [of] the Begin government and parts of the American Jewish community" for interfering with White House actions aimed at benefiting America as a whole. President Carter warned of "the danger of a third worldwide oil shock," and that "tensions in the Middle East make disruption of oil supplies a constant threat. We seem about to repeat the same errors that left us unprepared for the second oil shock of 1979."

Never had so many members of Congress broken so openly with the Israel lobby and its publicly declared wishes.

California Representative Paul (Pete) McClosky told reporters, "We've got to overcome the tendency of the Jewish community in America to control the actions of Congress and to force the Congress and the President not to be even-handed in the Middle East."

Never had the criticism of Israel and its lobby been so open or intense from mainstream publications which had traditionally been the staunchest supporters of Israel.

Flora Lewis of the New York *Times* wrote that the paper had been flooded with "an unusually large number of letters from readers, mostly irate and, in some cases, shrilly insulting and even menacing. Many of the letter writers take the position that any criticism of Israeli policy or leadership automatically makes one pro-PLO, anti-Israel, even anti-Semite. There is a tone of desperation to this outpouring, as though it cloaked a secret sense that things really are going so badly for Israel on its present course that reason can no longer help and only frenzy will serve."[7]

Joseph Kraft of the Washington *Post* wrote, "Intense supporters of Israel make their views known all over the country, and especially in the White House. They often identify opposition to their views with approval of the Holocaust. They frequently turn a blind eye to the excesses committed by Israel, especially under Prime Minister Menachem Begin."[8]

Never had the forces of the emerging Arab industrial complex so efficiently applied pressure at the grass roots level in fifty states—

causing entire blocks of senators to reverse their stands and vote in favor of a measure they previously disagreed with.

Senator Edward Zorinsky of Nebraska explained, "I've never seen a full court press like this before . . . this is something else . . . I've got everyone who's got a vested interest economically, both in the State of Nebraska and nationally, who's got bucks to make or lose in the event that the sale is turned down." Zorinsky voted in favor of Saudi Arabia.[9]

Senator Edward M. Kennedy said, "In my nineteen years up here, I have never seen such 180-degree turns on the part of so many senators."[10]

Never had the Israel lobby conceded in public that it had, finally, come up against a new power capable of matching its previously invincible hold on Congress.

Hyman Bookbinder, lobbyist for the American Jewish Committee, told reporters, "There was a time we didn't even like to talk about it, because we didn't want to make it any more real than it was. But there is no question that [American] policy toward Saudi Arabia has been affected by a fear of incurring its wrath on oil prices and supply."[11]

And never had the Arab world had occasion to celebrate such a profound, far-reaching triumph as that toasted and retoasted that October 1981 night at Ali Hedda's banquet.

"I was expecting victory from the first day," Saudi Ambassador Faisal Alhegelan told the applauding crowd in Hedda's dining room. "The moment of truth came in the Senate."[12]

Nor was it to be the last such moment. In less than a year, Alhegelan would savor yet another as he helped unseat a U. S. Secretary of State who declined to soften his pro-Israeli view.

In 1980 as he prepared to make the final selections for his new cabinet, President-elect Reagan was reported to have narrowed his choices for Secretary of State to two: George Shultz and Alexander Haig. Shultz, who had served as Treasury and Labor Secretary in the Nixon administration and was well-respected in the international business and diplomatic communities, was thought to have the edge. Shultz had been a close friend and adviser to Reagan during the campaigns and was equally close to other key advisers of the

President-elect. For instance, Shultz was vice president of the Bechtel Corporation and had previously been the boss of Caspar Weinberger, chief counsel of Bechtel. Weinberger, who was an economic adviser to Reagan prior to the election, was named Secretary of Defense.

Like many others who surrounded Reagan in his run, both Weinberger and Shultz were sympathetic to Arab historical perspectives in the Middle East. Bechtel was one of the largest contractors in Saudi Arabia and other Muslim oil nations, and had long been a leading proponent of Arab causes in the past. For instance, Bechtel's legal department fought a protracted battle in U.S. courts in an attempt to overturn the laws which impose fines on American corporations cooperating with the Arab boycott of Israel.

Just before Reagan announced his cabinet choices, Shultz disagreed publicly with a speech the President-elect had made to a Jewish group in which he stressed the continuing American support for Israel. Shultz's comments resulted in a storm of reaction from the Jewish lobby in Washington and from congressmen heavily dependent on Jewish voting blocs.

In short order, Shultz bowed out of the contest as Reagan sought to soothe ruffled feathers in the capital. Shultz was almost immediately named president of Bechtel. Alexander Haig, an ardently pro-Israel veteran of the Nixon administration who had launched an unsuccessful bid for the Presidency in 1980, was named Secretary of State instead.

From the very first days, the new Secretaries of State and Defense bickered constantly. Immediately after he took office, Defense Secretary Weinberger announced his support for additional sales of advanced, high-tech weaponry to Arab states. He was publicly rebuked by Haig, who disputed the Arab states' need for such weaponry.

Weinberger became one of the leading advocates of the AWACS sale to the Saudis. Haig soft-pedaled the issue and spoke favorably of arrangements which would prevent full Saudi ownership or use of the planes. Weinberger became one of the most outspoken critics of Menachem Begin; Haig, one of his most strident supporters.

For eighteen months, the animosity between Haig and other top Administration officials, such as Weinberger and National Security Adviser William P. Clark, grew. They differed on nearly every major issue confronting the Reagan White House: European trade, the handling of the Falkland Islands War, relations with the Soviet Union, arms limitations talks, procedural policy at the U.N. and similar matters. But the single issue which rankled most bitterly and most consistently and became "the bone in the throat of the White House" was Haig's pro-Israeli stance. This, even as Israel incurred the increasing wrath and condemnation of other world leaders for an escalating campaign of raids into surrounding Arab lands: bombing a nuclear reactor in Iraq, annexing Syria's Golan Heights, bombing and strafing the densely populated Palestinian refugee camps across southern Lebanon.

And it was Israel which brought the seething White House rivalry to a flash point in June of 1982, when Menachem Begin's armies invaded Lebanon and besieged Beirut. That Israeli June blitzkrieg began as President Reagan toured Europe on a round of economic and defense talks. In the opening days of the offensive, Prime Minister Begin called Haig, who was traveling with the Presidential party in West Germany. Begin asked the U. S. Secretary of State to fly to Israel for an official visit—a tacit show of American support for the invasion-in-progress.

Defense Secretary Weinberger and National Security Adviser Clark immediately urged that Begin's request be denied and that Haig be restrained from traveling to Israel. Haig threatened to go to Israel anyway, even if the White House did not approve it.

That argument became part of the larger one which enveloped the Oval Office and the Cabinet. Haig argued that the President should support the Israeli war effort, the announced goal of which was the liquidation of the military and political leadership of the Palestinians. Weinberger and Clark argued that the President should flatly rebuke Begin, call for an immediate end of the invasion and take the unprecedented step of withdrawing the U.S. ambassador from Tel Aviv.

Reagan took the middle road. He declined to approve Haig's visit to Israel, dispatching special envoy Philip Habib to the Middle East instead. Habib, a retired State Department official who had been employed by the Bechtel Corporation since 1978,[13] was instructed to seek a halt to the fighting and assess the situation. Clark and the White House staff took special measures to ensure that Habib's daily cables on the situation were not routed to Haig at the State Department.

Another confrontation between the State Department and the White House occurred over the question of what to do about a previously planned state visit by Menachem Begin to Washington. Haig argued that Reagan should keep the engagement with Begin. Clark and Weinberger argued that such a meeting could be construed as an act of tacit approval for the Israeli leader's war-making policies. But Haig won. Reagan elected to follow the Secretary of State's suggestion and try personal diplomacy. Begin was invited to visit the White House during his trip to the United States. But even these plans became snarled in acrimony when Haig hurried to New York for a preliminary huddle with Begin and told the Israeli leader that he, Haig, was "Israel's only friend in the White House."

Even as Begin arrived in Washington, his armies in the field continued to grind down villages and towns in Lebanon, ignoring earlier U.S. pleas for a halt. The city of Beirut was shrouded in smoke and encircled in a closing ring of Israeli steel. The American TV networks were broadcasting panoramic scenes of civilian carnage. Republican Senator Mark Hatfield, in one of the rising crescendo of such outbursts, asked angrily, "Can Israeli children live in peace only if Lebanese children die in war? I will not countenance that bargain, and I do not believe this nation can afford to be a silent partner to it."

The Haig-arranged luncheon between Reagan and Begin was described as "more of a collision than a conference." A White House aide explained, "What bothered us is that Begin didn't end the killing. When he sat here, they were bombing a hospital. You get the feeling he will use any excuse to start the killing again. It was the first time that an American President has really let a Prime Minister of Israel know that we're goddamned unhappy."

For openers, Reagan refused to accord Begin the normal courtesy of a toast. Instead, he called for an end to the fighting and killing. Reagan demanded, and got, a pledge from Begin that Israeli troops would not invade the city of Beirut where the Palestinian leadership and hundreds of thousands of civilians were trapped. The President told Begin he wanted Israel to cease its encroachment and settlements on the occupied West Bank and wanted "progress" on the issue of self-government for Palestinians there and in the other occupied zones.

Begin also met with a group of thirty-six senators. He caustically argued that the 60,000 troops, hundreds of tanks, fleets of attack jets and round-the-clock artillery barrages that were still pouring into Lebanon "was not an invasion." He began a lecture on the atrocities committed by Germans against Jewish Europeans in the 1940s, but was cut short by a senator who said that European atrocities forty years ago did not justify the Israeli "killing and wounding of hundreds and thousands of Lebanese and Palestinian women and children" in 1982.

Participants in that closed-door session said only three of the thirty-six senators spoke favorably to Begin. Republican Senator Larry Pressler said it was "the first time I have seen such a confrontation between the Prime Minister of Israel and senators in terms of head-to-head disagreement." In fact, Begin's verbal attacks on individual senators became so vitriolic that Israel's Ambassador to the United States, Moshe Arens, later offered a personal apology to each for Begin's behavior.

Meanwhile, the efforts of the local Arab and Israeli lobbies aimed at influencing the U.S. response to the invasion reached a level of activity approaching that of the previous AWACS battle. In New York and at the Israeli Embassy in Washington, Begin encouraged Jewish-American groups to turn on the pressure in support of the Israeli military adventure. At the Fairfax Hotel and the Saudi Embassy in Washington, Ambassador Faisal Alhegelan and Prince Bandar once again coordinated the national activities of Arab-American groups protesting the invasion. The immediate concern of both lobbies was the White House position on the siege which had trapped Yasir Arafat and the Palestinian leadership in Beirut.

One of the Arab world's most unique and most effective activist groups evolved during this period: the Arab Women's Council of Washington. Comprised of more than a hundred prominent Middle Eastern women in Washington, it included the wives of two dozen ambassadors. Organized by Nouha Alhegelan, wife of the Saudi diplomat, the council quickly became one of the most vigorous Arab political groups involved in the Lebanon fray. Retaining the prestigious public relations agency of Gray & Company—a firm run by Robert Gray, a long-time personal friend of President Reagan—the council launched a national TV campaign, a newspaper advertising blitz, a series of nightly vigils in front of the White House and rounds of woman-to-woman meetings with wives of U.S. congressmen.

The group's boldest and single most important action in June of 1982 was a woman-to-woman meeting between Nouha Alhegelan and First Lady Nancy Reagan. That encounter set in motion a series of events which directly resulted in the ouster of the Secretary of State and altered the course of the war for Beirut.

After Mrs. Reagan agreed to meet with Mrs. Alhegelan, the White House arranged for a senior official—National Security Adviser Clark—to be present with the First Lady. Mrs. Alhegelan was escorted to her appointment by her husband, the Saudi Ambassador. After the Alhegelans were ushered into the family quarters of the executive mansion, two dialogues eventually resulted. The first was the scheduled one between the two women. The second was the initially incidental one between Clark and Ambassador Alhegelan. Both discussions concerned the war-in-progress in Lebanon.

Mrs. Alhegelan spoke with the First Lady for forty minutes, giving a detailed presentation on the civilian casualties as well as an extensive report about how the Israeli invasion forces were blocking efforts to rush food, medicine and relief supplies to the survivors throughout the devastated areas. The Washington *Post* reported that "Mrs. Reagan was shocked" by the presentation and other information Mrs. Alhegelan provided about "the elderly, the children, the women" being killed throughout the region by the Israeli military.

The exact details of Clark's and Ambassador Alhegelan's exchanges are not known; but that meeting, which began as a sidelight of Mrs. Alhegelan's visit, opened a new channel between the White House and Arab leaders who objected to Alexander Haig's policy of publicly supporting the Israeli siege. *Time* magazine later reported: "Clark appeared to the Arab leaders to be much more sympathetic to their general views, which naturally were anti-Israel."

Four days later, Clark and Alhegelan once again met in secret. The Saudi diplomat urged the Reagan administration to play a more direct role in the Beirut crisis and to exert maximum restraining pressures on Israel at the same time that it made contact with Yasir Arafat inside Beirut. The ambassador offered to provide the confidential conduit for such contacts between the White House and the PLO chief.

Shortly thereafter, both Alhegelan and Prince Bandar were acting as liaisons between the Oval Office and the Palestinians bunkered in Beirut. The route of communication was from the White House to Alhegelan or from Bandar to King Fahd in Saudi Arabia, who remained in continual phone contact with Arafat.

The public position taken by the U.S. during the siege of Beirut was of crucial importance to the ultimate outcome of that fighting. The Israelis had surrounded the city and were poised for a final, all-out attack; they were threatening to annihilate the Palestinians and Lebanese there if Arafat did not unconditionally surrender the city. If the trapped Palestinians thought the U.S. was exerting pressure on Israel to stave off a final assault on the city, Arafat would have no reason to seriously consider an unconditional surrender.

Secretary of State Haig was issuing public statements which indicated that the U.S. could not restrain Israel from attacking and inferred that the Palestinians had no option but unconditional surrender.

But suddenly the White House began to directly contradict Haig by releasing statements such as the one which detailed the pledge Reagan had obtained from Begin—that there would be no final invasion of Beirut by the Israelis.

From his own contacts in the Middle East, Haig learned that the Saudis and Palestinians had been assured by National Security Adviser Clark that "the United States would achieve an Israeli withdrawal" from around Beirut and actively seek to protect the Palestinians from total defeat. Haig exploded when he investigated further and learned the details of the secret meetings between Clark and Alhegelan. He demanded that President Reagan halt all communications with the Arab world except for those approved by the Secretary of State.

Reagan called Haig into the Oval Office and announced that his resignation had been accepted.

But Haig had not submitted a resignation. His associates explained that he had been "in fact, fired."

Reagan immediately named George Shultz, President of Bechtel, the new Secretay of State.

Haig's abrupt departure sent seismic shocks through Israel's political and military establishment and resulted in a cease-fire which did not ultimately hold, but which did break the momentum of the siege.

And a farewell dinner with two hundred senior aides on the eighth floor of the State Department, an embittered Haig quipped, "I only today had to quell the rumor that Cap Weinberger had closed the Pentagon cafeteria for Ramadan"—a sarcastic reference to the high Islamic holy days which require Muslims to fast during daylight hours.

In his confirmation hearings before Congress, George Shultz assumed the same stance which had, only a year and a half earlier, disqualified him as a potential Secretary of State. He made the plight of the Palestinians the keynote of his remarks, telling Congress and the nation that "the crisis in Lebanon makes painfully and totally clear a central reality of the Middle East: the legitimate needs and problems of the Palestinian people must be addressed and resolved —urgently and in all their dimensions."

Twenty-four hours later, Shultz was confirmed by a unanimous vote in the full Senate.

Within two months, dramatic changes in U. S. Middle East policy were evident. The White House announced it had completed a "comprehensive assessment" of relations with Israel and found "very profound differences."[14]

In a public and protracted bare knuckles confrontation with the Begin government, the Reagan administration thwarted the planned invasion of Beirut and engineered the agreement which allowed the trapped Palestinians to evacuate the city—protected by a contingent of American Marines. Yasir Arafat went directly to Athens, Greece, and was given a tumultuous welcome as a statesman and hero. From there, in yet another diplomatic coup, the Palestinian leader proceeded to the Vatican to be received by Pope John Paul II.

As Arafat left, President Reagan went on television to announce that the United States would not support Israeli annexation of the West Bank or Gaza. Reagan also indicated that the United States did not recognize Israel's claim to the Old City of Jerusalem seized in 1967. The President said that the final status of the city holy to Muslims, Jews and Christians "should be decided through negotiations."[15]

And the Beirut adventure further accelerated the Israel lobby's decline in prestige and power in Congress.

James Reston of the New York *Times* wrote: "At no time since the formation of the state of Israel has its support on Capitol Hill been as weak as it is now."

Explained another veteran capital politico: "Since 1947, the 'special relationship' between the U.S. and Israel has had its ups and downs. There has been a certain cyclical quality to it. But that's not what we're witnessing now—a mere fluctuation. The fear expressed by many during the F-15 and AWACS debates became an unavoidable fact during the siege of Beirut. There has been a fundamental change in the American perception of Israel. The 'special relationship' is never going to be the same again. We have reached the end of an era."

In 1947, when—in the midst of a presidential election campaign —the White House and the Congress became the patrons of a new state for European refugees in Asia, the United States was the unchallenged ruler of the world. In 1948, when that new State of Israel was officially declared, it emerged directly from a womb of U.S.-dominated international systems.

The "special relationship" between the United States and Israel— that bond which allowed Israel to sustain itself as an isolated fortress island in a sea of hostile Asians and Africans—was a function of the U.S. control of the world's industrial machinery, financial systems, military prerogatives and diplomatic options. From the very first days, Israel's prospects for ultimately surviving were only as bright as America's prospects for maintaining dominance in those world politico-financial systems.

But in the 1950s American power reached its inevitable global peak.

Throughout the 1960s America's exclusive hold on the lines of global power appreciably declined.

In the 1970s America's exclusive hold on those same lines had all but dissolved.

And, by the opening years of the 1980s, both Americans and Israelis were struggling to adjust—or, in some cases, even admit—to the new order of the international power structure. The signs of these new global realities were everywhere, as disturbing as they were unavoidable.

Americans no longer ultimately controlled the webs of machinery which were the sinew of their nation's domestic life and industrial might.

Asian and African oil powers did.

Americans no longer ultimately controlled the world's financial grids or even their own economy or currency or banking systems.

Asian and African oil powers did.

Americans no longer exercised dominant control over the United Nations or the international matrix of diplomatic systems which stretched out from that agency to girdle the continents.

Asian and African oil powers did.

Americans no longer commanded the obedience of such industrial and political powers as Japan or Britain or France.

Asian and African oil powers did.

Americans no longer even ultimately controlled the ability of their own military to operate in and around the most strategically important resource areas of the earth.

Asian and African oil powers did.

And, by the fall of 1982, it had become clear that Americans no longer controlled the international political momentum that will ultimately shape the outcome of the Middle East conflict.

Asian and African oil powers did.

The Western, Eurocentric world and the Asian and African Muslim world, though they use translators to speak the same words, talk in different languages. Each side's sense of imagery and inference comes filtered through such different cultural fabric that they remain unintelligible to each other.

One example of the different meanings resounding in the same word at either end of the world can be seen in the colloquial use of the term "European." In one place this term seems innocuous and is used to describe persons now living in a handful of countries north of the Mediterranean. In another place, however, this term is used to describe all white persons of European ancestry now living in nations scattered across several continents.

In the urban ghettos of the United States, where a deepening sense of African connection and a growing Islamic movement continue to alter cultural perceptions and even speech patterns, it is now a common matter of street parlance for many blacks to speak not of "whites" but of "Europeans." This even though the whites in question may be tenth-generation North Americans who live three blocks away and have never set foot in that zone they recognize on the map as "Europe."

The animosity reflected in this use of the term is also important. In the West, a presumption of superiority continues to linger in populations long accustomed to having their way with non-whites. In Asia and Africa, anger and the need for reassertion linger in populations which endured the humiliations of European colonial conquest. In this Third World, "European" is often a pejorative word and describes persons as diverse as Americans, Canadians, Afrikaners, Israelis, Australians or Italians.

In the Western, Eurocentric world the colonial era is largely forgotten by choice or glossed over in modern entertainments which emphasize its romanticized principles rather than its non-white victims. In Asia and Africa the atrocities of the colonial era remain a vibrant part of daily life and a populist political chord often used to unite otherwise divergent groups.

Events of the colonial era remain the pivot upon which many of the most disparate of the two worlds' historical perceptions hang. The Eurocentric societies, for instance, consider the Holocaust to have been the greatest atrocity ever committed by man upon his fellow man. However, throughout Asia and Africa, the Nazi Holocaust is perceived to have been unique only in terms of the relationship between victims and victimizers: the first time the practices of racial extermination commonly used by Europeans against colonized non-whites were used by Europeans against other Europeans.

For instance, the European Zionist movement remembers the pre-World War I era largely in terms of the sufferings of Jewish Russians in the final period of that collapsing empire: thick-soled Cossack boots splintering open hut doors; teen-aged female corpses frozen into the road mud and ripped up the front—like hastily butchered livestock; old men with skulls caved in, sprawled in the doorways of burning synagogues.

This same period is remembered differently by Muslims. It was a time when European powers surrounded and then systematically subjugated the breadth of Muslim civilization. This civilization comprised one sixth of all the human beings on earth and stretched across every geographical zone from arctic tundra to tropical rain forest and included cultural groups ranging from Nubian cattle herders to Pakistani spice brokers, Thai rice farmers and Arab silversmiths, to Burmese teak cutters and Tunisian sailors.

These geographically extended communities, joined by the same ritual language, same disgust for swine meat, same art forms, same daily prayers, feasts and fasts, and same life goal of an individual journey to Mecca, also came to be joined in the same helplessness, civil chaos, military impotence and personal shame as fellow victims of the mechanized onslaught of the industrialized European colonial regimes. By the early 1900s—when the frenzy of European colonial conquests had reached its fevered pitch—thirty-three of today's thirty-nine nations with majority Islamic populations had come under European control.

Today more than 366 million people—or nearly half the globe's Muslims—live in twenty-five countries which had been dominated by the British Empire. The sort of psychological lesions left by that relationship can be better appreciated with a brief flip through some of Britain's archives. Stored there are voluminous collections of photographs and etchings used by the British to record activities of all sorts in their far-flung colonial assemblage of non-white lands. One of those sepia photographs is a picture of human bones, some still ragged with flags of sinew near the joints, scattered willy-nilly about the stones of a minareted courtyard, the remains of Muslims trapped in a panicked, screaming mass as a line of British regulars with twenty-eight-inch razor bayonets on their rifles advanced like a brightly colored necklace of plunging, jabbing, flashing steel pulled ever tighter about the crowd and then left the debris to be dismembered by dogs and flesh-scavenging birds.

Another picture is of a sun-scorched parade ground where soldiers in white sashes and stiff hats stare forward in unison at the officers about to order the cannon to commence firing, each weapon having been fitted with a spread-eagled Muslim lashed across its muzzle mouth so that the explosion will tear out the man's center in a smoking geyser of red flames, spewed metal and trailing entrails.

The third picture shows a village gallows dangling with an oddly wrapped body—a Muslim who watched as a live pig was shot dead, slit up the belly and peeled of its skin by British regulars who then entwined the mess around the condemned man's head so that his last two sensations would be the snapping of his vertebrae and the gasped taste of God's most abominable animal: His defiled body was then left on display by a British commander determined to make a lasting impression on his ever-troublesome Islamic subjects.

In the chaotic aftermath of World War I, the European colonial powers launched their final wave of land seizures in Africa and Asia, rounding out their empires. It was during this time that Europeans completed the consolidation of their hold on the broad band of Islamic lands along the southern and eastern extremes of the Mediterranean, where oil deposits had been found in numerous places.

It was also at this time that, as a result of political maneuvers in London, the European Zionist movement was given rights by the crown to a portion of ancient Judah which was now Islamic Palestine.

Three decades later the United States rose to assume the mantle of world leadership and began exercising its new power in an attempt to reshape the world. It declared a tiny island in the Taiwan Straits to be China and Chiang Kai-shek to be its leader; it encouraged the French to reinvade their former plantation colonies in Vietnam; it approved the bid by European refugee and Jewish American political groups to establish a new European colony state along a coastal strip of Asia.

In this same post-World War II period the broad swath of Islamic populations across Africa and Asia began wrenching free from European domination. In some cases Islamic independence occurred only after protracted and savage wars against European occupational armies, such as Algeria's war against the French or Indonesia's war against the Dutch. In other cases Islamic states gained final sovereignty when European powers peaceably withdrew the old colonial control mechanisms, as was the case with countries like Kuwait and Nigeria.

Over the next thirty years all the Islamic territories, except Palestine, were able to regain their independence from European colonial rule. In the new Arab Islamic nations of North Africa and eastern Asia this did not bring peace or harmony. On the contrary, they erupted in a near-constant string of civil wars, coups, revolutions, invasions, mutinies, border skirmishes, assassinations, tribal vendettas, palace intrigues and other bits of blood-laced acrimony.

However, throughout all these conflicting levels of the Arab world there ran two emotional currents which served as common links between even the bitterest Muslim rivals: an overwhelming sense of Islamic identity capable of transcending all ideological disputes, and a visceral disdain for what is today the last remaining vestige left by the receding tide of European colonial powers—Israel.

This radically different sense of historical perspective in the Third World has traditionally been an academic issue of little interest to the press and public in the West. Not until the early 1970s did Asian and African nations begin acquiring the power to bring their point of view to the attention of the populations of the West. And, even then, those messages were often ignored because Westerners did not understand the alien gestures contained in apocalyptic Muslim pronouncements.

The most important of these announcements occurred in October 1973. An elderly tribal chieftain stepped out onto the sun-broiled pavement in front of a conference center in Kuwait, drew out a sword and announced his intention to hold the citizens of the United States of America responsible for the continued Israeli occupation of Islam's third most sacred city, Jerusalem. Faisal Ibn Abdul-Aziz al Saud, his face weathered by seven decades of wind and desert glare and resembling nothing so much as the face of one of the killer falcons he bred, proclaimed that the decision had been made to "unsheath the sword of oil."

The Western world's news media made very little of Faisal's gesture. To them, the Saudi monarch's actions were those of a caricature potentate using a bit of figurative language in the midst of the Muslim world's latest bungled attempt to destroy Israel.

In the Eastern world, Faisal's words had a different impact. Eight hundred million Muslims concentrated in more than forty countries across Asia and Africa heard Faisal's as the voice of the Keeper of the Holy Cities of Islam—a position analogous to that of the Pope. On the rare occasions the voice of the Keeper of the Holy Cities of Islam invokes its full authority, it rebounds down fourteen hundred years of history through the courtyards of thousands of mosques.

For the Keeper of the Holy Cities of Islam to mix oil and the unsheathed sword in a single declaration of action was a stunning gesture. In the West, a sword is a sword: a sharpened length of metal with a handle at the end. In the Islamic East, a sword is the most potent cultural and religious symbol: simultaneously signifying the essence of God's will, frontal attack, tribal duty, family honor, personal fortitude and vengeance rightfully taken.

And the unsheathed sword has also been the traditional signal used to launch *jihad*. There is no English word that captures the full meaning of *jihad*—an Arabic term most frequently, but inadequately, translated as "holy war." It is a word that describes a unique coalescence of physical and emotional imperatives within Islamic society focusing all that society's resources into a single do-or-die struggle whose importance has been raised to the level of a celestial command.

The essence of jihad—as a past, triumphant, physical event and an ultimate future possibility—has provided the thread of Islamic historical continuity for fourteen centuries. Today, jihad remains one of the civilization's most potent emotional chords—capable of energizing the collective imagination of the Muslim world like no other.

The broadest outlines of the history of the Islamic world can be summarized with a brief review of its numerous jihads—each being an event which drastically altered the course of history in both the Islamic and non-Islamic worlds.

The first jihad was launched in the year A.D. 624 by Muhammad, the theocratic revolutionary who overturned the political and social orders of the Red Sea area and set in motion a broad regional battlefront.

Riding in the shadow of the sword of their Prophet, Muhammad's men pushed outward to take control of Iraq and Persia to the east, Palestine, Lebanon, Jordan and Syria to the north, and Egypt and Libya to the west by A.D. 670.

It was in jihad that Umayyad and Abbasid Muslim dynasties plunged warrior hordes across Afghanistan and north to take all the central Asian lands ruled from Samarkand, and also pushed west to take Tunisia, Algeria and Morocco.

It was in jihad that the Muslim war machine rolled across Gibraltar to take most of the lands of Spain, where Islamic rule became a fact of life for nearly seven centuries.

It was in jihad that the Kurdish rebel Saladin led the Muslim armies against the trans-Mediterranean invasion forces of Richard the Lion-Hearted in the battles of the late 1100s that drove the Europeans out of Palestine for the last time, ending the Crusades.

And it was in jihad that Turkish Muslims plunged deep into the heart of Hindu India to the borders of China and later, pushed west, breaching the wall of Christian Constantinople, beginning the campaign in which Ghazi—warriors for the faith—slashed and blasted their way to control of Balkan Europe up to the outer walls of Vienna.

The most recent jihad, launched in 1973 by King Faisal, was historically noteworthy both in its revolutionary approach to weaponry and its unprecedented logistical scope: riding in the shadow of the sword of oil, waves of modern-day Ghazi moved out and began systematically to seize control of most of the planet earth.

2

TOWARD NUCLEAR MASADA

Even as it came into existence in 1948, the new State of Israel looked forward to a future shadowed by a threat of potentially unstoppable force: a surrounding sea of native Asian and African Muslims intent on driving the Europeans back to Europe. In the late 1940s that threat had yet to manifest itself. Disorganized bands of native inhabitants armed with muskets and swords did battle the incoming Europeans in Palestine, but the action was hardly more than symbolic. Muslims were still a conquered people, living in technologically backward societies dominated by the European military powers which had controlled the region for centuries. But those same societies were showing signs of revolutionary change: regaining sovereignty, developing fledgling petroleum industries, shipping off large numbers of sons to European schools and beginning to coalesce slowly toward ethnic unity and cultural renaissance.

And from the very first days of its formation, the European government in Tel Aviv noted these trends and began preparing for the inevitable day of confrontation. Even before they had fully organized their new government, Polish-born Premier David Ben-Gurion and Russian-born President Chaim

Weizmann launched a secret program aimed at providing their military with the only tools capable of ultimately holding back two continents of Muslims: atomic bombs.

The story of Israel's atomic weapons production programs has been a tightly held secret for most of the country's history. However, during the last eight years details of those programs have been made public in a series of disclosures by U.S. congressional committees, top Israeli military officials, the former head of the French Atomic Energy Commission, two directors and top staff members of the U. S. Central Intelligence Agency, former operatives of the Mossad and investigative reports by such authoritative international news organizations as *Time* magazine, the New York *Times,* ABC-TV, the BBC network and others.[1]

In much the same way U.S. atomic weapons scientists pursued two routes when perfecting their "Manhattan Project" bombs in the early 1940s, Israel's atomic weapons scientists began two seperate bomb research projects in the late 1940s. One method involved the use of enriched uranium—uranium purified and concentrated into its most volatile form. The other method involved the use of plutonium—a man-made substance which occurs when uranium is exposed to intense radioactivity, such as that found at the center of a nuclear reactor.

Much as a conventional iron shrapnel bomb can be made with either dynamite or TNT at its core, atomic bombs can be made with either enriched uranium or plutonium at their cores. Each sort of bomb is constructed and triggered somewhat differently, but the overall result is the same. It was an enriched uranium bomb that destroyed Hiroshima; a plutonium bomb destroyed Nagasaki. Israel wanted both.

The hardest part of an atomic bomb-building project is the production of either variety of core explosive. Once enriched uranium or plutonium has been produced, the rest of the process is relatively simple and involves the machining, fabrication and assembly of routine metal, plastic and electronic parts.

The processes for producing either enriched uranium or plutonium begin with low-grade uranium ore—harmless-looking mineral dirt of the sort found in numerous spots around the earth's crust. But each process then employs very different and extremely complex mechanical and electronic devices and chemical procedures which laboriously convert that powder into one of the two most poisonous and explosive substances known to man.

Israel's first bomb project depended on either obtaining large quantities of enriched uranium from another country or developing facilities in Israel for enriching the substance. The second project depended on obtaining a nuclear reactor to produce plutonium and then obtaining the additional reprocessing plant required to purify and concentrate the plutonium.

Because both methods produce only tiny amounts of either bomb substance from large amounts of low-grade uranium, enormous quantities of uranium are required. And in 1948, even as the Israeli militia was still engaged in emptying out Muslim towns in the new European zone, crews of Israeli scientists were foraging across the Negev Desert surveying and cataloging the deposits of uranium-bearing phosphates in that wasteland south of the Dead Sea.

In 1952 Israel set up its Atomic Energy Commission—that agency charged with overseeing the development of nuclear-powered electrical generating stations. Immediately after its creation, the AEC began purchasing enriched uranium from the United States for "research."

In 1953 the Israeli Government's atomic scientists and military planners entered into a secret agreement with France in which the Israelis were allowed to take part in the French atomic weapons tests in the Sahara Desert in return for turning over the details of the new Israeli process for extracting uranium from phosphate sands.

Four years later, in the wake of the failed Israeli-French-British invasion of Egypt, the Israelis and French formalized and broadened their secret atomic weapons cooperation pact. France first sold Israel the plans and parts for a plutonuim-producing reactor. Then the French firm Saint Gobain, which built plutonium reprocessing facilities for the French military, provided the Israeli Government with a complete set of plans for constructing a plutonium reprocessing plant for extracting the weapons material from spent reactor fuel.

In a top-secret operation, the Israelis began constructing the reactor and weapons-production facilities at Dimona—an isolated site in the Negev Desert near a complex of phosphate mines. Premier David Ben-Gurion repeatedly told inquiring reporters and representatives of the U. S. Government that the heavily guarded construction site was "a textile plant."

In 1960 the Egyptian Intelligence Agency publicly identified the Dimona facility as a nuclear reactor. U.S. spy planes with special radiation sensing devices confirmed that report and, under pressure from President Dwight Eisenhower, David Ben-Gurion admitted that the facility was not a textile plant but a nuclear reactor.

Time magazine reported that in 1963 intelligence sources detected a small underground nuclear explosion beneath the Negev Desert.

In 1965, U.S. inspectors found more than two hundred pounds of enriched uranium missing from the Nuclear Materials and Equipment Corporation plant in Apollo, Pennsylvania. U. S. Central Intelligence Agency investigators found that NUMEC had previously been retained as the "technical consultant" and "training and procurement agency" in the United States by the Israeli Atomic Energy Commission. Investigators found that NUMEC's president, Dr. Zalman Shapiro, routinely used an electronic scrambler to code his phone calls with Israeli officials and that the records detailing the company's dealings with Israel were "incomplete, inaccurate or missing." Carl Duckett, deputy director for Science and Technology of the CIA, reported to a Senate investigating committee that the 208 pounds of enriched uranium "had been diverted and has been used by the Israelis in fabricating weapons."

In 1966, President Lyndon Johnson attempted to slow down or stop Israel's atomic bomb-building activities. Johnson agreed to provide Israel with large quantities of offensive conventional weapons systems, such as A-4 attack jets, thereby ensuring Israel's military superiority and diminishing the need for ultimate weapons. However, shortly after the U.S. jets were delivered, the CIA reported to the White House that Israel had begun a new program and was training pilots in the special A-4 maneuvers used exclusively for carrying and dropping atomic bombs.

In 1967, after the war campaigns in which Israeli troops seized the Old City of Jerusalem, Sinai, Gaza, Golan and the West Bank, France cut off shipments of uranium and further technological and military assistance to Israel.

At the same time, the Israeli seizure of the Old City of Jerusalem —the third holiest spot in the Islamic world—resulted in the formation of a new anti-Israel coalition of Muslim nations led by King Faisal of Saudi Arabia.

Israeli Defense Minister Moshe Dayan, who had administrative control over the country's atomic weapons programs, ordered the mass production and stockpiling of the nuclear bombs necessary for simultaneously striking all surrounding Muslim capitals.

Dayan explained to reporters that "Israel has no choice. With our manpower, we cannot physically, financially or economically go on acquiring more and more tanks and more and more planes. Before long, you will have all of us maintaining and oiling tanks."

As it began preparing for full-scale bomb production, Israel also pushed ahead on the development of a new missile system for carrying those weapons. The new system was a two-stage, solid-fuel rocket made with parts and technology previously acquired from France. The new atomic missile was named the "Jericho" by Israeli military authorities. "Jericho" is both a place and an event of deep significance to Israelis. Currently located on the occupied West Bank, the city of Jericho is the oldest known population center in the world and is thought to have been the place where man first stepped toward civilization. It was also the first town attacked by the Hebrews when they began their conquest of Palestine in biblical days. The Old Testament recounts that Joshua, a warrior chieftain and successor to Moses, wielded a magical force which caused the walls of the fortified Jericho to disintegrate. The Hebrews then killed every living human and animal in the city, tumbled its buildings and burned the piles of carnage as an offering to God in celebration of their victory.

In 1968, Israel's newly expanded weapons production programs required enormous new amounts of uranium—quantities far beyond that which could quickly be obtained from the phosphate deposits surrounding Dimona. Cut off from its former sources in France, under scrutiny by the CIA for its thefts in America, blocked from making outright purchases on the open market by international nonproliferation protocols, Israel's military turned to piracy on the high seas to get what it needed. Their target in November of that year was the *Scheersburg A,* a ship carrying two hundred tons of uranium from West Germany to Italy. The vessel never arrived. In mid-Mediterranean it was halted by Israeli ships and its cargo removed and transported to Dimona.

In December 1968, Israeli officials were negotiating for the purchase of fifty Phantom jets from the United States. The Israelis requested that the planes be equipped with the special wing pylons required for carrying nuclear bombs.

The Johnson administration refused.

Then-Assistant Secretary of Defense Paul C. Warnke demanded that Israel sign the nuclear nonproliferation treaty. Parties to the treaty were required to open their nuclear facilities to international inspection.

Israel refused.

And, in a city of tunnels beneath the Negev, the Israeli atomic weapons production programs proceeded at full speed. Israeli technicians laboriously constructed both enriched-uranium bombs and plutonium bombs. Then each bomb was partially disassembled so that it was not a "bomb" but a collection of "bomb parts." This allowed the Israeli Government to issue public statements denying it was stockpiling "atomic bombs" because, in fact, it was stockpiling "atomic bomb parts."

It was Israel's intention, according to U.S. intelligence specialists, to remain just "a screwdriver's turn away" from functioning bombs.

And so it would be until 1973, the year the nuclear enclave of Israel would face off against the force it had both prophesied and dreaded for three decades: two continents of native Muslims gone wealthy and worldly and able to march modern, well-equipped armies against the last beachhead of Western civilization in Islamic Asia.

This epochal event in October 1973 would bring the world to the brink of nuclear holocaust and ultimately wrap the fate of the United States and the West around the ancient stones of that city both Israelis and Muslims are determined to control no matter what the price, that city which has become the pivot on which the tortured history of the twentieth century now hangs:

Jerusalem.

3

JIHAD FOR JERUSALEM

The last military jihad for Jerusalem began shortly
after noon on October 6, 1973. Then Egyptian,
Syrian, Iraqi, Jordanian, Saudi Arabian, Moroccan
and Palestinian soldiers uttered a prayer, laying
aside their grenade belts and Kalashnikov assault
rifles, removing their boots and prostrating themselves toward Mecca. Their helmets and uniforms
and the sides of their Soviet-supplied T-54 tanks,
half-track Zil trucks, needle-nosed MIG jets,
armored personnel carriers and patrol boats were
stenciled with the golden eagle of Saladin, the
insignia carried by the Muslim armies whose jihad
recaptured Islamic Jerusalem from the invading
European crusaders in the twelfth century.

Moving out into the sky, onto the water and across
the sands, these twentieth-century Eagles of Saladin
flung themselves en masse at the lightning-swift
and space-age-modern Israeli military machine which
had, three times previous, reduced their ranks to
quiet tangles of twisted metal and flayed meat.

In 1956 and 1967 the Middle East wars began
with massive, multipronged Israeli air and ground
invasions into neighboring Muslim lands. Flying the
most sophisticated American jets, guided by state-

of-the-art fire-control technology and supplied with the latest United States satellite reconnaissance reports, the Israeli Air Force had devastated the airfields and planes of the Arab countries in surprise attacks.

In the two previous wars the Israelis had then pushed out in their American- and British-supplied M-60, M-48 and Centurion tanks to crash through the defensive formations of the miserably equipped Arab armies.

The Arab attack in 1973 was different. It was the first time the Arabs fielded forces drilled in the disciplines of modern battle tactics and equipped with up-to-date integrated weapons systems for coordinated ground, air and water operations. Although the Soviet-supplied tanks, jets, rocketry and radar systems were still technologically inferior to the American equipment of the Israelis, the Arabs had the advantage of numerical superiority and the complete surprise with which they launched their attacks into the occupied territories.

Across the Suez Canal the first line of defense erected by the occupational Israeli forces was a system of "hell-pipes." These were a series of pipelines connected to reservoirs of volatile liquids and positioned to empty into the canal. Capable of spewing high-pressure flows of gasoline and naphtha, the system was designed by Israelis to create an instantaneous maelstrom of flame capable of incinerating large, densely packed masses of men attempting to cross the water on portable bridges or rafts.

Beyond the hell-pipes lay the Bar-Lev line—a man-made barrier mound erected against tanks and troop attacks and made of sand spines studded with bombproof steel and concrete gun bunkers. Behind the Bar-Lev line were 290 American-made tanks ready to roll into immediate action. Behind that—within minutes of an alert —were squadrons of Phantom jets. Each Israeli Phantom was a flying, computerized arsenal of antitank, antiplane, antiradar, antimissile and antipersonnel ordinance without equal.

For twenty-five years Israel was the invincible military power of the Middle East: Its overwhelming air power, its superbly disciplined and electronically coordinated tank corps and its intelligence system and sense of national vigilance made a successful Arab attack close to impossible.

But the October 1973 jihad began with a phenomenon new to Arab warfare: frogmen. Swimming silently across the Suez and operating close enough to Israeli bunkers to hear the voices inside, Arab divers methodically sealed off the mouths of the hell-pipes. Returning as quietly as they had come, their work went unnoticed by the Israelis—until, in the turmoil of surprise attack, the Israelis attempted to activate the canal incineration equipment. Nothing happened.

Chanting "Allahu Akbar, Allahu Akbar . . . [God is great, God is great]," the first wave of 4,000 Muslim shock troops paddled across the water in dinghies and stormed the Israeli bunkers. The occupational Israeli garrisons along the Bar-Lev line were completely overwhelmed.

Next came the missiles—missiles in trucks roaring across special bridges thrown across the water, missiles piled in pontoon ferries, missiles pulled by half-tracks, missiles in self-propelled vehicles, missiles on ground sleds and missiles hand-carried by crews of individual soldiers. Before the stunned Israeli nation had mobilized its response to the Muslim attacks into the occupied territories, the banks of the Suez had been turned into a thicket of electronically guided antiaircraft missiles. When the formations of Israeli Phantoms and Skyhawk fighters shrieked west seeking to locate and destroy the Arab squadrons they assumed had provided air cover for the canal crossing, they found no planes. Instead, they found a desert lit with the fire blossoms of launched missiles. During the first day of battle fifty-one Israeli planes—more than 10 percent of the entire Israeli Air Force—were ripped from the sky by Muslim missilery.

Following the first stage of Arab attackers came the barge-mounted water pumps, each nozzled to function as a high-pressure water gun. These water cannon were able to cut into the Bar-Lev mounds much like a garden hose cuts into a sand castle. And they quickly opened large, muddy gaps through the sand barriers which were wide enough for tanks to roll through. During the post-World War II decades, tanks had continuously grown larger and thicker-skinned in an attempt to thwart increasingly sophisticated antitank weapons systems. Those antitank systems, in turn, became more powerful and versatile. Tanks, in turn, developed complex electronic systems for detecting, tracking and targeting the now ponderous antitank mobile cannon, antitank armored vehicles and antitank missile batteries towed behind half-tracks through the desert.

In preparation for the 1973 October jihad, the Arabs had disassembled the large, Soviet-supplied "Sagger" antitank missile-launching batteries mounted atop armored trucks. The clusters of stubby missiles were taken one by one and fitted into individual suitcases along with a small impromptu aiming- and firing-control box. Once the assault across the canal had begun, hundreds of Arab soldiers—each carrying a single suitcase—were sent walking into the deserts toward 290 Israeli tanks, which were spread out and moving cautiously toward the battle zone. All the tanks' systems were activated for detecting and immediately honing in on enemy tanks, antitank vehicles and antitank aircraft sorties from above. None of the Israeli equipment or human observers were programmed to recognize an individual enemy soldier walking in the desert as anything more than a minor, momentary diversion along the route to the combat zone.

Imagine what it is like to be a single man on foot, in a flat place offering no shelter, and to be confronted suddenly by an enemy M-60 tank: forty-five tons of computerized, flesh-shredding equipment operated by four members of the world's elite killer-tank corps, wheeling around in your direction like a steel-hide rhino preparing for the final charge.

Imagine the scene repeated over and over in those October deserts east of Suez: a lone Muslim man, still shaking from the adrenaline rush of the encounter, walking solemnly away from the spot where, with a one-shot, do-or-die hand-held device, he faced off against an Israeli M-60 tank, and left that machine blurting flames, its sides peeled outward, like the blackened skin of a burst metal melon.

In October 1973 the Israelis lost 840 tanks—or over 49 percent of their entire 1,700-strong tank corps—to the new and savagely effective Muslim antitank tactics. One third of all those losses occurred within the first seventy-two hours of the war.

By October 11 the Israeli occupational garrisons had been pushed back off the Suez, the Arab armies and tank corps had taken the critical "Artillery Road" behind the Bar-Lev line and were consolidating to continue their push outward across the occupied Sinai.

In the occupied territories to the north—around the Golan

Heights—Syrian, Jordanian, Moroccan, Iraqi and Saudi Arabian forces had swept across Golan, driven the occupational Israeli forces from the observation and command post atop the strategic Mount Hermon and were rolling their tanks across the territory to the very banks of the Sea of Galilee—the northern border of Israel.

In his journal of the opening stage of the war, Egyptian Chief of Staff Major General Saad El Shazly recorded that within the first day "The battle of the crossing had been won. The three armored brigades and one infantry brigade defending the Bar-Lev line had been virtually annihilated . . . the enemy forces were in chaos, effectively without armor in the tactical zone. . . . In twenty-four hours we had put across the canal 100,000 men, 1,020 tanks, and 13,500 vehicles—the largest first day crossing in world military history."[1]

In his memoirs President Richard Nixon recounted that "I was stunned by the failure of Israeli intelligence. . . . By the third day . . . it was clear that the Israelis had been over confident about their ability to win a quick victory. The initial battles had gone against them. They had already lost a thousand men—compared with fewer than 700 lost in the entire 1967 war—and they were on the way to losing a third of their tank force."[2]

In a recently published biography, an aide to Israeli Prime Minister Golda Meir described the scene as Defense Minister Moshe Dayan delivered his report from the field:

"Golda closed the door behind him and wept openly. [An aide] watched as the tears streamed down the prime minister's face.

" 'What's the matter?' she asked Golda.

" 'Dayan wants to talk about the conditions for surrender,' she sobbed, brushing away her tears."

The Prime Minister at that time indicated to her aides that she would commit suicide rather than surrender.[3]

She ordered that Israel prepare for a nuclear Masada—an atomic holocaust which would consume Israel as well as the surrounding Islamic capitals and oil fields.

Time magazine reported, "Israel's 13 [atomic] bombs were hastily assembled at a secret underground tunnel during a 78-hour period at the start of the war. At the time, the Egyptians had repulsed the first Israeli counterattacks along the Suez Canal, causing heavy casualties, and the Israeli forces on the Golan Heights were retreating in the face of a massive Syrian tank assault. At 10 A.M. on October 8, the Israeli commander on the northern front, Major General Yitzhak Hoffi, told his superior, 'I am not sure that we can hold out much longer.'

"Moshe Dayan solemnly warned Premier Golda Meir: 'This is the end of the Third Temple.'

"Mrs. Meir thereupon gave Dayan permission to activate Israel's Doomsday weapons. As each bomb was assembled, it was rushed to waiting air force units."[4]

High above those Middle Eastern battlefields cruised one of the world's most secret and elusive airplanes. Like a thirty-five-yard-long titanium dart, the craft moved back and forth across the war zone. Egyptian radar picked it up even as they were consolidating their hold on the Suez Canal. Egyptian Chief of Staff El Shazly recorded in his journal:

"This morning a dot appears on our air defense screens in Center Ten, moving swiftly north over the canal zone and out over the Nile Delta. . . . I watched its track for a few minutes, then called General Fahmy to ask why his SAM crews were letting this thing promenade over us. He replied giving me the speed and altitude of the dot —Mach Three plus and 20 miles plus. Then, of course, we realized what it was: an SR-71A."[5]

The Egyptian SAM missile crews made no attempt at the SR-71A, better known as "The Blackbird." It would have been fruitless. The indigo-blue spy craft moves so fast that even missiles fired at it can only trail behind until their fuel is gone and they fall back to the earth, like arrows short of their mark.

The Blackbird, which began flying in the late 1960s, is the United States' ultimate spy plane—the space-age successor to the old U-2. It is routinely used to overfly Soviet facilities in the flights which keep the CIA, the Defense Intelligence Agency and the White House apprised of Soviet nuclear and non-nuclear developments and deployments.

Flown by pilots from the 9th Strategic Reconnaissance Wing of the U. S. Air Force's Strategic Air Command, the planes kept a constant vigil on developments below throughout the 1973 Middle East war. Among the equipment packed on the plane are cameras so accurate they can record the graffiti stenciled on the side of an individual tank and radiation sensors so acute they can detect nuclear materials hidden underground in concrete bunkers or stowed in the lowest holds of a ship.

The Blackbird swept across the Israeli fields as the hastily assembled atomic weapons were being loaded for launching.

Time magazine reported, "The plane was spotted by Israeli air defenses and two Phantom jets scrambled to intercept it. 'I have it on my radar,' the Israeli pilot radioed. 'It is an American Blackbird.' Back to him came a direct order from a high-ranking Israeli Air Force Commander: 'Down it.' The SR-71A, flying effortlessly at 85,000 feet, easily outclimbed and outdistanced the Israelis and returned to its base with significant readings."[6]

On October 12 the Nixon White House, then totally entangled in the debilitating debacle of the Watergate proceedings, was provided with the hard evidence that Israel had loaded atomic weapons onto both airplanes and Jericho missiles.

That same day Prime Minister Golda Meir dispatched a message to President Nixon indicating that the war situation was "critical." She asked for massive airlifts of American military equipment and arms needed to push back the Arab forces.

Also on that same day the chairmen of Exxon, Mobil, Texaco, and Standard Oil—the consortium which owned the Arabian-American Oil Company—delivered an urgent message to President Nixon. Their message contained a communication from King Faisal of Saudi Arabia to the President. The exact text was never released, but the gist of the message is known: Faisal indicated that oil and the issue of the now partially liberated occupied territories were inseparable. Confirming this, the oil executives told Nixon, "We are convinced of the seriousness of the intentions of the Saudis. Any action of the U. S. Government at this time in terms of increased military aid to Israel will have a critical adverse effect on our relations with moderate Arab [oil] producing countries. Much more than our commercial interests in that area are at hazard. The real stakes are both our economy and our security."

Faisal also sent other messages to Nixon through both his son, Saudi Foreign Minister Prince Saud al Faisal, and his Oil Minister, Sheik Ahmed Zaki Yamani. Their messages to Nixon were the same: a demand that the Nixon administration take "a more even-handed approach to Middle East policy" and a threat of an oil cutoff if America provided new weapons, supplies and supports to aid Israel in halting the Arab military thrusts which were retaking the Muslim lands occupied by Israel in 1967.

The White House was faced with making a choice between two awesome threats: an oil cutoff, which would devastate industrial America, or an atomic war launched by a defeated Israel.

Richard Nixon did not respond to, nor even acknowledge, the messages from King Faisal. That 1973 day in the White House would mark two historic events: the last time a President of the United States would ever totally ignore a communication from the King of Saudi Arabia and the beginning of the largest single airlift of military weapons, supplies and support equipment in the history of America.

By the first light of morning, the skies above the United States were crisscrossed with Air Force planes flying to and from twenty-nine military bases in California, Nevada, Utah, Oklahoma, Missouri, Colorado, Illinois, Ohio, Louisiana, Georgia, North Carolina, Texas, Virginia, New Jersey and Delaware to scoop up tens of thousands of tons of material to be flown to Israel. Landing at Tel Aviv, the U.S. planes disgorged tanks and other armored vehicles, which were driven out across the runways, out across the border of Israel and into the battle zones of the occupied territories where they began firing at Muslim troops with guns still wet with the dew of the American Southwest, machines whose sides were emblazoned with the insignia of the United States. During the next thirty-four days the gargantuan American Starlifter jets and other cargo planes made 569 flights to Israel, off-loading entire armies' worth of supplies and weaponry.

One of the problems encountered by the U. S. Military Airlift Command was the refusal of every country in Africa as well as Britain, Spain, France, Italy, Greece and Turkey to allow either their airspace or ground facilities to be used by planes involved in the operations. West Germany, which initially allowed American ships to be loaded with tanks and equipment stripped from the U.S. military bases in Europe, also asked the United States to cease using its airspace or ground facilities for the Israeli supply operations. In the end only Portugal consented to allow the United States to use ground facilities—the Azore Islands—for a needed refueling and staging stop in the Atlantic.

Incomplete lists available in partially declassified Pentagon documents indicate that the American equipment flown in to be used by the Israelis against the Arabs included "Skyhawk aircraft sections, M-60 main battle tanks, M-48 main battle tanks, self-propelled howitzers, Maverick missiles, Chapparel missiles, Shrike missiles, Walleye missiles, Hawk missiles, Rockeye missile bombs, helicopters, Hawk radar, communications trucks, tents, wheels, fuel trucks, cargo trucks, aircraft engines, fuel tanks, clothing, power supply vans, Vulcan cannon" and thousands of tons of bombs and assorted ammunition. A study later done for the U. S. Congress noted that "Aerial delivery of combat tanks and other outsize cargo by C-5s was an impressive use of airlift capability, and it is impossible to assess the psychological impact of those flights."[7]

Nixon wrote, "With our infusion of new supplies [the Israelis] were able to push all the way to the outskirts of Damascus and were close to encircling the Egyptian forces in the Sinai."[8]

But at the same time the Nixon administration was attempting to offset the Israeli atomic threat with massive supplies of conventional weapons, the Soviet Union was receiving demands from Egypt for the nuclear weapons needed to match and neutralize the political leverage of Israel's arsenal.

Since late 1971 the Soviet Union has been using MIG-25 "Foxbat" reconnaissance planes to monitor Israel's atomic weapons facilities in the Negev. The Foxbat is the Soviet counterpart to the U. S. Blackbird: a high-level, mach-three spy plane capable of outflying both missiles and Phantom jets. Packed with sensors similar to those of the American military, both the Foxbat and the Soviet Cosmos spy satellite detected the deployment of Israel's nuclear weapons during the opening days of the war.

This intelligence was passed on to Egyptian President Anwar Sadat, whose armies were being supplied and advised by the Soviets and whose government had signed a nuclear contingency pact with the Kremlin. This had been the bottom line of that agreement: If Israel should ever introduce atomic weapons into the Middle East conflict, the Soviet Union was pledged to provide Egypt with atomic weapons of equal force.

On October 13, the day after the Nixon administration began the massive rearmament of Israel, crews at a Soviet Navy base at Odessa, on the Black Sea, loaded a Soviet warship with a cargo of atomic weapons. Most of the cargo consisted of atomic warheads to be fitted on the long-range Scud missiles, which were already in Egypt. Accompanied by an armada of Soviet submarines, missile frigates and cruisers, the ship set sail for Alexandria, Egypt.

On October 15, as it was passing through the Bosporous Straits at Istanbul, the ship's atomic cargo was detected and reported by an American Blackbird spy plane flying overhead.

Shortly after that, the ship docked in Alexandria harbor, and Anwar Sadat, like Golda Meir, had atomic weapons at his command.

The White House now faced the possibility that *either* side might launch an atomic strike rather than accept defeat at the hands of a passionately hated adversary.

At the same time on October 15—the third day of a nonstop sky train of American cargo planes stretching across the Atlantic—the Israeli armies began to turn the tide of battle against Muslim forces. By October 16, with their U.S.-supplied Phantoms, Skyhawks, self-propelled artillery, Shrike antiradar missiles, Maverick television-guided missiles, Hawk pulsed-radar homing missiles, Chapparel infrared guided missiles, Walleye laser-guided rocket bombs and Rockeye laser-guided cluster bombs, the Israelis were effectively cutting into the Arab missile thickets. Breaking a corridor through to one section of the Suez Canal, they began pouring M-60 tanks across into Egypt for counterattacks behind the Muslim lines. To the north, in similar actions, the Israelis began the counterattacks which would ultimately retake Mount Hermon and the Golan Heights.

In Kuwait, where the Muslim oil ministers and heads of state had gathered for a strategy session on oil and war, all awaited the decision of King Faisal. Saudi Arabia's massive oil reserves and production capacity were the deciding factors which would make or break any attempted oil embargo against the West.

On October 17, 1973, after the day's reports—on Saudi Arabian and other Muslim troop casualties in the Golan Heights and the continuing American cargo flights into Tel Aviv—Faisal stepped outside the Kuwait conference center to announce his decision. The Sword of Oil would be unsheathed. The jihad for Jerusalem—previously waged as a ground war against Israeli troops in the occupied territories—would now be expanded to be a world war in which money and oil, rather than tanks and missiles, would be the weapons. Faisal indicated that the Muslims would wage jihad against the people whose continued support made the Israeli occupation of Jerusalem and the seized territories possible: the government and the 220 million citizens of the United States. Faisal said the United States would get no oil from the Muslims, whose third holiest city America had tacitly bequeathed to Israel.

Meanwhile in the field, the war continued. It went increasingly badly for the Muslim forces. Nixon wrote, "The Arab countries were fanatically determined to regain the occupied territories from Israel. . . . Any such high hopes were dashed by the Israeli counteroffensive made possible by the American airlift. For the second time in six years, the Arabs lost most of the Soviet equipment that had been sent them."[9]

On October 22 a cease-fire was arranged by the Soviet Union and the United States. Before the day was over, it had broken down.

The Israelis, now on the offensive and beyond the control of the White House, had begun further invasions of Egypt, surrounded the Egyptian Third Army, which had stopped for the cease-fire, and were attempting to seize both the town of Suez and the main Egyptian oil port at Adabiya.

Not only had the Arab armies failed to liberate Jerusalem or the other occupied territories, but now they were about to lose even more territory—including key Egyptian industrial facilities—to the U.S.-armed Israelis.

Egyptian Chief of Staff Major General El Shazly wrote, "By October 24, our military position was about as bad as could be. The Third Army—two reinforced divisions, about 45,000 men and 250 tanks—was completely cut off. They had four days food and water. They were dominated by enemy armor on top of our west bank ramparts. Out of range of our surviving SAM units, they were open prey to enemy air attacks. They could not fight their way west; air strikes had already destroyed most of the Third Army's limited stock of crossing equipment. They could not be relieved: enemy air and armor superiority was such that we could not break through. And after the enemy air force started systematic work, the Third Army soon had 600 casualties needing evacuation. Hopeless."[10]

Anwar Sadat had only one final threat capable of turning back such a total humiliation: his newly acquired arsenal of atomic missiles.

The Middle East once again danced to the very edge of nuclear war.

Soviet Premier Leonid Brezhnev sent a message to the White House. It arrived at 10:45 P.M. on the twenty-fourth. It said, "We strongly urge that we both send forces to enforce the cease-fire, and, if you do not, we may be obliged to consider acting alone."

The Soviet Union put six airborne divisions on alert for immediate airlift to the Middle East. To forestall Egypt's use of nuclear weapons as a last desperate act, the Soviets were prepared to send in their own troops to halt further Israeli penetration of Egypt.

Nixon sent Sadat an urgent message: "I ask you to consider the consequences for your country if the two great nuclear countries were thus to confront each other on your soil."

Sadat's top aide issued a statement charging that "Israel is cheating on the cease-fire and the United States is helping it to cheat."

On the morning of October 25 the Israeli attacks into Egypt continued. Major General El Shazly wrote, "Today, the enemy turned to air power and artillery. Third Army now suffered the latest fruits of the American airlift. Enemy fighter-bombers launched Maverick TV-guided, air-to-surface missiles . . . our losses climbed. Meanwhile, enemy artillery systematically set about reducing the town of Suez."[11]

That day the United States ordered its forces around the world to mobilize for nuclear war. The action was taken so quickly that not even America's closest allies were informed.

European leaders, for instance, awoke on October 25 to be informed by dumbfounded aides that the American bases on their soil had invoked wartime security measures during the night and were now raising their missile launchers into firing position.

Some 2.2 million American military personnel were mobilized. At the Strategic Air Command Headquarters underground city near Bellevue, Nebraska, the SAC atomic warfare battle staff was assembled. Arriving officers were tersely informed, "This is not a drill." On the airfields across America, and in American bases around the world, B-52s with armed atomic weapons in place were wheeled into take-off position with their crews in position inside.

At Fort Bragg 12,500 paratroopers of the 82nd Airborne Division prepared for airlift into the Middle East, as did the Army's 3,500-man "quick reaction" team in West Germany. A Marine battal-

ion of 1,800 men was flown into the Sixth Fleet in the Mediterranean as additional U.S. aircraft carriers and submarines converged
on the area.

By October 26, under the enormous international political pressure created by the nuclear emergency, the Israeli advances into
Egypt stopped. A 7,000-man United Nations peace-keeping force
arrived to separate the combatants, and a tense, but solid, cease-fire
finally took effect.

Israel emerged as the clear military victor. The Arabs had not liberated Jerusalem or even held on to any substantial part of the occupied territories. The Muslim armies were in tatters. Israel had
regained the whole of the Sinai and now controlled territory thirty
miles deep inside Egypt proper.

The nuclear stalemate had abated. Israel retrieved its atomic
weapons from the field and returned them to the Negev arsenal site,
where they were partially disassembled and stored again.

The Soviet Union retrieved all atomic weapons it had provided to
Egypt and removed them from the country, leaving the nation once
again a conventional military power.

Israel's introduction of atomic weapons into the Middle East
conflict forever altered the participants' future combat options. It
was no longer possible for Muslim leaders to think in terms of
rebuilding their militaries for another full-scale conventional war
against Israel. Future campaigns which might succeed in recapturing
Jerusalem might also succeed in achieving the atomic incineration of
all surrounding Islamic population centers.

And the Israeli nuclear monopoly in the Middle East had also altered the context of that country's relations with its Western allies,
particularly the United States. As a new atomic superpower whose
leaders had already demonstrated a willingness to accept nuclear
suicide rather than military defeat or compromise on Jerusalem, Israel could neither be easily manipulated nor ignored.

On the surface in that first week of November 1973 it appeared
that the Arab world had lost it all.

But on November 14, the same day the United States made its last
airlift delivery of weapons and heavy supplies to Israel, the nature of
that regional conflict took yet another wild turn.

That same day American naval commanders cruising their ships
through the Indian Ocean and South Pacific were astounded to find

that the refineries in southern Asia would not sell them the fuel oil they required to continue their normal operations. And similar events were occurring on all continents around the world.

The world's pumps had slowed and then stopped. The pipelines had emptied and echoed. Tankers en route were ordered to circle at sea. Refineries' cracking towers went cold. Deep-water ports went vacant. Deliveries of oil from the Middle East into the Western petroleum distribution system were first reduced and then squeezed off to a trickle.

It had taken nearly four weeks for the oil embargo declared by King Faisal at the height of the war to take effect along the far-flung petroleum supply grids. But by early November, even as the media in the West was heralding the end of one Middle Eastern war, another one was beginning.

In the United States factories were silent, skylines were black, schools were empty and stores were closed. There were hours-long waits at available gas stations that quickly deteriorated into street-corner fistfights, shoot-outs and riots. Turnpikes went barren as truckers created blockades, hundreds of rigs deep, to protest their inability to obtain fuel. Commuters left their cars and switched to public transportation systems—which quickly broke down for lack of adequate equipment, maintenance or fuel. Airlines were grounded, assembly lines silent, the stock market plummeted, the cost of living soared, the economic indicators registered earthquake levels of disruptions and dislocation. The blinking, flashing, clanking, whooshing, neon wonder of machineAmerica spasmed to a halt in what became the single most traumatic national experience since World War II.

The global petro-jihad—planned by the House of Saud for more than a decade—had begun.

By harnessing gargantuan amounts of money and oil, King Faisal had fashioned a new sort of weapon as politically potent as that which the Israelis had fashioned by harnessing uranium.

The Muslim-Israeli war for Jerusalem, which had previously been an isolated conflict confined to the deserts of the Middle East, had suddenly moved onto the streets of Western cities. Faisal's Holy War would reach out to become a force dramatically affecting every facet of daily life in America. At the same time it drastically altered the international political position of Israel.

But that was only the beginning.

Even as the lights were dimming across the United States and Muslim dead were still being retrieved from the battle zones of the occupied territories, Saudi Arabia, Libya and Iraq were dispatching emissaries on top-secret missions to Paris. There Iraq would open discussions with the French military and government. The Saudis and Libyans would meet with officials from Pakistan.

Those Paris meetings would remain a closely guarded secret for more than six years. And those sessions witnessed some of the most important discussions and decisions of modern times, leading directly to the agreements which launched two separate atomic bomb-development projects involving four Muslim nations.

The Arabs, who were about to reach out to take control of the world's petroleum, industrial and financial networks in the 1970s, were also reaching out with equal determination toward atomic weapons parity with Israel.

One hundred years after it had begun with sticks and swords, the battle for Jerusalem was on the verge of going completely nuclear. By 1982 this was the terrifying prospect evolving for America and the West: The next full-scale war between Muslims and Israelis may not only disrupt our daily world but destroy it.

4

RISE OF THE SWORD

In 1880 Abdul-Aziz ibn Saud, founder of the modern Arab dynasty which would eventually harness the global petroleum supply system as the ultimate weapon against Israel, was born in a land whose physical realities are beyond the imagination of most Americans.

It was a place of indescribable desolation whose primary sights were of endless horizons, gravel gullies and solitary palm silhouettes. It was a place whose primary sounds were those of hoofs clopping hurriedly over sharp rock, tattered tent felt fluttering in the night's wind and the wet-chunk noise made as a clear-swung blade cut hard into living neck bone.

Before he was eleven years old, Abdul-Aziz ibn Saud—his name meant Servant of the Mighty of the House of Saud—had hacked another human to death, taking part in a clan massacre of a rival tribe's leaders. Those rival leaders had originally invited the Saud tribe to a feast at which they intended to kill all its male members. But the Saudis struck first, allowing coffee to be served, then leaping upon their hosts in a throat-slitting, skull-splitting melee.

The decade of Ibn Saud's birth was one of great turmoil around the world. John Rockefeller was consolidating his oil-control apparatus in an America suddenly burst upward in steam engines and steel beams. Czar Nicholas II was leading Russia's armies and police squads in new waves of anti-Semitic thuggery as that nation convulsed toward collapse. European petro-baron Edmond Rothschild had placed his oil fortunes behind the "Zionist movement"—a new colonial movement seeking to establish European control around Zion Hill in Palestine. And, at this same time, Ibn Saud was a small boy packed into a leather pouch, bouncing wildly about the sweat-smeared haunches of a galloping camel. Although the Saud clan had defeated one rival tribe, another had invaded and seized the Saudi oasis headquarters—a collection of melon patches and mud huts called Riyadh.

That ignominious retreat into exile—first into the open desert and then to the squalid waterfront slums of neighboring Kuwait—ended an era for the House of Saud, which had been the dominant tribe in the northeastern portion of the Arabian Peninsula for 150 years. In 1744 that dynasty began when a Bedouin chief, Muhammad ibn Saud, joined with a wandering religious scholar, Muhammad ibn Abd al-Wahhab and began a jihad in the name of Wahhabi Islam, which conquered large tracts of territory. Conquest, at that time, largely involved small but vicious sword-and-dagger battles for control of the few oasis sites around which all life—and power—was centered in Arabia.

From one of those sites—Riyadh—the House of Saud came to rule throughout the 1800s. By the end of that century they had lost several battles, most of their prestige and most of their followers and were driven into exile. Huddled in shame, hunger and rags, the Sauds remained in Kuwait for a decade while young Ibn Saud grew to manhood.

Ibn Saud grew to be, physically, an extraordinarily large man, towering over six feet in a region where males normally averaged about five and a half feet. This was no small asset in a society of swordsmen, where the physical advantage which turned battles and toppled kingdoms was often an extra stretch of arm no longer than the width of a throat vein.

At age twenty-one Ibn Saud gathered together forty remaining clan members and set out on four dozen scraggly camels back toward Riyadh to stage a surprise attack on the walled settlement. Before the sun had cleared the horizon on the morning of the attack, Ibn Saud had killed the rival tribal leader, taken control of Riyadh and sent couriers out to contact and recruit booty-seeking warriors from surrounding tribal encampments.

Couriers were also sent to retrieve the rest of the Saud family from Kuwait, and, in a ceremony at Riyadh, Ibn Saud's elderly father passed over authority and possession of the clan's most prized possession—the sword of their ancestor and founder of the Wahhabi sect of Islam.

So began the reign of the pauper-bandit-turned-king, who, with a mix of discipline, cunning, ruthlessness and religious fanatacism, would lead a camel-mounted jihad through thirty years of blood-spattered campaigns in which he would eliminate all rivals and extend his theocratic rule across nearly the whole of the Arabian Peninsula. It would soon become the land where "no camel was mounted, no opinion voiced" without the approval of Abdul-Aziz ibn Saud.

In those first years, as warrior encampments encircled the mud huts at Riyadh and Ibn Saud thrust out in nearly continuous warfare in all directions, he also began to sire the first of more than forty children he would have. As was traditional, the males would be given names after previous leaders of the Saud dynasty. The third son born within these crude pack fortifications would be called what was both the name of an ancestor and the word for the instrument of God: The Sword. This third male's title would be The Sword, Son of the Servant of the Mighty of the House of Saud.

Faisal, Ibn Abdul-Aziz al Saud, would transform the late twentieth century.

King Faisal, the man who overturned the existing world order in 1973, began his education at age eight as the prince of an Islamic warrior sect.

Turned over to his mother's father—a scholar of the Koran—he began the regimen of training traditional for a Bedouin boy in his position. He was tutored by rote and by age ten had memorized the Koran.

Faisal was eleven years old in 1917 when his father's court in

Riyadh began buzzing with rumors and consternation over news of the Balfour Declaration, an agreement between two British noblemen about the manner in which the Muslim lands at the eastern end of the Mediterranean would be sectioned up among European interests after the all-but-finished World War I. The letter of agreement was exchanged between the about-to-retire patriarch of the Victorian colonial regime, Arthur Balfour, and Lionel Walter Rothschild, a private zoologist, museum keeper, collector of rare beetles and head of the London branch of Europe's richest family. The Rothschild family had previously begun establishing private settlements in Asia. The document expressed the London colonial government's sympathy for a plan to expand those embattled Rothschild settlements in Palestine into an officially sanctioned British colony to be peopled by several million Russian refugees.

Faisal was twelve when he began warrior training with stallion, edged steel and musket. That same year British forces swept into Palestine as the world war ended. Major James Rothschild, son of oil magnate Edmond Rothschild, accompanied the British command staff as it took over the region. Rothschild was appointed President for Life of the Jewish Colonial Association, overseeing the European settlement-building programs. Also arriving with the British forces was the 38th Battalion of the Royal Fusiliers, a British legion hastily formed at the close of the war and comprised of Jewish volunteers from Europe. Appointed as first British High Commissioner of the Palestine Colony was Herbert Samuel—son of a prominent London banking family, member of the British cabinet and the leading Jewish lobbyist promoting the establishment of a beachhead colony for expanding British interests in the Middle East oil regions.

When Faisal was thirteen he took his first trip abroad, to Europe, where he passed through Versailles as the final details of the World War I peace treaty and resulting colonial realignments were being negotiated. There thick-whiskered continental gentlemen gathered in gilded archways beneath tapestries of Napoleon the Conqueror and divided up the land and populations of Asia and Africa among themselves as casually as they might have dissected a round of cheese.

Faisal was fourteen when Muslim leaders reported to England's Prime Minister, Lloyd George, that they would accept the European peace decrees but had one absolute condition: that the three holy cities of Islam—Mecca, Medina and Jerusalem—would remain under Muslim administration and the direct purview of the Keeper of the Holy Cities.

In 1922, at age sixteen, Faisal rode into battle for the first time. His father, Ibn Saud, took him into a skirmish in the Red Sea highlands as the Saud clan continued its fight against a rival clan then in control of the western end of the Arabian Peninsula—including the cities of Mecca and Medina.

When he was eighteen years old and a novice lieutenant, marching his father's Al Jihad Camel Corps as it moved for the *coup de grâce* that was to provide the capstone of the Saud empire, the Red Sea coastal provinces, Faisal was abruptly put in charge of 40,000 Bedouin warriors and instructed by his father to die or take Mecca. Employing a tactic which would later return to haunt the dynasty, Faisal infiltrated the Holy City with corps of riflemen disguised as pilgrims, hiding their weapons beneath their robes. Inside the Sacred Mosque, they unsheathed their swords, brandished their guns and took over the center of the ancient Islamic world in the name of Wahhabi Islam and the House of Saud.

In 1925, at nineteen years of age, Faisal was left in charge of administering Mecca and the Red Sea provinces. He established the office in which he would work the rest of his life in a walled villa compound in Jedda. Jedda is a port city on the Red Sea a short distance from Mecca and was the kingdom's primary point of contact with the outside world. There, in rooms airy with the odors of sea salt, Faisal settled in as the third most powerful person in the realm, behind the King, and his other brother, Saud, the crown prince. Mecca became the project that drew most of Faisal's attentions.

His villa was turned into a seminar site for Islamic scholars with whom Faisal began studying and planning. Eventually, his self-designed educational programs would be expanded to include intense studies of the Western world and, in particular, Western industrial and government systems of organization. Faisal had still been a teen-ager when he took Mecca—then a crumbling, bandit-ridden backwater of debris that had once been the capital of an empire flung across half the world. Fifty years later, when he died, he left behind one of the most modern cities in Asia, each year hosting the largest gathering of human beings on earth.

From those early years Faisal was a man caught between the medieval society into which he had been born and the modern machine age in which he would mature and rule. He was never able completely to step into or out of those disparate worlds. He was, for instance, determined to preserve the texture and exterior trappings of ancient Islam and to insulate his country from the cultural influences of Westernization, yet he was the man responsible for creating the programs under which tens of thousands of Saudis—including his own sons—were schooled in places such as Oxfordshire, England, Boston, Princeton and Berkeley. Ironically, it was one of these returning foreign-trained students who eventually killed Faisal.

Faisal was an avid world traveler who took great pains to master the intricacies of European imperial etiquette, and moved with cosmopolitan graciousness and ease through the capitals of the Continent. He also pursued a lifelong avocation as a connoisseur of classical poetry—both Arabic and European—and became fluent in both English and French. Fond of quoting George Bernard Shaw in private conversations, he also transcribed the oral verse he collected from Bedouin storytellers. Rigorously maintaining his public image as an oriental potentate, he deigned to communicate with Europeans only through his royal interpreter, despite the fact that he understood every word spoken by Frenchmen, Englishmen and Americans.

He was also one of the kingdom's leading adherents of falconry, the Bedouin sport of hunting with trained killer birds. Often, Faisal rode out on one of his stallions for such hunts in the desert. There a trained falcon loosed from a forearm perch would soar aloft and, suddenly, like a stone, drop from the air and rip the throat from a wild gazelle passing at full gallop.

After studying it to conclude that it violated no Islamic principles, Faisal developed an interest in the alien sport of soccer. He became one of its primary patrons as teams were established throughout the kingdom in later years.

Faisal was twenty-three in 1929 when Jerusalem erupted in riots and warfare between native Muslims and European colonists. The controversy was originally sparked over questions of control of the ruins which are both the foundations of the destroyed Jewish Temple of biblical times and the base of two of Islam's oldest shrines— the Dome of the Rock and Al Aqsa Mosque. Muslim mobs, whipped into a frenzy during nationalistic rallies, ran a butcherous rampage through the European settlements, hacking infant children in half and leaving European hut clusters tangled with mutilated bodies and flaming rubble. British occupational troops declared martial law as Muslims began a six-month strike in protest of the expanding European presence. The House of Saud provided what would become a continuous stream of moral, monetary and military support to the revolt against the Europeans in Palestine.

In 1932, when the polyglot of confederated tribal zones under the rule of Ibn Saud were officially united as the modern state of Saudi Arabia, Faisal was named the country's Foreign Minister. He set off on a tour of Western capitals for diplomatic formalities, which included intensive lobbying for the end of the European occupation of Palestine.

The next year Faisal was on hand with his father to greet the engineers of Standard Oil of America who were arriving in Saudi Arabia to pay gold coin for the privilege of poking holes in the sand and salt crust along the Saudi shore of the Persian Gulf.

In 1934 Faisal, who had become the most popular commander of the Al Jihad Camel Corps and its most acclaimed marksman, undertook his most controversial military campaign—a foray along a disputed border zone with Yemen, south of Mecca. Ibn Saud ordered Faisal to secure a disputed section and remain in place as negotiations on the problem continued with leaders of the neighboring sheikdom. Ignoring his father's orders, and rallying his men, Faisal led an invasion force, sweeping through the border zone and into Yemen. After rolling easily over the poorly organized defenders, he was on the verge of seizing the capital and claiming the territory for the House of Saud when his campaign abruptly halted. Faisal had suddenly been handed a terse message from Ibn Saud. The message said that if Faisal did not immediately return to the border zone, he would be decapitated by the royal executioner upon his return to Riyadh. Faisal abandoned his invasion.

A short while later he was walking with his father in the courtyard of the Sacred Mosque in Mecca when three dagger-wielding assassins leaped from the crowd in an attempt to kill Ibn Saud. Faisal hugged his own body around that of his father, providing his own back to the attackers and suffering severe knife wounds of the shoulders and torso before the would-be killers were subdued and shot to death by the royal guards.

In 1937 Faisal was thirty-one when the British Peel Commission concluded—in the wake of the continuous and widespread bloodshed in and around Jerusalem—that the original British plans to sponsor a mixed community of European colonists and native Muslims in Palestine was "not workable."

Faisal was thirty-three when Standard Oil crews from California struck major oil deposits and began pumping them in small but steady commercial quantities that provided the kingdom with a quantum leap in income. The year was 1939.

It was the same year that riots and full-scale Arab revolt—supported by the House of Saud's pledge of troops and whatever arms could be had—erupted throughout Palestine, turning Jerusalem into a war zone in which British occupational forces, Jewish European guerrilla units and Muslims massacred each other in a three-way, all-out struggle for control of the territory.

It was the same year that Faisal, as leader of an Arab summit conference in Cairo, issued a demand in the name of all Islamic peoples of the Middle East for Britain to stop the tidal flow of European colonists then being shipped by the thousands into Palestine. He also demanded that Palestine be made into a majority-rule, independent state inhabited by Arabs and only those Europeans already present.

Later, after the war, as events moved toward a continuing European presence in the Middle East, Faisal's Islamic nationalism grew more and more fervent. But his determination to stop the immigration couldn't stop the formation of the State of Israel. Indeed, as the Jewish presence became more entrenched, Faisal's desire for retribution became more urgent.

5

ROOTS OF CONFLICT: OIL, ISLAM AND ZIONISM

In 1947 a Bedouin rider coming off an inner-desert trek and seeking the quiet solace of the Persian Gulf shoreline near Dhahran would have been jolted by the sudden apparition which appeared beyond the last sand dune. Peering through the rippling heat waves and trying to hold his animal steady, this is what he would have seen: solitary hawks soaring in great arcs toward the far waterline; sooty fires and resting camels and clusters of black wool tents; ancient dhows beached and turned sideways, like drying fish; and suddenly, wildly incongruously, a stark-white, Levittown-like development of split-level homes with swimming pools, carports and barbecue pits laid down inside a huge rectangle of metal fence.

This was the American settlement built by the U.S. oil companies in conjunction with the U. S. Army Corps of Engineers to house what had become, overnight, a large self-contained city of American workers and oil executives. It sat like some odd piece of suburbia, lifted intact—complete with hairdressers, grocery shops and hamburger stands—to the barren surface of an alien, desert planet.

This American installation received almost no publicity back in the United States at the time. There were so many more newsworthy things happening in those postwar years. Yet it was here that the real future of America was being determined. Here between the Bedouins and the barbecue pits and the killer hawks soaring toward the horizon.

Shortly after America's entry into World War II, the War Department had quickly established military missions in the two Middle Eastern countries judged to be crucial to the Allied war effort: Iran and Saudi Arabia. Iran's older and more-developed oil fields were critically important as the primary source of fuel for the British Army and Navy, then locked in battle with the Nazi desert corps in northern Africa.

In Saudi Arabia the newly discovered oil fields were a potentially rich target for the Nazi desert armies. Although the Saudi fields had been producing for only three years, they quickly became extremely important for supplying the Allied fleets engaged in fighting throughout the Pacific theater.

The U. S. Army Corps of Engineers had built the largest airport in the world at Dhahran in Saudi Arabia to serve the sprawling new construction zones of wells, pipelines, refineries and tanker wharves. President Roosevelt visited Saudi King Ibn Saud during the war and presented him with the gift of an airplane.

The King also asked for, and received, a replica of Roosevelt's wheelchair. Chairs themselves were something of a novelty in the feudal desert kingdom, which was devoid of furniture. Chairs with wheels were perceived as status symbols, and Ibn Saud, possessor of the only wheeled chair in the kingdom, frequently caromed up and down the paved airstrip, his robes flowing wildly in the wind behind him.

In less than four years' time, the deserts of Ibn Saud had moved from the back of beyond to center stage in the plans for the future of the United States. Both the Pentagon and the American oil conglomerates had launched massive new projects which, in effect, yanked the mother root of the petroleum supply grid out of the North American continent and replanted it at the western end of the Persian Gulf. There they had found oil which was as endless in quantity as it was cheap in extraction.

These moves were cause for a substantial bit of controversy. For one thing, many government officials called for the creation of a new national oil company which would put the control of petroleum supply directly in the hands of Congress and the White House. Interior Department Secretary Harold Ickes greeted President Truman when he took office on the death of President Roosevelt with strong warnings about the dangers of moving the primary oil supply lines into the Middle East. Ickes' point was this: The Western world was about to embark on a crash program for rebuilding three continents with petroleum-intensive industrial societies. If the taproot of the world's oil production apparatus was to be placed in the middle of Arabia and kept beyond the direct administrative control of the U. S. Government, then obviously that taproot—and the entire civilization which depended on it—was vulnerable to disruption by Arabians.

The Truman administration ignored its own voluminously documented evidence of pervasive corruption throughout the oil industry during the war, refused to consider tighter government controls on oil companies as requested by the Joint Chiefs of Staff and, working through the State Department, aggressively encouraged and assisted U.S. oil companies as they set up a global oil distribution monopoly centered in Saudi Arabia, protected by the U. S. Army, pampered by the U. S. Congress, funded by the U.S. taxpayers but ultimately beyond the control of the White House.

During the first weeks of 1947, and as his campaign for re-election was getting into full swing, Harry S. Truman also opened another campaign aimed at gaining the friendship and loyalty of the Islamic countries whose oil deposits he had declared vital to the security of the United States.

At Truman's personal invitation, Ibn Saud's son and immediate heir to the throne, Crown Prince Saud, arrived in America for an extended tour. The Prince's first stop on his official state visit was at the White House, where he presented the President with a jeweled sword and a letter from the King. In a series of letters and communications during this period, King Ibn Saud was the spokesman for the Arab League and repeatedly called on Truman to drop his support for proposals to allow further immigration by European refugees to Palestine. The House of Saud, simultaneously, was continuing its support in the form of money and arms to the Muslim militia, then clashing with the militia of the European refugee community and the occupational British Army in Palestine.

Crown Prince Saud, before flying off in Truman's personal airplane—"The Sacred Cow"—was taken on a whirlwind tour which included a stop at the Empire State Building. There the Prince, who had never seen a skyscraper before, was photographed by newsmen as he clapped his hands in childlike glee on the observation deck of the building.

Avoiding publicity and photographers and remaining a low-profile personality handling the actual nuts and bolts of the relations between Washington and Saudi Arabia was Saud's brother, Prince Faisal. Faisal, forty-one, was Foreign Minister of Saudi Arabia as well as its representative to the United Nations. He had spent long periods traveling through America, was particularly interested in visiting farms and factories for in-depth discussion about the arcane subjects of machinery and agriculture and served as the primary representative between his father's court and the White House.

Dean Acheson, Acting Secretary of State at the time and present at meetings between Faisal and Truman, wrote that Faisal, "striking in white burnoose and golden circlet, which heightened his swarthy complexion, with black, pointed beard and moustache topped by a thin hooked nose and piercing dark eyes, gave a sinister impression, relieved from time to time by a shy smile. . . . As he talked with President Truman, it seemed to me that their minds crossed but did not meet. [Faisal] was concerned with conditions in the Near East, the President with the conditions of displaced Jews in Europe. . . . [Faisal] impressed me as a man who could be an implacable enemy and who should be taken very seriously."[1]

As Truman was beginning his campaign in the 1947 presidential primaries, in which he was a hopeless underdog attempting to form a new political coalition of minority ethnic groups, the World Zionist Organization and the Jewish American lobby mounted a desperate, now-or-never push calling for the White House to use its postwar powers to create a new sovereign nation for Jewish Europeans in Palestine, where Europeans and native Muslims had been fighting each other since the turn of the century.

By the beginning of 1947 all of Palestine was a riot of mayhem and murder. Muslim militia turned mosque minarets into deadly sniper's nests and manned the fortlike walls of Jerusalem and other cities. Meanwhile marauding Muslim bands attacked British truck transports and European refugee strongholds.

Jewish European bomb squads—particularly those under the personal direction of terrorist leader Menachem Begin—became notorious in their ability to engineer innovative killing tools from the most mundane materials. One of Begin's groups' routine devices was the large metal milk can. Filled with explosives, these were often placed in the middle of crowded bazaars. Their detonation cut through the crowds of Muslim women and children like a buzz saw of shrapnel, scattering severed legs and upper torsos here and there about the stones. One of their most famous weapons—they sent diagrams and photographs of it to newspapers after it exploded—was a fifty-gallon oil-barrel bomb fitted with special wheels and launched from a moving truck into the heavily fortified British police headquarters in Haifa. The device, designed to "grab" the first wall it struck, was dropped over the high fence, rolled down the hill, locked itself onto the front of the building and exploded. Ten persons were killed and fifty-four injured, including both soldiers and cafe patrons next door.

Meanwhile, in 1947, in a drafty, cavernous rink temporarily serving as headquarters of the United Nations in New York, the U. S. Special Commission on Palestine submitted its final report to the General Assembly. The commission noted that "The claims to Palestine of the Arabs and Jews . . . are irreconcilable. . . . The basic conflict in Palestine is a clash between two intense nationalisms. . . . Jewish immigration is the central issue in Palestine today and is the one factor, above all others, that rules out the necessary cooperation between the Arab and Jewish communities in a single state."

In Palestine, Muslims declared "Zionists must not have an inch of this country" as their terrorist teams continued assassinations in the streets and bombed the U. S. Consulate in Jerusalem to protest American backing of the Zionist movement at the UN proceedings.

Jewish Europeans declared a step-up of their terrorist attacks aimed at "nullifying the local Arab factor" and also increased their street-corner assassinations and bombings of British police and military installations.

In the White House, Harry Truman—rated by the Gallup Poll a bare 51 to 49 percent favorite in the presidential race against New York Governor Thomas E. Dewey—watched as Henry Wallace took the podium in Detroit to announce the opening of a third-party candidacy that would split the Democratic Party and destroy Truman's hair's breadth edge against Dewey. Both Dewey and Wallace would run campaigns aimed at winning the critical nod of the Jewish American urban electorate with repeated charges that Truman did not wholeheartedly support the Zionist side of the Palestine struggle. Wallace, who left for a tour of Jerusalem shortly after announcing his third-party candidacy, lambasted Truman for his "sellout" of Zionist interests to Arab oil interests.

This at the same time Truman was under siege from the new Defense Department, the State Department and the oil lobby for his public statements of support for a Jewish state in Palestine. Defense, State and the oil companies charged that Truman's pro-Zionist position was antagonizing the Muslim states whose cooperation was necessary to build the trans-Arabian pipeline and the foreign-based oil-supply system—which the White House had just approved.

In November 1947, at Lake Success on Long Island, the question of the ultimate control of Palestine was put to a final vote before the fifty-seven nations which then comprised the United Nations. The Truman administration turned the full political heat of its international powers to the task of swaying the vote in favor of the Zionist cause.

In addition the Zionist lobby pulled out all stops in the final drive to line up the needed number of votes in the General Assembly. Truman's presidential papers of the period document what is described as "high pressure being exerted by Jewish Agencies. There have been indications of bribes and threats by these groups. In the case of Liberia, certain groups have informed the Liberian delegation that if they do not go along, the [U.S. economic aid] pact with Liberia will be cancelled."[2]

Harvard historian Dr. J. Bowyer Bell records, "At five in the afternoon, with speeches still to come, the General Assembly decided to recess until Friday, because Thursday was Thanksgiving. For forty-eight hours, with the help of the Americans and their other friends, the Zionists shored up their position. Antonio Vieuz of Haiti, who had spoken eloquently against partition, received instructions to vote for it. Pressure was turned on Liberia and Greece. General Carlos Romulo of the Philippines suddenly departed on an Atlantic voyage, and his replacement agreed to abide by the wishes of Ambassador Elizalde in Washington and vote yes. Belgium, the Netherlands and New Zealand, instead of abstaining, reluctantly agreed to vote yes. Paraguay finally received instructions to vote yes. The new revolutionary regime in Thailand removed its old ambassador. Thailand did not vote. France remained uncertain. Ambassador Alexandre Parodi on Friday requested a further delay of twenty-four hours. Apparently Paris wanted to show her Islamic colonies that every avenue was being explored, but this gave no clue to the ultimate intentions of France. Washington had indicated further aid might depend on her vote."

The vote that evening was 33 in favor of a Jewish European state, 13 opposed and 10 abstentions, and one absent. The Zionists, who needed a two-thirds vote won by a single vote margin. Palestine would be split in half. Half would be given to the Europeans. The other half would be given to the native inhabitants.

As the news of the Zionist victory flashed across America and around the world via radio, there was wild rejoicing in the streets of New York. In Tel Aviv they danced the hora on rooftops. In the displaced persons camps throughout Europe, Jews with numbers tattooed on their forearms knelt on the ground and wept.

At the New York UN site, the overwhelmingly Jewish American crowd of spectators erupted in jubilant thunder as flash bulbs popped and newspaper reporters scribbled in their pads and radio announcers squawked details of the victorious pandemonium into the metal halos of their microphones.

In the middle of all this, in one of the hardly noticed details of the day, six Muslim delegations—Saudi Arabia, Egypt, Iraq, Yemen, Syria and Lebanon—rose from their seats and walked out of the proceedings. Leading this action was a six-foot-tall, sharp-faced man whose striking black robes and gold-braided white burnoose stood out against the crowd. This was Faisal Ibn Abdul-Aziz al Saud, the most vociferous opponent of the proposal of a European state in Muslim Palestine.

Faisal moved quickly away from the shouting, chanting, boisterous crowds thronging the hall and, through an interpreter, issued a terse, two-sentence reaction to the vote. It was couched in the polite formalities of diplomatic jargon, but its message was quite short and simple.

Faisal said that one day he would get even.

6

KING OF OIL: KEEPER
OF THE HOLY CITIES

The last day of the 1964 presidential campaign
ended with each candidate in his home state. Lyndon Johnson's last appearance was a hand-pump-
ing, stetson-waving celebration on the steps of the
capitol in Austin, Texas, where he proclaimed,
"The path of progress stretches in front of us."

Barry Goldwater's last appearance was in the
dusty streets of a tiny town overlooking the Grand
Canyon and a Navaho Indian reservation in Arizona,
where he charged that "American prestige has been
sinking slowly out of sight."

On that same day in 1964—half a world away
and far beyond the glare of the klieg lights, the whir
of the tape recorders and the excited chatter of the
teletype—another event was occurring which would
ultimately be as significant to Americans as the
year's presidential election. In the ancient mud-
walled oasis town of Riyadh—recently gone grand
with paved roads and furniture and chandeliers and
electricity—the House of Saud was ending a traumatic two-year power struggle and installing a new
king. King Saud, the portly, profligate son of Ibn
Saud, who had ruled since the patriarch's death in
1953, had been deposed. Taking over as new King

of Saudi Arabia, controller of the largest oil reserves on earth and Keeper of the Holy Cities of Islam, was the acerbic, sharp-featured, fifty-seven-year-old Faisal Ibn Abdul-Aziz al Saud.

Since 1962, incredibly, Saudi Arabia—a place where wealth oozed out of the ground—had been on the brink of bankruptcy. Ibn Saud—the Wahhabi Islamic monarch who had risen to power on his pledge to purge the deserts of sinful luxury and ostentation—had left behind a country awash in money but totally devoid of a system for managing that vast wealth. There was no financial system save for the practice of keeping trunks and crates of gold bars hidden beneath the bed or buried in the sand. There was no government other than the network of kinsmen who served the King.

After Ibn Saud's death in 1953, his eldest son, Saud, ascended to the throne and, during the nine years of his rule, became the arch-stereotype of a bloat-faced, lamb-dainty, silk-wrapped, wild-spending oil sheikh. The kingdom's quickening inflows of money were apportioned out to court members as fast as they were accumulated. Saud isolated himself behind a royal army whose primary purpose was to protect the King from his subjects. He had a taste for palaces of delicately veined marble, knickknacks of rare ivory and the finest jade, sword hilts encrusted with diamonds and Cadillacs from America on which the traditional chrome trim was replaced with solid gold.

A gadabout traveler, Saud gloried in nibbling Parisian delicacies, lolling about on satin pillows and spewing bagsful of golden coin and jewelry to the doormen, elevator operators, maids and passersby in the ultraposh European hotels he frequented for relief from the Arabian heat. He was also famed for the hordes of women and young girls he collected from across the kingdom for the entertainment of himself and his extensive royal entourage. One of the palaces he built in Riyadh had the second-largest air-conditioning plant on earth, topped in size only by the installation that cools the Pentagon in Washington.

By the opening years of the 1960s the court's spending sprees had outstripped the income of the kingdom from its oil royalties. Undaunted, Saud took increasingly larger loans from Western financial consortiums and oil companies to support his life-style. For the first time Saudi Arabia—which had avoided the Western economic penetration and domination suffered by neighboring Muslim states for more than a century—began mortgaging its future to pay for its gold-plated daily operating expenses.

King Saud came under increasing pressure from a faction within the House of Saud that wanted Saud's brother, Faisal, to take over the throne. Faisal's life-style and outlook provided a sharp contrast to those of his older brother. His personal habits were as decorous as those of a Jesuit; his approach to government and fiscal matters as abstemious as a Boston Brahmin. And sexually, Faisal was notorious as the single most conspicuous case of royal monogamy in the kingdom's modern history.

As Foreign Minister during the postwar years, Faisal had been the kingdom's connection to the outside world. When his brother Saud had become King, Faisal had taken over much of the country's loosely knit tribal administrative apparatus.

For more than fifteen years Faisal had brought an endless stream of American and European engineers, architects, urban planners and other consultants through his Jedda office where he was formulating an organizational master plan that called for the transformation of a Bedouin tribal state into a modern industrial nation. He envisioned the country taking control of its own oil reserves from foreign oil firms and creating a government system patterned along the lines of Western bureaucratic institutions, which he had been studying since the 1940s.

Faisal also envisioned his country physically isolated from Western cultural intrusions and socially and legally organized around strict Islamic forms. For instance, Faisal was responsible for the decrees which continued to make women's veils and segregation in public places mandatory. On the other hand, in 1960 he brought in army troops to disperse the fundamentalist demonstrations aimed at halting the opening of his new national system of modern, Western-style schools for girls.

By 1962 Faisal's programs—as well as the rest of the kingdom's government operations—faced imminent collapse as the court's money ran out and King Saud finanaced his binges by taking loans against future oil earnings.

The council of religious and family elders, who by tradition invest the occupant of the throne with his ultimate authority, moved to strip Saud of many of his powers. He remained King in title, but lost most of the control of court finances and daily operational matters.

Two years later—in 1964—the council deposed Saud, providing him with a $20-million-a-year pension to ease the pain of his forced exile to Europe, and granted Faisal full powers and title of King.

The draconian reform measures taken by Faisal—disruptive and highly controversial within the tribal circles of the House of Saud—revolutionized the kingdom. Faisal ruthlessly cut off the tidal outflow of the kingdom's money and overturned the methods previously used by the ruling court to collect and disperse oil revenues. He quickly amassed the reserves needed to pay his brother's Western debts and removed control of oil wealth from individual family members, institutionalizing new controls in a new group of government fiscal ministries. Overseeing all matters of finance throughout the court and the country was the new Saudi Arabian Monetary Agency—the government's central bank. A new Royal Planning Commission took over the large-scale organizing functions which had previously been headquartered in the patio room of Faisal's villa.

Faisal introduced the general population of Saudi Arabia to television, telephones, printing presses, air conditioning and frozen foods. He also made the Sharia—the ultrastrict code of classical Islamic precepts—the nation's official constitution.

He decreed a justice system which maintained the traditionally harsh punishments for crimes against the Faith, banned all political parties or group activities except those approved and controlled by the monarchy and closed the nation's borders, social institutions, fiscal systems and blossoming government departments to outsiders.

Along with this drastic reorganization inside Saudi Arabia, Faisal simultaneously turned his attentions to four other areas which had been the focus of his planning seminars and Islamic conferences throughout the 1950s:

—The revivification of the Pope-like aura of spiritual authority and physical vitality which had, in the eras of Muslim empire, been vested in the Keeper of the Holy Cities of Islam.

—The consolidation of the loosely knit political initiatives he had been personally seeding and nurturing throughout Asia and Africa during a decade of quiet diplomacy with other Islamic governments.

—The rapid expansion of the program under which waves of Saudi males were being transported to universities, military academies and industrial institutes in Europe and America for their government-funded training in international finance, business administration, chemical engineering, computer technology and similar fields.

—And the unification of the rival factions within the newly formed Organization of Petroleum Exporting Countries. The region's other oil producers—Iraq, Iran, Kuwait, Bahrain, Syria, the United Arab Emirates, Qatar, Libya and Algeria—were often at odds with each other and Saudi Arabia, split over various religious, political, philosophical and tribal conflicts.

These oil nations moved toward increased cooperation along the general lines of three themes emphasized by Faisal: gaining control of their own oil reserves from Western firms, keeping the influences of Western culture at bay and mounting the broad, regional actions necessary to liquidate the European enclave of Israel.

Saudi Arabia, by the weight of its oil reserves and massive production capacity, was evolving into the central power among the Middle Eastern Muslim states. During the previous years Saudi Arabia's reserves were proven to be vast beyond even the wildest expectations of the American oil crews who pioneered their development. Every day those crews were hooking ever-larger sections of the world's oil-supply system to their wellheads.

By 1964, the year Faisal took full power, these Saudi oil facilities had become the pivotal force in the global oil-distribution grid which the Americans had started building in 1947. Now Texaco, Socal, Exxon and Mobil were able to routinely phone a few commands to the pumping stations at Dhahran and affect both the price and overall supply balance of the oil flowing to market around the world on any given day.

During Lyndon Johnson's first two years in office—as the country became accustomed to the sight of crew-cut teen-agers walking boot-deep in rice shoots; as the first Marine battalions splashed ashore at Da Nang; as the 173rd Airborne choppered north across I Corps, and as the First Cav thrust west toward Laos, the weapon which would ultimately devastate the American homelands was being fashioned without publicity in Riyadh.

The weapon was *Nahda*—the striving for unified action by the Arab world. Since World War II this ideal—of the political unification of Muslim nations of the Middle East—had been a constant but elusive goal. Nahda is the central point of much of the postwar rhetoric of the Arab world and a popular theme throughout all levels of their society. From the past it draws its populist appeal by way of the romanticized memories of the great Islamic empires of the Middle Ages. From the present it derives its power from the obvious fact that large groups of small nations acting in political concert represent a potential force beyond the sum of their individual numbers.

During the postwar decades a number of attempts were made to forge the checkerboard of Middle Eastern Arab countries into some larger entity which could act as a single force. The first attempt in the 1940s resulted in the formation of the Arab League, an organization daubed together with speeches but frequently burst apart in endless squabbles among member states.

Another—and probably the most publicized—attempt to unify was that of Gamal Abdel Nasser, who championed a Pan-Arab movement—the idea being that Arab countries should officially confederate as a larger nation, not unlike the states within the United States. This began shortly after Nasser, a soldier-turned-social revolutionary, overthrew the Egyptian monarchy, assumed power in 1952 and began nationalizing the remaining holdings of the French and British colonial regimes, including the Suez Canal.

Nasser succeeded in achieving a merger of sorts between Syria, Yemen and Egypt, but that attempt at federal union fell apart in a roil of feuds destroying both the United Arab States and the Pan-Arab movement.

The approach to Middle East solidarity which finally did achieve a high level of success was begun in the 1950s and was quietly pursued throughout the 1960s by Faisal Ibn Abdul-Aziz al Saud. His Pan-Islamic unification plan—controversial from its inception and a product of the extensive studies which had made Faisal an Islamic scholar in his early thirties—proposed to establish an organization that would bring not only Arabs but the entire world of Islam into loose confederation. Although Arabs are geographically and culturally at the center of Islam, they constitute a numerical minority in the community of more than three dozen Islamic nations across three continents.

Faisal proposed that those countries form an international body of representatives which could, for the first time in more than four centuries, speak as the single voice of 800 million Africans and Asians.

In the 1950s Faisal was openly ridiculed for this grandiose idea, which was discounted by other Arab leaders as a preposterous, utopian fantasy. One of the most vociferous opponents to the Pan-Islamic movement was Egypt's Nasser, who, along with other Arab heads of state, objected because of the idea's obvious mechanical problems. How could Arab leaders who had proven unable to cooperate on even the most rudimentary level of common interests among neighboring states be expected to achieve any level of unity with a larger clump of disparate countries strung from Gibraltar to the south of China?

The House of Saud, making the same claim as Nasser to the mantle of regional leadership, did not take such criticism lightly. Then-King Saud offered £2 million to a Syrian intelligence agent for the assassination of Nasser.

The plot was foiled. Nasser lived and continued to champion his own Pan-Arab movement over Faisal's more ambitious plan.

Faisal persisted with his call for an Islamic world coalition, with the Saudi throne at the titular center. This became an obsession to which Faisal devoted the last two decades of his life and billions of his kingdom's petro-dollars.

As Faisal assumed the throne of Saudi Arabia in 1964, he also began moving throughout Africa and Asia on diplomatic missions. Stumping country by country, he sought to have other Muslim nations align themselves with Saudi Arabia as well as with each other.

At the same time, many of those Muslim nations were supplying ever-larger amounts of the daily oil needs of the United States. Since 1947 the Western oil consortiums had continued to extend their operations deeper into the Persian Gulf region while cutting back their drilling and explorations in America.

For instance, in 1956—the year fifty-year-old Foreign Minister Faisal watched squadrons of Dakota airplanes dropping British, French and Israeli paratroopers for the invasions of Egypt aimed at restoring European supremacy to the region—there were more than 2,860 oil-drilling rigs in operation throughout the continental United States. That year America produced 48 percent of all the free world's oil.

In 1964—when Faisal became King and his government extended support to the newly formed Palestine Liberation Organization in Jerusalem—the number of active oil rigs operating in America had fallen to 1,500. That year America produced 35 percent of all the free world's oil.

In 1967—when Muslim armies, largely funded by Faisal, Keeper of the Holy Cities of Islam, were crushed by crack Israeli units seizing new segments of Palestine and Islam's third Holy City, Jerusalem—there were 1,100 rigs providing Americans with American oil. That year America produced 28 percent of the free world's oil.

And in 1969—when the world's oldest mosque, Al Aqsa, atop the ruins of the Jewish Temple in Jerusalem, was set afire by an arsonist from an Israeli kibbutz—there were fewer than 990 rigs in America drilling for oil. That year America produced 26 percent of the free world's oil.

At the same time, other aspects of the oil supply-and-demand patterns were changing at a similar rate. In 1964, when Lyndon Johnson was elected and Faisal became King, America consumed a record 3.9 billion barrels of refined petroleum products a year.

In 1969, when Johnson—his presidency shredded by an out-of-control Southeast Asian war—left office, America was demanding 5.1 billion barrels of refined petroleum a year.

In Johnson's memoirs, *The Vantage Point, Perspectives on the Presidency, 1963–1969,* there are fewer than seventeen pages devoted to a mention of the Middle East. Virtually all that tiny section is focused on an intense few weeks in June 1967 when the White House attempted, unsuccessfully, to head off another Israeli-Muslim war.

Nowhere in the 636 pages is there a single mention of Saudi Arabia—the country whose government spent the years 1963 to 1969 systematically organizing toward the petro-campaign which would shortly devastate the interior foundations of American society.

7

IN THE FLAMES
OF AL AQSA

In 1967—as race riots gutted entire sections of America's major cities and General William Westmoreland was asking for 200,000 more troops to add to the half-million GIs already in Vietnam—King Faisal and a consortium of other Muslim leaders attempted their first oil boycott against the West.

In May 1967, after months of escalating border skirmishes, raids, reprisals and general military mayhem between Muslims and Israeli troops along the borders, the Muslim states moved to close off the port of Aqaba—one of Israel's most important military and commercial facilities and its only outlet to the Red Sea and the Asian oceans beyond.

In the vicinity of Aqaba, which sits at the head of a narrow tongue of water, Saudi Arabia massed 20,000 troops along with Egyptian and Jordanian troops. Egypt announced that any ships attempting to carry oil or other strategic materials to the port would be shelled and sunk.

Israel informed President Johnson that he had a "week or two" to use whatever diplomatic pressures he could muster to open the port again or Israel would launch attacks on the neighboring Muslim states. Ten days after that, war broke out. Johnson wrote, "The Israeli Cabinet decided to move. Only the Israelis themselves can describe and assess the reasons for their decision. . . . The Israelis may have concluded that it was necessary for Israel to solve the crisis on its own rather than rely on the United States and the international community."[1]

In a blitzkrieg of troop thrusts, aerial sorties and mechanized sweeps, the Israeli military moved simultaneously on all fronts, smashing the Muslim armies massed on the borders and then rolling onward to seize all the Sinai Peninsula and the Gaza Strip from Egypt in the south, the Old City of Jerusalem and the broad western banks of the Jordan River and the Golan Heights from Syria in the north. The United States Government also confirmed that "American technicians were in Israel in connection with the sale of war planes" during the 1967 battles and that "numerous Americans had served in the Israeli armed forces in the past few years."[2]

Virtually overnight, Israel tripled the size of the territory it controlled.

Menachem Begin, the Polish former leader of the Zionist terrorist underground, was brought into the Israeli Government in 1967 as a cabinet member. Russian-born Moshe Dayan was appointed Israeli Defense Minister. This is the same Dayan referred to by former Israeli Foreign Minister Moshe Sharett, who wrote in his 1956 diary, "Dayan's words are clear . . . [Israel] must calculate its steps narrowmindedly and live by the sword. It must see the sword as the main and only instrument with which to keep its morale high. And above all, let us hope for a new war with the Arab countries, so that we may finally find our space."[3]

Ukrainian-born Premier Levi Eshkol announced that the occupational Israeli forces that had taken the Muslim Old City of Jerusalem would not leave and that the city would be "reunified" to Israel. Reacting to sharp criticism from around the world, Eshkol said that the "reunification" of the Arab city was not "annexation" but rather "integration of Jerusalem in the administrative and municipal sphere."

The Israeli Government also announced plans to build four settlements within the other territories seized during the war. The Premier's office said these were not "permanent settlements" but "designed solely for military security." At the same time, Israeli military

demolition crews bulldozed and dynamited Muslim towns throughout the occupied territories. In the occupied West Bank—in the
town of Jiftliq—eight hundred buildings were destroyed. The Israeli
Government said this was required for security reasons.

Throughout the Old City of Jerusalem, the Gaza Strip, the West
Bank and the Golan Heights, Muslims by the thousands ran amok—
burning, bombing and stoning vehicles and personnel of the Israeli
forces erecting garrison fortifications in Arab communities.

The Palestinian guerrilla underground, a relatively docile and disorganized movement up until 1967, pushed out in waves of attacks.
Its members bombed seventeen sites, shot up eleven others and
killed or seriously injured 102 persons.

In Baghdad—sitting witness to the most disastrous and humili-
ating defeat they had yet suffered in their war against Zionism—the
leaders of Iraq, Qatar, Bahrain, Kuwait, Libya, Algeria, the United
Arab Emirates, Syria, Lebanon and Egypt awaited the crucial decision of King Faisal on the proposal for a cutoff of oil to the West in
retaliation for the European and American support of Israel and its
military. Faisal called for Saudi Arabia's massive oil shipments to be
stopped and launched the first petroleum boycott against the West.

That 1967 action was a complete failure.

There were two primary reasons for this failure. The Muslim oil
states did not have physical control of their oil or its shipment—
Western oil consortiums did. And, despite the rapid shifts of con-
sumption-and-supply patterns throughout the decade, the West
could still supply itself with oil from outside the Middle East. The
United States produced enough oil from its own fields to meet its
own needs in an emergency, and the American-dominated oil consortiums could reroute oil supplies from other regions of the global
oil-supply grid. Because of these surplus supply sources, the West
could circumvent the Arab supply lines.

At an Arab summit conference in Khartoum, Sudan, Faisal and
leaders of the other oil states admitted failure and called off the oil
embargo. The meeting turned out to be a watershed event in other
aspects, though. Faisal and Gamal Nasser—whose rivalry had split
the Arab world into separate camps throughout the 1960s—agreed
to settle their differences and cooperate toward "common goals."

Saudi Arabia pledged to lead a new program in which oil-producing Arab states would use portions of their now substantial oil roy-

alty receipts to help fund the rebuilding of the cities, fortifications, armies and morale of the border states surrounding Israel. Saudi Arabia and the oil states of which it had become the undisputed leader additionally resolved to use their resources in a manner aimed at unifying "efforts at the international and diplomatic levels to assure the withdrawal of Israel from Muslim lands."

Faisal publicly vowed never to rest until he had once again walked across Muslim ground and prayed at Al Aqsa Mosque in a once-again Muslim Jerusalem.

Eyewitness accounts of King Faisal's behavior during this period indicate that he was personally so distraught by the seizure of the Old City of Jerusalem by Israel that, when the subject came up in his court, the normally poised and aloof Keeper of the Holy Cities of Islam was unable to talk coherently and, at times, displayed physical reactions so intense they rendered him speechless.

In 1969 the Israeli Government continued to consolidate its hold throughout the Old City of Jerusalem, the Gaza Strip, the West Bank, the Sinai and the Golan regions seized during the 1967 war. This despite the rising criticism of these actions by Israel's previously staunch allies in Europe. The Israeli Premier announced that the original four "security settlements" which had been erected in those occupied Muslim areas were being expanded into a "string of paramilitary settlements." A short time later the Premier's office announced that the string of paramilitary settlements would be further expanded by occupational forces to include "construction of three Israeli towns." A short time later the Premier's office announced that those settlements and towns on Arab lands had been officially decreed "Israeli territory."

The Israeli Agricultural Ministry announced plans to build an additional six farming settlements in the occupied Golan region, the West Bank and the Sinai. The government also decreed that Israel law and court jurisdiction had been extended over all legal matters in Golan, superseding indigenous Islamic legal codes. The Israeli Government said this was necessary to "settle land disputes" in the zone seized from Syria.

The Israeli Government also announced it was expropriating 838 acres of Muslim properties—farms, pastures, shops and homes—outside the occupied Old City of Jerusalem in order to make room for the planned construction of "public institutions, roads and parks" in a project centered around the erection of 1,400 new housing units for Israeli families being moved into the Arab territories.

Shortly after that the Israeli Government announced that another park project had been started and would involve constructions encircling most of the outer walls of the Old City. Israeli Government spokesmen said that several "Arab slums" would be removed by bulldozer to make way for "clusters of hotels and commercial developments" that were to be part of the park.

Defense Minister Moshe Dayan announced that "sterner measures" were to be taken by Israeli military forces against Muslim residents in the occupied territories in an effort to stem the tide of Palestinian terrorist attacks. Dayan said that under the new Israeli policy a system of "neighborhood punishment" would be implemented: every home in a neighborhood would by dynamited or bulldozed if any one of the neighborhood's inhabitants failed to "cooperate in investigations" or was judged to be sympathetically involved with the Palestine Liberation Organization. Dayan demonstrated the new policy by removing the Muslim families from villages in sections of the occupied West Bank and dynamiting 140 houses.

Palestinian guerrillas blew up the Trans-Arabian Pipeline where it crossed a river in the Israeli-occupied Golan Heights, cutting off the flow of oil to American terminals and processing plants on the Mediterranean Sea. Palestinian guerrillas also attacked airliners in Zurich, Athens and Damascus, bombed shops and offices in London, Brussels and Athens, attacked Israeli embassies in the Netherlands and West Germany and increased their attacks in and around Israel. Throughout 1969 they bombed forty sites around the world, shot up twenty-eight others and killed or seriously injured 513 persons.

The Israeli Government decreed in 1969 that all persons of Arab ancestry would be required to apply for special permits and licenses if they wished to continue their trades and businesses in and around the occupied Old City of Jerusalem. Persons of Arab ancestry who failed to register with the occupational authorities were subject to the "loss of their enterprises and practices."

The Israeli Government moved the headquarters of its National Police from Tel Aviv to the Old City of Jerusalem. One of the first tasks of the new police force was enforcing the Israeli Government decree expropriating twenty-nine acres of Muslim properties and evicting six hundred Muslim families from their homes. The Israeli Government issued a statement explaining that this was necessary to combat the "dilapidated, unsanitary conditions" of the area around the central plateau of the Old City.

With cliff-like walls, this central heft of rock rises majestically out of the jumble of Jerusalem's crooked streets and arched alleyways and smoky bazaars below. Its top is flat: a thirty-five-acre trapezoid of elevated ground enclosed by walls and overlooking the surrounding city and the fields and hills beyond.

And it is here, at this plateau, that the Middle East conflict reaches its most vicious and uncompromising intensity. Muslims call this place "The Noble Enclosure." Jews call the same place "The Temple Mount." Both call it theirs. Both are determined to have it, no matter what. The historical and emotional momentums of their separate cultures appear to leave them little choice.

Nearly 2,000 years ago, when Christ was born, a large squarish building of white stone and cedarwood stood on this plateau. It had been built thirty-one years before Christ's birth by the Jewish civilization that ruled along the Jordan River. That temple stood for another seventy years—a total of 101 years—before it was tumbled off the plateau by the Roman legions which also disassembled the surrounding Jewish state.

In the 600s A.D., another religion worshiping the same God as Judaism and Christianity arose in the deserts south of Jerusalem and quickly enveloped that city. Jerusalem became one of the three poles employed by the Prophet Muhammad to delineate the new religion's holy grounds. That sacred zone was measured from Mecca and Medina in the south to Jerusalem, its farthest point, in the north. On the empty heights of Jerusalem's central plateau, a mosque was erected to mark that farther point and called "The Farther" Mosque —in Arabic, "Al Aqsa" Mosque. Near Al Aqsa Mosque, on the top of the plateau, Muslims also built the Dome of the Rock—a shrine which enclosed the small outcropping of rock at which the Prophet Abraham is said to have laid the philosophical foundations which evolved into the monotheistic religions of Islam, Christianity and Judaism. This same outcropping of rock—sacred for the same reasons to Muslims, Christians and Jews—is thought to have been the altar stone used by Jews when their Temple covered the same site during the time of Christ.

Al Aqsa Mosque—which is now both the oldest mosque in the world and the building containing the root designs which evolved into the distinctive architecture of the Islamic world—has stood on the site for fourteen centuries. In the Middle Ages, European crusaders invaded and attempted to seize the Old City of Jerusalem and its central plateau but were ultimately repulsed by Muslim armies. When the European movement to colonize Asian Palestine again became popular in the 1880s, the central plateau of Jerusalem became a major target of the colonists. French oil-baron Edmond Rothschild, who was sponsoring the colonial movement with his personal fortune, attempted to purchase the central mountain of Jerusalem. Islamic authorities refused his offer.

In the 1948 war between Europeans and Muslims for control of Palestine, European Jewish militia attacked the Old City of Jerusalem, attempting to breach the walls and seize the central plateau. Some members of the Jewish militia carried explosives with which they intended to blow up the two Islamic shrines on the plateau so that the Jewish Temple could be rebuilt. However, Muslims who lost much of the rest of Palestine put up a ferocious fight and repulsed the Europeans at the walls of Jerusalem.

In the 1967 war the Israelis attacked the Old City of Jerusalem in massive force and, finally, overcame the Muslim defenders. Five months after Israeli forces occupied the city, Israeli officials made inspections and issued a report that the fire-fighting equipment in and around Al Aqsa Mosque and the Dome of the Rock atop the central plateau was inadequate by modern standards.

In July of 1969, Israel transferred the headquarters of its National police to Jerusalem and began evicting entire neighborhoods of Muslims living in the vicinity of the central plateau.

Twenty-one days after that operation began, a fire broke out inside the Al Aqsa Mosque and gutted major portions of the ancient structure. Muslims immediately began rioting throughout Jerusalem, Egypt, Jordan, Lebanon, Syria, Iraq and as far away as the Philippines, where Muslims fire-bombed the car of the Israeli ambassador to Manila and attempted to sack the Israeli Embassy.

The Israeli police announced they had arrested a kibbutz worker, Denis Michael Rohan, and indicated that he had set the fire by carrying three large containers of kerosene in a rucksack into the mosque, splashing the liquid across the walls and torching the building. At the kibbutz Mishmar ha Sharon, Rohan had worked tending citrus orchards and gladioli gardens and studying Hebrew.

The Israeli police said Rohan was twenty-seven years old and had come to Israel from Australia. They said he was a member of the American-based Church of God. The Israeli Government said Rohan had set the fire because he had a "religious obsession that Jesus would return to earth when Jerusalem became completely Jewish and the Third Temple was built, replacing the Second Temple destroyed by the Romans in A.D. 70."

The American-based Church of God, a Protestant denomination, issued a statement from its headquarters saying that the kibbutz worker, Rohan, was not, and had never been, a member of that sect.

The Israeli court—convened in the midst of what had become an international incident involving even the Vatican and the United Nations Secretariat—ultimately found Rohan guilty. Later the court declared that the kibbutz worker would not be subject to punishment because he had "acted under an uncontrollable pathological impulse" when setting fire to the oldest mosque in the world.

The August 1969 arson in the Al Aqsa Mosque was not perceived as a particularly momentous event by the Western news media, which gave it small mention. The riots, demonstrations and official outcry throughout dozens of Muslim Asian and African countries were hardly reported at all and, even then, presented as random, incomprehensible incidents and disturbances among the natives of obscure countries most Americans could not easily locate on a large map—even if they cared to try.

In the basement of the White House, in the office that was being turned into a command post for a new, top-secret war being launched by the United States against the nation of Cambodia, the new presidential assistant on National Security Affairs, Henry Kissinger, was worried primarily about news leaks involving those new Southeast Asian invasion strategies. The transcripts of the first phone tap he had ordered had already begun coming across his desk for review. That first bug he had ordered was placed on the home lines of his own aide, Morton Halperin. This was the beginning of a growing tangle of electronic activities which emanated from his office and would soon be consolidated in the hands of a new White House group which would come to be known as "The Plumbers."

At that time the Middle East conflict was a back-burner concern in and around the executive mansion. Kissinger wrote that "For the moment, the White House and State Department were in rare accord on doing nothing, diplomatic activity could be expected to resume in the fall."

Kissinger noted that "In August, fighting flared up again on all fronts, especially dangerous along the Suez Canal. It was not calmed by the burning of the Al Aqsa Mosque in Jerusalem by a deranged Australian. The Arabs predictably blamed Israel; both Nasser and King Faisal of Saudi Arabia called for a holy war to liberate Jerusalem. Terrorists hijacked a TWA jetliner to Damascus, where Israeli passengers were held for several weeks. Israel's Labour Party, gearing up for the fall elections, proclaimed its intention of keeping parts of the occupied territories whatever the peace terms. This grim scene called for another policy review."[4]

During the ten days following the arson in the Al Aqsa Mosque, a number of events occurred which would have profound and far-reaching implications for Americans.

One event occurred in Libya. There twenty-seven-year-old Army Captain Muammar el-Qaddafi, who had planned the overthrow of the Libyan monarchy with a group of cadets while studying in Britain's Sandhurst, a military academy, had twice scheduled and twice postponed his planned coup because of general apathy and lack of populist support. Immediately after the Jerusalem fire, and riding atop a wave of anti-Zionist hysteria which swept Libya, the Muslim revolutionary launched "Operation Palestine"—the intricately planned coup which overturned the Libyan Government of the placid and pro-Western seventy-nine-year-old King Idris. Qaddafi's first move was to seal off the country, dissolve parliament, assume power over the armed forces and the oil ports. Then he closed down the United States Wheelus Air Force Base and announced the beginning of a new regime, pledged to dedicate "all its resources and energies" to the cause of "Pan-Arab, Pan-Islamic, Anti-Zionist brotherhood" and whose national goal would be "the liberation of Palestine."

At the same time—and even as Muslim volunteers began sifting through the charred debris of the Al Aqsa Mosque seeking to recover and preserve even splinters of the remaining, ancient woodwork—an emergency session of the Arab League's Council of Foreign Ministers met in Cairo. Expectations at the meeting's opening were that Egypt's Nasser—who had been the Arab world's most visible and volatile spokesman against Israel and the West—would get what he wanted: the creation of a new all-Arab political and military apparatus pledged to new initiatives in Palestine and aimed at retaking Jerusalem.

Instead, the League members openly rejected the traditional Nasser approach and voted to support the plan put forward by King Faisal. Faisal proposed that the Arab states collectively call upon all Muslims of the world to "raise up and liberate their profaned sanctuaries in Jerusalem." And Faisal proposed that call be used to convene the modern age's first international summit of Islamic heads of state. The Saudi King, who had already established a working system of cultural and religious cohesions between Mecca and the far Asian and African ends of the Islamic world, was able to organize and open that historic session of Muslim presidents, prime ministers and kings in less than three weeks in Rabat, Morocco.

Government heads representing 450 million Muslims from nations as geographically diverse as Guinea and Senegal in southwest Africa to Malaysia and Indonesia in Southeast Asia attended the meeting, which endorsed a broad body of programs whose basic goals had not changed during the twenty years in which Faisal had been publicly and privately lobbying for them:

—The recognition that Islam—revitalized as a vibrant world force —represented the single most potent organizational tool available to the Third World nations of Asia and Africa.

—The creation of a global network of Muslim political mechanisms capable of making Islam an irresistible force within the international and domestic political systems of the Western industrial powers.

—The erection of barriers against Soviet expansion—particularly in the Middle East oil regions—and the expulsion of Soviet influence in those places where it had gained footholds in Asia and Africa.

—The mobilization of the entire Muslim world and all its resources in a campaign aimed at returning the Old City of Jerusalem to Muslim rule.

One of the actions of this body of Muslim governments was to provide the public forum, the political endorsement and the pledges of future monetary backing necessary to transform the Palestine Liberation Organization from a loose-knit gaggle of quarrelsome guerrilla squads into an international presence whose demands were backed by the weight of the wealth and resources of the Islamic world.

It was at this meeting—and from under the protective wing of King Faisal—that an unknown, Jerusalem-born civil-engineer-and-magazine-editor turned-demolition-expert was catapulted into the position from which his name—Yasir Arafat—would become a household word in the West.

That 1969 Islamic summit would be the first in a rapidly expanding web of international Islamic organizations spinning outward from Jedda and Mecca during the next few years. There would be the officially chartered world Islamic body of national leaders known as the Organization of the Islamic Conference, the International Islamic News Agency, the Islamic Broadcasting Organization and the Islamic Solidarity Fund. This last was begun with a $10.2 million initial contribution by King Faisal and was the starting point of what became an annual multibillion-dollar series of foreign aid programs extended throughout the world.

Within one year of this Pan-Islamic summit in Rabat, the Arab oil states would begin the wave of oil-well and production-facility seizures that would break the hold of the Western consortiums and transfer physical control of Middle East petroleum reserves from American and European executives to Muslim ones.

All of these grand global designs and Pan-Islamic political strategies, which began evolving in 1969, completely depended upon a single reality for their fulfillment: the growing wealth and power being generated in the East as a result of the growing demand for petroleum in the West.

Mere demand for Middle East oil—because it was then the cheapest and most profitable source for Western companies to produce—provided the Arab world with some wealth, but not real power. That fact had been demonstrated graphically during the abortive 1967 embargo attempt. Real power could come only with desperation and real need. Real power could come only when Western nations were not able to circumvent the Middle East oil supplies in times of emergency, when Western nations had outstripped their own supplies and had no alternative to the Muslim oil that would be required to maintain the daily operations of those Western industrial societies.

In 1969, even as the flames were leaping through the roof of the Al Aqsa Mosque, a crucial change in the patterns of world petroleum supply and demand had occurred. This was to be the turning point for the history of both the Eastern and Western worlds.

It was to be the point at which American policy-makers were faced with what would prove to be the single most important decision they would make in the nation's modern age.

It was a point at which the government could have taken a number of actions which would have completely changed the outcome of events in the 1970s. But those actions were not taken or even seriously contemplated.

Because, in 1969, Richard Nixon didn't feel such measures were really necessary.

It was in the midst of the political and emotional turmoil caused by the Nixon administration's escalation of the Vietnam War that the White House and Congress encountered another new development which was not as controversial. It did not make headlines. It was not raged over, marched for or passionately editorialized about. No television station presented the broad facts of the issue conveying the extraordinary significance of the government decisions about to be made about it.

The issue was oil.

In 1969 the United States experienced one of the most important watershed developments in its history. That year America's mills, malls, lawnmowers, movie theaters, generating stations, turnpikes, hair dryers, pool filtration systems, ice-makers, vibrators, factories, foundries and assorted neon canyons burned up more petroleum than all the petroleum pumped from every oil well in every state in the union. The American output, for the thirteenth year in a row, was down. America, for the thirtieth straight year, increased its daily use of oil—by more than 3 percent.

The shortfalls and growing supply pressures caused the largest seller of gasoline in America—Texaco—to increase its prices by six tenths of a cent per gallon, pushing the price of a gallon of gasoline in New York to $.19. Senator Edward Kennedy of Massachusetts termed this price hike "outrageous" and made a major public issue of his demand that the Nixon administration take steps to lower gasoline prices by increasing supplies. The only supplies of additional oil were those of foreign countries. Kennedy charged that gasoline at $.19 per gallon was "propped up to extraordinarily high artificial levels" and repeatedly told TV cameras that the Nixon administration "has not only the right, but the obligation, to prevent those prices from going even higher" by increasing the amount of oil transported from foreign countries into the continental United States.

In the White House, Richard Nixon was faced with a decision not about price but about the long-term security of a nation and the viability of the continental sprawl of machinery which was its core force: the machinery on which every other aspect of its daily life and international dominance depended. This was the same sprawl of machinery that had, twenty-five years before, operated as an isolated, independent arsenal in a global sea of war: fueled on Texas crude, smelted with Ohio coke, lathed and mass-assembled with Detroit zeal and pouring out tidal waves of material and technological innovations that allowed the United States to both win the war and seize control of the evolving new world order.

Up until 1969 this blinking, booming, boundless apparatus of machineAmerica was totally self-contained—propelled by fuel provided by feeder lines plunged deep into the shale rock and dome crust throughout the southern plates of its own landmass. MachineAmerica's global power relied on the fact that its operations were impervious to outside interference.

In 1969 machineAmerica's billions of moving parts needed more petroleum every day than the wellheads—working full-tilt—could produce. The physical reality of this situation provided President Nixon with two options:

One: He could address the crisis as the national emergency it was, and take measures to retool machineAmerica's systems to restore the balance between the amount of oil used and the amount of oil available from American wells—thereby maintaining the invulnerability of the nation's machinery, or

Two: He could quietly unplug the feeder lines from the American landmass and run them out across the borders, out across the potential war zones, out across the political storm warnings and into the hands of foreign governments which would then physically control machineAmerica's ability to continue operations on any given day.

Nixon went for option Two. He lowered the barriers which had previously restricted American machinery from running on foreign oil in any substantial quantity. At first the White House announced that 10 percent of the foreign oil to be supplied to America's machines would come from the Middle East. This, at a time when Israeli military units were engaged in a series of ferocious border skirmishes with Syrian, Egyptian, Lebanese, Jordanian, Iraqi and Palestinian forces, and the world press was reporting that there appeared no prospect for peace in the region in the foreseeable future.

That was the start of a rapid spiral as the Nixon administration routinely approved the extension of ever-thicker feeder lines out of America's industrial centers and north into Canada, south into Latin America and east into the Persian Gulf as overall imports—and national vulnerability—zoomed upward.

This issue—the fuel integrity of machineAmerica's core—was handled as an item of secondary concern in a White House whose primary attentions were directed at those events it said posed the generation's gravest threat to the security and future of the United States: the civil wars in Southeast Asia.

At the same time, the staggering costs of those Southeast Asian entanglements were drastically altering other aspects of America. Its moral grip on the world—that post-World War II aura of eminent benevolence synonymous with its name—had drained away, spilled like blood from a sudden gash, lost forever in a swirl of screaming peasants and burning thatch.

And its physical grip on the world was loosening as well. In 1969 President Nixon announced that his administration was making cuts of unprecedented size in the allotments of money and technical assistance provided to less-developed nations throughout Latin America, Africa and Asia. Nixon's original proposal lowered the total of those programs to $2.6 billion. Congress chopped that amount to $1.9 billion—the lowest amount ever authorized in the history of American foreign aid programs.

These three seemingly unrelated developments—the extension of machineAmerica's fuel feeder lines beyond its borders, the collapse of its international prestige and the wholesale emasculation of its systems of foreign aid to poor countries in Africa and Asia—were, almost immediately, seized as opportunities by King Faisal of Saudi Arabia. The three trends would serve, intertwined, as principal strands in the noose Faisal was patiently fashioning—and which he would suddenly yank tight as he stood amid the 1973 wreckage of the Muslim world's failed military jihad for Jerusalem.

By the time of the second Arab oil embargo the noose had been tightened. The Muslim world—under Faisal's leadership—had assumed control of oil production and distribution. Indeed, the second embargo was so effective that many observers argued that Israel's victory in 1973 was one of the most costly victories in the history of armed conflict.

8

THE UNSHEATHED
SWORD

In November 1973 Secretary of State Henry Kissinger began a frantic round of shuttle diplomacy aimed at ending the debilitating oil embargo launched by King Faisal in revenge for American aid to Israel during the war. Kissinger was unable immediately to negotiate a solution and, instead, issued a warning that the United States might consider using its military forces against Saudi Arabia and the other Middle Eastern Muslim states unless they began oil shipments to America again.

In response, the refining and depot centers in Singapore—serving the vast oil fields of the Islamic Southeast Asian nations of Malaysia and Indonesia —suddenly ceased supplying fuel to United States military forces. Those petroleum facilities on the Straits of Malacca constitute the third-largest conglomeration of oil refineries in the world outside of Houston and Rotterdam. They also serve as the main source of fuel oil for the U.S. fleets cruising the South Pacific and Indian oceans: the same fleets which would launch any attacks by American forces against Saudi Arabia or its neighbors.

Pentagon documents released later indicate that the cutoff of military fuels caused all branches of the American military throughout the world to experience an immediate 18 percent rollback in all mechanized operations. The United States Navy experienced a 20 percent decrease in fleet steaming hours around the globe.

By December the Pentagon invoked wartime emergency powers to requisition fuel from American oil companies after those companies refused to sell the Pentagon more petroleum in violation of Faisal's prohibition against such sales.

At the same time, the Organization of Arab Petroleum Exporting Countries issued a statement indicating that the oil embargo would end after the United States took actions aimed at implementing the United Nations resolutions calling for Israeli withdrawal from the occupied Old City of Jerusalem and other territories seized in the 1967 war. The statement also announced that, in cooperation with the Organization of African Unity, the Arabs were cutting off oil shipments to the white supremacist colonial regimes of South Africa and Rhodesia. Ethiopia became the sixteenth African country to announce it was breaking off diplomatic relations with Israel.

In Iran, Henry Kissinger sought to have Shah Riza Pahlevi use his growing power to back an American-sponsored solution to the crisis in the occupied territories. The Shah told Kissinger that his Islamic Government "will not be able to support any measures which do not provide for a return of the Islamic holy places of Jerusalem to Islamic rule."

In Europe, France was basking in a certain notoriety after the Arabs announced that because the Paris Government had indicated its intention to shift toward the Arab cause, it would be exempted from the worst impact of the oil embargo, which had darkened the streets throughout the rest of the continent.

At an emergency two-day meeting in Brussels, the ministers of the European Economic Community unanimously voted to approve a statement pledging their nine countries' support of the principle that Israel must "end the territorial occupation which it has maintained since the conflict of 1967." The Netherlands—Israel's most ardent continental supporter and hardest hit by the oil embargo—requested that the EEC issue an additional statement in which the European nations would agree to form a common oil pool to thwart further Muslim attempts to selectively embargo specific nations. The EEC refused the request.

In London, at the 1973 Conference of the Socialist International
—the organization of laborite political parties and the milieu from
which Zionism originally evolved—laborite Israeli Premier Golda
Meir gave a speech in which she said that Israel was "going through
a deadly difficult period" and called for the European countries to
provide "their all-out support." Her remarks were followed by si-
lence and then criticism by West German Chancellor Willy Brandt,
chosen to speak for the European parties, who chastised the Israeli
Premier for "holding on to the territories occupied in the 1967 war."

After a twelve-hour emergency meeting of its top political leaders
in mid-December, Italy issued a public statement emphasizing its
government's determination to seek "closer relations with the Arab
oil-producing countries."

In Austria, Chancellor Bruno Kreisky agreed to meet Muslim
demands and closed the transit facilities through which Russian
Jews were processed when immigrating to Israel.

In Japan, Tokyo announced its intention to establish the new
Japan-Saudi Cooperation Organization to seek new economic links
with the Middle East oil producers. By year's end Japan had
dispatched a team of government negotiators to the United Arab
Emirates, where it signed an eight-year contract for oil supplies. The
contract was the first of its kind, completely eliminating any involvement of the Western oil companies and establishing the principle of
government-to-government oil sales in which petroleum allotments
were just another part of the overall political and diplomatic relationships between a Middle Eastern and an industrialized nation.

Saudi Arabia, which, earlier in the year, had taken over partial interest in its oil facilities, announced that it would assume controlling
interest of all American oil-firm operations in the country. For thirty
years Saudi Arabia had been building up both a modern army and a
population of highly trained Arab professionals capable of running
large portions of the nation's sprawling petroleum apparatus. The oil
companies received polite requests to either renegotiate their contracts and turn over administrative control of the oil industry to
their hosts or please evacuate the country. The oil companies faced
the option of either capitulating to the Arab requests or attempting
to physically hold on to their facilities—turning their corporate security police into a private army battling for possession of large sections of industrial territory inside a sovereign Asian nation. The

companies capitulated and sought the best deal possible under the new circumstances. They had little choice. The entire global apparatus of their extended corporations had been organized in a manner totally dependent on the continuing daily flow of oil—and money— from their Persian Gulf operations.

In the last week of December 1973 King Faisal—now the focus of worldwide publicity and attention—led the assembled leaders of the Arab world into the strategy session and summit conference at Algiers. Moving slowly past the crowds of Western reporters and television cameras, Faisal walked side by side with Yasir Arafat. Inside, the delegates voted to reiterate—for the benefit of the now-attentive world—their previous resolution recognizing the Palestine Liberation Organization as the "sole, legitimate voice of the Palestine people."

In the United States the television screens and front pages were riveted not on the Middle East but on the Watergate hearings, which were inexorably marching toward the ouster of President Nixon. The price of energy had increased 400 percent almost overnight and the oil embargo continued to send shock waves through the emotional, industrial and financial foundations of American society. Richard Nixon sequestered himself in the residential suite of the White House, leaving the major decisions of government to his top aides. Henry Kissinger stepped forward as the major spokesman of the Administration at this time, functioning as de facto head of state in his pronouncements on both international and domestic affairs. He again indicated that the United States might be driven to using military force against the Arabs because "The early warning signs of a major economic crisis are evident. The world's financial institutions are staggering under the most massive and rapid movement of reserves in history. And profound questions have arisen about man's most fundamental needs for energy and food." Kissinger again warned that the United States was seriously considering the use of military force to prevent the "strangulation of the industrialized world."[1]

The Muslim oil producers issued a statement indicating that they were wiring their oil fields and petroleum-processing and transportation facilities with explosives and would detonate them if the United States attempted to invade any of the Middle Eastern states. The Muslim nations' joint statement said that "lifting the oil measures is still linked to Israeli withdrawal from occupied Arab territories and the restoration of the rights of the Palestinian people."

A study of the feasibility of an American invasion was commissioned by Congress and concluded that while "terrain in the Saudi core area is well suited for parachute assaults and airmobile operations," even massive U.S. invasion forces would have great difficulties seizing "essential oil fields and facilities intact." The report indicated that "wells, pipelines, pumping stations, power plants, storage tanks, refineries and loading installations were all vulnerable. Amateurs with little experience handling explosives would find lucrative targets. [Explosions] . . . would play hob if they hit oil facilities before our landings." If a hundred wells around the Persian Gulf were hit simultaneously with such explosions, the report concluded, the oil fields that were the target of the invasion would be totally destroyed.[2]

Kissinger called a Washington conference with the foreign ministers of Great Britain, France, West Germany, Italy, Ireland, Japan, the Netherlands, Norway and Canada and called for the formation of a new relationship aimed at "dealing with world problems cooperatively." Specifically, Kissinger called for the Western allies to join together to present a united front against the attempt by Muslim states to use an oil embargo to create international political pressures aimed at forcing the Israeli evacuation of the Old City of Jerusalem, the Gaza Strip, the West Bank and the Golan Heights territories seized during the 1967 war. The conference was marked by some of the most acrimonious public debate between Western leaders since World War II years. European critics, led by France, charged that the United States was attempting to "dominate the relationships of Western Europe and Japan."

Back in Europe, ministers of the nine European Economic Community countries announced the formation of a new program offering European economic, technological and cultural exchanges with twenty Arab countries as the beginning of new diplomatic relationships between European countries and the Middle Eastern Muslim states.

French President Valéry Giscard d'Estaing said the oil embargo had created a catastrophe, presaging an "enduring crisis" in the world economic system. He defended France's political shift in favor of the Muslim states, who, he said, were taking "revenge on Europe

for the nineteenth century." French Foreign Minister Jean Sauvag-
nargues was dispatched to Beirut, Lebanon, for a highly publicized
meeting with Yasir Arafat—the first meeting of a high-level European government official and the head of the Palestine Liberation
Organization. France announced that it had signed agreements to
supply nuclear power plants, steel mills, a subway system, twelve
new oil tankers and urban electrical systems to Iran in return for oil;
an aluminum plant, military base, television system and petrochemical complex to Iraq in return for oil, and a refinery complex and $110 million in government loans to Qatar in return for
oil.

In West Germany, Gerhard Schroeder, leading Christian Democratic Deputy in Parliament, embarked on a trip for a meeting with
PLO chairman Arafat in Damascus. The West German Government
announced that it had signed agreements to provide refineries and
petrochemical plant constructions to Iran in return for oil, and technicians, equipment and funding for petroleum exploration and development projects in Algeria in return for oil.

Italian President Giovanni Leone, traveling for meetings with government leaders in the Middle East, in Cairo loudly proclaimed his
government's intention to "improve economic and political relations
with Arabs and to insure a continuous flow of oil." Italy also announced it would supply steelworks, shipbuilding yards, petrochemical plants, agricultural projects, oil tankers and technological assistance to Saudi Arabia in return for oil; desalinization
plants, steel mills, aluminum plants and petrochemical complexes to
Iran in return for oil, and agricultural programs, urban public works
projects and technological training facilities to Iraq in return for oil.

Japan announced it would begin construction projects involving
oil refineries, aluminum smelters, cement plants, fertilizer factories,
tanker-ship construction and technological training programs in Iraq
in return for oil.

Great Britain announced it would supply textiles, steel facilities,
paper products, petrochemical technology and technological training
to Iran in return for oil; shipyards and drydock works to the United
Arab Emirates in return for oil, and had also negotiated a government-to-government oil agreement with Saudi Arabia.

Swedish Premier Olof Palme traveled to Algeria for discreet discussions with Yasir Arafat. The Netherlands Foreign Ministry issued

a statement emphasizing the country's sincere desire to "stimulate the development of good relations between the Netherlands and the Arab world."

A delegation of representatives of the British, French, Swedish, Italian, Dutch, West German, Austrian and Japanese labor parties of the Socialist International—led by Austrian Chancellor Bruno Kreisky—traveled on a fact-finding mission to the Middle East. The delegation proclaimed its intentions to open "permanent contacts" in the Arab world and issued a statement in Egypt declaring that "the political and humanitarian problems of the Palestinians could leave no socialist indifferent."

Elsewhere around the world in 1974, Zaire, Nigeria, Venezuela and Qatar assumed control of their oil fields and facilities—inviting Western oil consortiums to comply or evacuate their sovereign borders. Kuwait, Ecuador, Saudi Arabia and the United Arab Emirates completed takeovers-in-progress.

In October—following an earlier strategy session with Asian and African leaders attending the Islamic Foreign Ministers Conference in Lahore, Pakistan, where Yasir Arafat's arrival had been greeted with a twenty-one-gun salute—nineteen Arab leaders met in Rabat, Morocco. Led by King Faisal, that assembly announced plans to:

—Establish a new world monetary system whose new realities would be reflected by the "petro-dollar," a unit of currency which physically looked like an American dollar but which was tied in value to the worth of oil.

—Launch the largest, most complex and expensive programs of city building, industrial development and capital construction ever undertaken.

—Begin massive investment programs throughout America and the industrialized West in a manner aimed at establishing Arab nations as "pivotal financial factors" and "viable political powers" within the fabric of those Western societies.

Out on the sun-seared parade grounds during the conference, King Faisal made an inspection tour of Moroccan troops and their new armaments. Faisal, the former desert marksman, hefted one of the sniper's rifles for the benefit of the assembled photographic corps of the Western press. Peering through the telescopic sight, Faisal swung the weapon in a westerly direction—toward America—as the photographers clicked away. Nearby, Faisal spokesmen pointed out in English that "We don't want to ruin America any more than you want to take military action against us. There is no reason why a compromise can't be worked out."

Within five months of that Rabat planning session, Faisal would be dead—assassinated by a nephew just returned from school in California. Those bullets ended the sixty-nine-year *hajj* of The Sword, Son of the Servant of the Mighty, a journey which began in the mud hut of a medieval war lord and ended in the marble audience hall where humble requests from the President of the United States, the Queen of England and the Emperor of Japan were routinely entertained. Faisal's years as King ran the exact length of the Vietnam War—a period during which he would inflict far greater damage on America than Ho Chi Minh could have even contemplated. During those years Faisal dramatically altered the lives of more of earth's inhabitants than had even the man on whose birthday he died: Muhammad.

Faisal's half brother, Khalid, became the new King of Saudi Arabia, Keeper of the Holy Cities of Islam and controller of the largest petroleum deposits in the free world. In an impassioned speech before the Sixth Annual Conference of Islamic Foreign Ministers, attended by forty-three African and Asian nations, Khalid declared of Faisal, "The best way to honor his memory is for all of us to be determined to follow his lead and what he sought in the solidarity and unity of all Muslims, and to strive to achieve the greatness of the Muslim nation. Above all is to fulfill his most earnest hope; for us to pray, by God's Grace and Will, in Al Aqsa Mosque, the first of the two Quiblahs and the third holiest shrine, with Jerusalem once again Arab, free and dedicated to the service of God and his religion."

That 1975 conference voted unanimously in favor of a resolution calling for the establishment of an "independent national authority" in the territories occupied by Israel since the 1967 war. The conference ended with the creation of a thirteen-member committee charged with coordinating new global diplomatic efforts to augment those already under way in and around the United Nations, championing the cause of "Muslim rights in Jerusalem."

In the wake of that meeting, Saudi Arabian Oil Minister Sheik Ahmed Zaki Yamani issued a statement saying that "the Palestinian question cannot be solved, nor a Middle East settlement gained,

without the involvement of the Palestine Liberation Organization."
Yamani said that if Israel did not vacate the occupied territories—
and, in particular, the Old City of Jerusalem—Saudi Arabia would
support moves aimed at isolating Israel in both the United States
and the world economic community and would also seriously consider further oil actions against America and those of its allies which
continued to support the Israeli occupation of the territories seized
in 1967.

Throughout America public attention was no longer centered on
the Middle East but on the extraordinary spectacle in Washington,
where the country's first nonelected President was attempting to
manage the hurricane of controversy caused by the pardon granted
his criminally indictable predecessor. Gerald Ford, speaking in the
midst of this domestic political trauma—and incongruously back-
dropped by the bunting and hoopla of an imminent bicentennial gala
—addressed the new threats against the country's oil supplies. Ford
indicated that a difficult decade lay ahead in which "the future of the
industrialized democracies" was at stake. He assured the American
public that this situation represented "one of the great creative moments in our nation's history. The whole world," Ford said, "is
watching to see how we respond."

Shortly after that the International Energy Agency—the organization of industrialized nations formed to coordinate energy policies
and present a united front against the Arab oil world—issued a
global report that ranked the United States last among all industrialized nations in terms of operational national policies aimed at
"conserving energy." The report said that the United States Government had "no standards, no incentives, and almost no taxes" aimed
at forcing its society to curtail petroleum use.

At the same time the office of Federal Energy Administrator
Frank G. Zarb released documents which indicated that the wells
throughout America were producing less oil in 1975 than they had
in 1973, that Americans were consuming record amounts of petroleum products of all types and that the United States and its allies
were more dependent on the oil controlled by the Keeper of the
Holy Cities of Islam than ever before.

In Israel the right-wing Likud Party, headed by Menachem Begin,
held its 1975 national convention in an Israeli-garrisoned settlement
that had been established on land expropriated from Muslims near

the occupied West Bank town of Hebron. Begin issued a campaign call for the "retention" of the "entire West Bank" as "part of the Land of Israel." The "Land of Israel" is a biblical term describing all of present-day Israel, all of the occupied territories seized during the 1967 war and large additional segments of several contiguous Muslim nations.

At the same time, in Israel, Gush Emunim—land raiders—a militant Israeli political group, began physically raiding and seizing Muslim homes, farms and pastures in the occupied territories and proclaimed the "rights of Jews to live anywhere in what they considered their historic homeland."

At the same time, Palestinian guerrillas carried out waves of violent attacks in both Israel and the occupied territories, hijacked or attacked planes in France and Kenya, attacked a train in the Netherlands and kidnapped diplomats in Vienna. Throughout 1975, Palestinian guerrillas bombed fifty-two sites, shot up another twenty-one and killed or seriously injured 340 persons.

And at the United Nations headquarters in New York events were proceeding in a similarly tumultuous manner toward a climax of revolutionary importance to both America and Israel. The Rabat summit of 1969 had laid the groundwork for the diplomatic jihad which, by 1975, would overturn the existing order within the United Nations.

9

REVOLUTION AT THE UN

When World War II ended abruptly in a geyser of glowing ash above Nagasaki, Harry S. Truman sat in Washington as de facto "King of the World." No other person in history had the range of unrivaled power enjoyed by Truman for the four years between 1945 and 1949—the four years between the heat of the old war and the chill of the developing cold war.

America's power was absolute. Truman, the only man ever to order atomic attacks, was the sole possessor of the ultimate weapon which made all other aspects of military power obsolete. Technologically, the United States was not just the richest, strongest and most productive nation, but the only major power on earth with a functioning industrial base untouched by war.

Economically, America's rule was unchallenged. London, which had for two centuries been the hub of the world's economy, lay blitzed to rubble. At the meeting of Allied governments at Bretton Woods in New Hampshire, the world's financial system had been rearranged in a new form, anchored to the U.S. dollar and revolving around the International Monetary Fund and the World Bank. Both institutions relied on the financial support of the U. S. Government.

At the new United Nations the General Assembly sat daily witness to America's unprecedented foreign aid programs. During the war the United States had become the architect and bankroller of the world's first comprehensive system of foreign aid. The idea itself was novel at the time: that one nation should tax its citizens and businesses to collect money it would hand over to citizens and businesses in less fortunate countries. By 1946 these American programs of giveaways had become the dominant factor in its relations with the rest of the world—providing the leverage the White House used to work its will. The U.S. aid program for the reconstruction of war-devastated Europe—the Marshall Plan—was the first international program which directly linked foreign aid payments to compliance with specific political demands. Countries willing to structure their societies on American-dictated economic and political principles received U.S. aid. Countries that balked at these principles, or otherwise displeased the White House, did not. The Marshall Plan was only the largest of the programs through which the United States was channeling aid of various sorts to societies throughout the world.

Imagine a tribesman-turned-soldier come to power in an underdeveloped country of Africa or Latin America. Imagine what local political power and control he would derive from being able to supply—with U.S. funds—food to villages previously starving and trucks and power saws to river trading posts previously dependent on dugout canoes or sharpened bone. Imagine what that political leader would do to retain that U.S. aid, the thoughts that would move through his mind when he received a personal request from the President of the United States to vote in a certain manner in the upcoming session of the United Nations General Assembly.

During the next thirty years after the United Nations voted to form Israel, dramatic changes occurred in both the ethnic configuration of the General Assembly as well as in the global foreign aid systems which were such an integral part of its internal political movements.

By 1959 other industrialized nations—notably France, Great Britain, Italy and Japan—had launched extensive aid programs, particularly in those regions of Africa and Asia from which they imported various raw materials. Meanwhile, the United States had begun to reduce the amount of money earmarked for foreign aid and to contract the overall spread of its programs. Slowly the U.S. aid system came to focus most of its funds into a handful of countries positioned like chain links against the borders of the Soviet Union and China: Turkey, Pakistan, India, Southeast Asia and South Korea.

By 1965, in the world rankings of nations by percentage of their gross national product devoted to foreign aid programs, the United States had quietly fallen to fifth place—behind France, Australia, Belgium and the Netherlands.

In 1969, in those same world rankings, the United States aid programs trailed in ninth place—behind France, Portugal, Japan, Australia, West Germany, the Netherlands, Belgium and Great Britain.

In 1969 those U.S. aid programs were further contracted by the Nixon administration, which shifted the bulk of all remaining foreign aid funds into Southeast Asia. The reason had to do largely with the fact that it was less politically troublesome to increase money for the war effort this way than by asking Congress—and the increasingly problematic electorate—to approve additional new money for the war. While sixty-nine different nations received some amount of U.S. aid in 1969, more than 70 percent of the total funds were spent in the war zone.

By 1979, in the world rankings of nations by percentage of their gross national product devoted to foreign aid, the United States had fallen to twentieth—behind Saudi Arabia, Kuwait, the United Arab Emirates, Qatar, Sweden, France, Australia, Austria, Belgium, Great Britain, Canada, Denmark, Finland, West Germany, Japan, the Netherlands, New Zealand, Norway and Switzerland.

That same year 85 percent of all the U.S. foreign aid funds budgeted were given to Israel and Egypt.

Meanwhile, the Congress had so cut the foreign aid programs and slashed U.S. contributions to the international development aid banks that America's eligibility for further participation in those institutions was threatened, and financial journals on three continents reported a rising international sentiment in favor of revoking America's traditional privilege of choosing the president of the World Bank.

The new front runners in foreign aid—Saudi Arabia, Kuwait, the United Arab Emirates and Qatar—had first laid the framework for their programs at the 1969 Islamic summit called by King Faisal immediately following the Al Aqsa Mosque arson. In 1973 those nations were virtually rocketed into the foreign aid business when oil price hikes provided them with unprecedented amounts of surplus national wealth.

In 1978 a report by the Chase World Information Corporation provided the first comprehensive details of the true size and worldwide patterns of the emerging Muslim foreign aid networks and indicated that during the first three years of their existence they channeled at least $19 billion in aid to Asian, African and Latin American countries. Those funds were distributed through several new agencies created by the oil-producing Muslim states including the Saudi Fund for Development, the Kuwait Fund for Arab Economic Development, the OPEC Fund for International Development, the Islamic Development Fund, the Abu Dhabi Fund for Economic Development, the Arab Bank for Economic Development in Africa, and others.

One of the larger of these Muslim foreign aid projects is a multibillion-dollar undertaking involving the construction of a vast sprawl of dams, cities, hydroelectric facilities, power transmission stations, road systems, irrigation networks, ore mining projects, mosques and schools along the Senegal River, snaking through all of western Africa. Other projects range from ice plants in India to fertilizer factories in Bangladesh to public electric systems in Brazil to sugar mills in Sudan to energy projects in Nicaragua to airports in the Maldive Islands.

In 1978 the United Nations Conference on Trade and Development issued a report on these foreign aid programs and indicated that, like the United States in the postwar era, the Muslim governments "attach strings to the bilateral aid they give" throughout Latin America, Africa and Asia.

Imagine, for instance, what goes through the mind of an African prime minister as he sits at his desk, poring over blueprints of a partially completed hydroelectric dam and receives a personal request from the King of Saudi Arabia to vote in a certain manner in the upcoming session of the United Nations General Assembly.

In 1967, as the third Israeli-Muslim war raged, the United States was still in firm control of events in the General Assembly. As the

United Nations convened in emergency session to deal with the Middle East war-in-progress, the United States and Israel led a vigorous lobbying effort to remove the subject from the agenda of the General Assembly and turn it over exclusively to the "upper house," the Security Council.

The Security Council has fifteen members, but its real power is vested in its five permanent members—the United States, the Soviet Union, Great Britain, France and China. Each of these five has the prerogative of a veto with which they can stop any Security Council action they oppose. The General Assembly—the "lower house"— provides no such special privileges. Every nation in the organization has one seat and one vote. There are no vetoes. Majority vote decides any given issue.

In the past the United States had frequently used its power to sway General Assembly votes to have certain issues removed from that body and passed on to the Security Council, where the American veto provided an absolute means of control and negotiation leverage.

This tactic was again used during the 1967 war as the United Nations met to attempt to set the terms under which the conflict might be halted. In a General Assembly vote of 63 to 26 with 27 abstentions, the United States succeeded in having the issue turned over to the Security Council. The plan which was formulated and approved by the Security Council became known as Resolution 242. It had three basic principles: that all Muslim states recognize that Israel had a right to exist; that Israel evacuate its troops from the Old City of Jerusalem, the Gaza Strip, the West Bank, the Sinai and the Golan regions seized during the war, and that there be a "just settlement to the refugee problem." This last clause was one of the most controversial sections of the resolution.

There are currently at least four million Palestinians—a group of people larger than the population of Ireland—scattered throughout the Middle East. They lost their ancestral lands when they fled or were forcibly driven out of Palestine during the 1947–48 war. In his memoirs former Israeli Premier Yitzhak Rabin detailed how the Israeli militia emptied entire cities of their Muslim inhabitants to make way for arriving Europeans. In one incident he detailed how 50,000 Palestinian Muslims in the towns of Ramle and Lydda were herded at gunpoint from their homes and into the street, where they were held prisoner before Premier David Ben-Gurion ordered his troops to "drive them out." They joined throngs of hundreds of thousands of other Palestinians also leaving behind their homes, farms and villages.[1]

The United Nations move to officially recognize these people as only "refugees" denied their claim, as indigenous inhabitants, to resettle after the war in the land in which their families had lived for as long as a thousand years or more.

In December 1969, three months after the first Pan-Islamic summit called by King Faisal in the wake of the Al Aqsa Mosque arson, the internal currents of the United Nations began to evidence a change. In a move noted by the Western press as a mild "surprise development," a Special Political Committee of the United Nations General Assembly passed a resolution affirming the "inalienable rights" of the Palestinians. The General Assembly committee vote was 50 to 20 as blocs of Asian and African representatives joined to overwhelm the opposition votes assembled by the United States and Israel.

Two of America's staunchest allies—Great Britain and France—declined to vote or officially take any position on the issue of the Palestinians.

In December 1970, in the first full General Assembly debate on the Middle East since the 1967 war, the Islamic nations of Afghanistan, Guinea, Indonesia, Malaysia, Mauretania, Pakistan and Somalia introduced a resolution asserting that the "people of Palestine" had the "inalienable right" to self-determination. In a battle which pitted the United States against a bloc of Asian and African nations coordinating both their votes and their lobbying efforts, the resolution passed by 47 to 22. Fifty nations abstained, including Great Britain and France. The United States was the only member of the Big Four powers that voted against the resolution.

In December 1971, as the full General Assembly once again turned to the Middle East issue, eighteen African and Asian nations sponsored a resolution which demanded that Israel withdraw from the Old City of Jerusalem and the other territories seized during the 1967 war.

The resolution passed 79 to 7 with 36 abstentions.

Israel's delegation issued a statement which said that the passage of the resolution "meant nothing" and that "nothing had changed."

In 1972, after Israeli occupational military commanders, citing "security reasons," dynamited, bulldozed or otherwise destroyed the houses of 15,855 Muslims in the Gaza Strip, the United Nations took up debate on the Middle East issue again. In the full General Assembly a resolution was proposed which urged all governments of the world not to recognize any changes carried out by Israel in the Old City of Jerusalem and other of the occupied territories.

The United States' spokesman condemned the African and Asian nations backing the resolution and charged that such actions "cannot render constructive assistance to the process of diplomacy."

The resolution passed by a vote of 86 to 7.

In 1973 in the United Nations Security Council, five of the rotating seats were held by the Muslim nations of Tanzania, Nigeria, Guinea, Algeria and Chad and proposed a resolution directing Israel to withdraw from the Old City of Jerusalem and the other occupied territories seized in the 1967 war.

Chad issued a statement calling on the upper house of the United Nations to recognize the "right of the Palestinians to recover their national heritage" and for the United Nations to grant official observer status to the Palestine Liberation Organization in order that the Palestinians would be directly represented in all United Nations actions determining their future.

Israel issued a statement charging that any attempt to deal with the Palestinian issue as anything other than a "refugee problem" would "create a complete void in the United Nations framework as far as the Middle East is concerned." Israel's representative said that "only the Jewish people" had a right to the "Land of Israel."

In July 1973, prior to adjourning for the summer, thirteen members of the fifteen-member Security Council voted in favor of a resolution "deploring" the continued Israeli occupation of the Old City of Jerusalem and the other seized territories. The resolution was killed when the United States exercised its veto power. U. S. Representative John A. Scali said the veto was necessary because the resolution "would have done irrevocable harm" in the Middle East.

Two months later the Muslim states launched the October jihad for Jerusalem and King Faisal announced that the "Sword of Oil" would be unsheathed against the United States and its industrialized allies.

In 1974—one year after the war and just as the industrialized nations began receiving their full supplies of oil again at prices 400 percent higher than before—the General Assembly took up the issue of "The Question of Palestine." In one of the most tumultuous sessions since those of 1947 that resulted in the creation of Israel by a one-vote margin, a vote was taken on a resolution to recognize the Palestine Liberation Organization as the official representative of the Palestinian people and to authorize the PLO to participate in all United Nations proceedings on the Middle East. The governments of 81 percent of all the countries in the world voted to officially recognize the PLO as "the representative of the Palestinian people" at the United Nations. Japan voted in favor of the PLO. Europe split its vote, France, Ireland and Italy recognizing the PLO and the other European nations abstaining.

Four nations out of 129—the United States, Israel, Bolivia and the Dominican Republic—voted not to recognize the PLO or allow representatives of the Palestinians to take part in debates involving the crisis in the Middle East.

By the end of 1974 the Palestinians and "The Question of Palestine" had become a ubiquitous presence throughout the broad fabric of the United Nations Organization. The UN Educational, Scientific and Cultural Organization (UNESCO) voted 80 to 2 to admit the PLO to its general conference with observer status. The two no votes were Israel and the United States.

The staid proceedings of the UN Conference on the Law of the Sea in Caracas, Venezuela, were disrupted by debate over whether the PLO should be seated as an official observer. Over the strenuous objections of the United States, it was.

The UN Economic and Social Council, which administers international economic, social and cultural programs, voted to allow the PLO to attend the World Conference on Food and Population as an official observer.

In the often-caustic General Assembly debate of 1974 on the Middle East, Great Britain, France and Italy called for immediate withdrawal of Israeli occupational troops from the Old City of Jerusalem and the other territories seized in 1967. Great Britain issued a declaration that the Palestinians had "just claim to the right to express their own identity within the territory with which they are historically associated."

United States Ambassador to the United Nations John Scali publicly called on Henry Kissinger and the Ford administration to resume negotiations in the Middle East in a manner which would take into account the "legitimate interests of the Palestinian people." By spring, Scali had been replaced.

In 1975 Switzerland convened a conference to update the 1949 rules of the Geneva Convention—the rules governing the treatment of civilian populations in territories occupied by alien military forces. The Netherlands, Finland, Norway, Australia and New Zealand sponsored a move which afforded the Palestine Liberation Organization official standing before the world body as a group fighting against "colonial and alien domination and against racist regimes in the exercise of their right to self-determination."

In November 1975 the United Nations General Assembly passed a resolution which established as official United Nations principle that Zionism—the nineteenth-century European philosophy which held that only Jews had a right to certain lands in Asia—was the same as apartheid—the nineteenth-century European philosophy which held that only whites had a right to certain lands in Africa.

In December, Israeli Phantom jets shrieked across southern Lebanon, bombing Palestinian refugee camps throughout the region. At least 91 persons were killed and 150 seriously injured. In some cases entire sections of villages and towns were obliterated.

Israeli officials described the dead as "terrorists" and said the raids had been preemptive strikes against known Palestinian groups located "in refugee camps."

Arab officials described the dead as "civilians including children" and said the raids were an attempt to disperse the Palestinians from the densely populated camps, which had become a focus of international attention and a primary political pressure point for Israel. Those 1975 air raids sparked widespread reaction around the world. Pope Paul VI issued a statement in the Vatican calling Israel's action an "inadmissible gesture of violence."

The fifteen-member United Nations Security Council, at the request of Muslim nations, took up official debate on the issue of Israeli air raids into Lebanon. After bitter public arguments, the Security Council members voted 9 to 3—with Sweden leading the vote against the United States—to admit the Palestine Liberation Organization as an official participant to the proceedings.

During the first week of July 1976, as America was celebrating the two hundredth anniversary of its revolution, the occupied Old City of Jerusalem and the West Bank exploded in tax riots, as Muslim merchants refused to keep records or collect the new "value added" tax imposed on citizens of the seized territories by the occupational Israeli military forces.

At the same time, the Israeli Government announced it would authorize the establishment of a new Israeli settlement on Muslim lands near the city of Nablus in the occupied West Bank—thereby officially sanctioning the program of vigilante land seizures begun as 1,500 Gush Emunim armed with machine guns crossed the border from Israel, forcibly took control of land near Nablus and fought off Muslim farmers seeking to retake it.

The Israeli Government additionally ruled that the stone plateau atop the Temple mount in the occupied Old City of Jerusalem—the area directly surrounding both Al Aqsa Mosque and the Dome of the Rock—was to be opened for unlimited use by Israelis as a "state-sanctioned Jewish worshiping site." The announcement touched off the worst and bloodiest Muslim riots, demonstrations and marches in more than three decades.

At the United Nations the 1976 General Assembly voted 122 to 2 to convene the Geneva Conference on the Middle East as a forum in which to seek a permanent peace settlement. Israel and the United States voted no. The United States said it could not vote in favor of the resolution because it called for Geneva talks which included "all parties to the conflict."

In the fifteen-member United Nations Security Council a resolution "deploring" Israeli treatment of civilians throughout the occupied Old City of Jerusalem, the Gaza Strip, the West Bank and the Golan Heights was passed by a vote of 14 to 1. Great Britain, France, Italy, Japan and Sweden were among those voting against the United States.

At the end of 1976 the Security Council opened further debate on the Middle East and entertained a resolution which would authorize the Palestine Liberation Organization—already an officially sanctioned observer—to be seated at the debate with all the rights of a UN member nation, entitled to full participation in all proceedings.

The United States criticized the resolution and called on its allies on the Security Council to reject it because it "eroded the influence and authority of the Security Council." In the vote the United States was the only nation to vote against the Palestine Liberation Organization.

In the United States in 1977 Jimmy Carter took office. On one of his first trips as President, Carter stopped for a major energy speech in Clinton, Massachusetts, and called for Israel to withdraw from the territories it had seized during the 1967 war. Carter also announced that his administration would work for the creation of a "Palestinian homeland."

In Israel in 1977 the right-wing Likud Party was voted into power, making Menachem Begin Premier. One of Begin's first public acts as Premier was to travel with TV and news crews across the border of Israel and into the occupied West Bank. There Begin scooped up a handful of dirt from the pasture of a farm seized from a Muslim farmer and declared that "We stand on the land of liberated Israel."

Begin, who appointed Moshe Dayan as new Foreign Minister, also announced that the capital offices of Israel would be moved out of Tel Aviv in Israel and into the seized Muslim neighborhoods of the Old City of Jerusalem.

New Foreign Minister Moshe Dayan announced that Israel would accept no peace treaty which required that it "relinquish" the Old City of Jerusalem or the other territories taken during the 1967 war.

Israeli Agricultural Minister Ariel Sharon made public a plan outlining a new government program for the erection of more "urban and agricultural" settlements throughout the occupied Muslim territories. The goal of the new program was to move "about two million Jews" onto lands taken from Muslims beyond the borders of Israel.

At the same time, Israeli Gush Emunim launched broad new attacks outside the borders of Israel, seizing more than 2,000 acres of Muslim lands and setting off long-term rioting throughout the occupied territories.

At the United Nations, President Carter delivered a speech calling for the recognition of human rights around the world. At a reception directly afterward, standing next to UN Secretary Kurt Waldheim and the U. S. Ambassador Andrew Young, Carter met and shook hands with Hasan Abdul Rahman, the UN representative of the Palestine Liberation Organization.

The General Assembly again took up the issue of the Palestinians and voted on a resolution which "strongly deplored" Israel's continued occupation of the Old City of Jerusalem, the Gaza Strip, the West Bank and the Golan Heights. The resolution also condemned the establishment of more settlements of Israelis in those occupied Muslim lands.

The Carter administration instructed its representative at the UN to abstain from voting.

The vote in favor of the resolution was 131 to 1. On the thirtieth anniversary of Israel's creation by the General Assembly, the government of Menachem Begin stood alone before that body, isolated from every other nation on earth.

10

PETRO-EMPIRE

Since the late 1800s, when the sticky subterranean stew first began gushing from man-drilled holes in western Pennsylvania and the shores of the Caspian Sea, oil has been the key to controlling the other systems of our civilization. During the hundred years they dominated the supply networks for this resource, United States and European oil magnates became more powerful than most of the governments of the world. A century of records of this industry evidences a history both colorful and bloody. On one hand that history includes some of the Western world's most intoxicating moments of triumph and creativity. And on the other it embodies some of America's and Europe's most shameful episodes of unbridled cruelty, criminality and debauchery.

In America oil power became synonymous with the name Rockefeller. John D. Rockefeller began his career as a lamp-oil salesman and by the 1880s had leaped into the new rock-oil refining business and taken it over. He pioneered a system based not upon control of oil in the ground but rather control of the machinery through which oil was transported and processed. From coast to coast in America, using bribes, threats, thugs and tubs of money, Rockefeller created his Standard Oil monolith. It drove out all competitors and came to control 90 percent of all the pipelines, railroad tankers, refineries, processing and packing plants and delivery systems through which oil moved from a hole in the ground to a final purchaser. His dream was to encircle the globe with his apparatus dominating the flow of all oil. He attempted to expand into Europe but was confronted by competitors whose name had become synonymous with oil power in Europe—the Rothschilds.

The Paris Rothschilds—Alphonse, Gustave and Edmond—were the richest men in Europe in the late 1800s and petro-barons with broad ventures centered around the vast oil deposits at Baku on the Caspian Sea. Like Rockefeller, the Rothschilds sought to control the transportation and processing systems for oil moving north into Russia, west into Europe and east into Asia, where the new industrial era of petroleum-intensive machinery was exploding across the landscape. The Rothschilds funded the first freight line carrying oil in ships up the Volga River. They controlled the railroad tanker networks that ran from Baku to the Black Sea. They controlled the pipelines, from the very first one built under their aegis by the construction firm of Dembo and Kagan across the neck of land between the Caspian and Black seas. And the Rothschilds also built the first fleet of oil tanker ships, which provided the real sinew for the lucrative transoceanic oil sales business. The tankers were operated by the new Shell Oil Transport and Trading Company, started by Marcus Samuel, a London businessman and partner of the Rothschilds. Shell Oil received all of its petroleum supplies from the Rothschilds' Baku operation. The Rothschild refineries were at Fiume—the Cleveland of Europe—on the Adriatic. And when competitors built railroads and other facilities at Baku, the Rothschild banking branch provided the funds in return for oil-field mortgages and long-term oil-supply contracts which further expanded their continental petro-clout. The Rothschild oil cartel crushed the Rockefeller cartel's attempts to scoop up substantial portions of the European and Far Eastern oil markets—boxing Rockefeller largely inside the confines of the United States, where his Standard Oil Trust was attacked by U. S. Justice Department trust busters. Meanwhile, in Paris, the youngest of the Rothschild oil magnates—Edmond—was employing increasingly larger amounts of his petro-fortunes to launch a venture that would come to eclipse all other aspects of his multifaceted life: the creation of a private European settlement colony for Russian refugees in the desert heartland of Islamic Asia.

Ninety years later, and employing much the same techniques as had the Rothschilds, a new group of oil barons would attempt to undo the Asian initiatives of their petro-predecessors.

Although it seemed incredible at the time he was announcing it in the 1960s, this was Faisal Ibn Abdul-Aziz al Saud's utopian vision: that Islamic nations which had been controlled by the Western oil powers could now coordinate their political moves, resources and capital wealth and rise up as industrial world powers in the 1980s as America and Europe had begun to do in the 1880s.

Ten of the thirteen members of the new OPEC were Muslim, including Nigeria in Black Africa and Indonesia in Southeast Asia. Overall, Muslim countries control the majority of all oil supplies on the planet. More than 67 percent of all currently known deposits of petroleum are located beneath the surface of thirty-two Islamic countries.

Considered in terms of either their direct physical importance to the petroleum-thirsty industrial community for the next fifty years, or their ability to generate unprecedented sums of capital, these Muslim oil reserves represent the richest potential development resource ever controlled by any single civilization in history. They dwarf those resources which enabled the United States and Europe to build themselves into industrial and political titans in past decades. And they have become the reason that the United States is losing its hold not only on the United Nations but on the other global institutions. And as American and European power declines throughout the world's industrial, commercial and financial networks, Muslim power within those same broad systems continues to rise.

Consider the events in the world's petroleum networks:

In 1960 the descendants of the petroleum colossus spawned by the Rockefeller and Rothschild systems—an American-dominated consortium led by Exxon, Texaco, Mobil, Chevron, Shell and British Petroleum—exerted enormous influence on the day-to-day operation of every nation in the non-Communist world. This consortium of corporations represented the most powerful financial-industrial apparatus ever assembled in the history of the planet. It was the first to wire almost all the nations of the globe into a unified grid of controls which allowed a handful of individuals to dictate the course of broad events on all continents.

The consortium itself was a hybrid. On one hand it was a free enterprise beyond the control of any single government. On the other it served as a global utility willing to "lend" its facilities in a manner which made those facilities direct extensions through which the Western governments exercised power around the post-World War II world.

In 1960 this consortium had come to encircle the globe like a web of iron. It controlled 90 percent of all petroleum being pumped, processed, shipped, refined, stored or sold in any form in the non-Communist world. It owned the oil fields, the drilling crews, the production facilities, the pipelines, the ports, the tanker fleets, the refineries, petrochemical plants and distribution systems—from tanker off-loading docks to corner retail outlets—through which petroleum products moved. Control of this system ever since the Rockefellers and Rothschilds pioneered it was one of the single most important aspects of the Western world's overall global power.

In 1970, Islamic governments that had been methodically employing their oil royalties to educate tens of thousands of their citizens in the science and machinery of the petroleum industry began to assume control of their own fields. Western corporations that previously depended on their vast capital and exclusive technological know-how to maintain monopoly control of the fields rapidly shifted their stance from patronization to partnership with the Arab governments. The same Muslim governments had also methodically acquired modern armies, navies and air forces as well as the other national systems required to enforce their sovereign rights within their own borders. The Western oil companies were "invited" to remain in the country and continue working the fields under the direction of their Arab hosts. Almost immediately dramatic changes began occurring throughout the entire global petroleum grid, which had, for thirty years, been anchored in the Middle East. After taking the wells, the Islamic governments began using their burgeoning petro-profits in campaigns aimed at expanding their hold to the drilling crews, the production facilities, the pipelines, the ports, the tanker fleets, the refineries, the petrochemical plants and the distribution systems which were the key not only to control of the world petroleum networks but the entire body of industrial civilization whose veins they formed.

By 1980 the Western oil consortiums—which once were the salesmen for more than 90 percent of all oil moving between nations—controlled less than 50 percent of world sales, and that figure was continuing to drop. Islamic governments were daily increasing the amounts of government-to-government sales—those transfers of oil from wellhead to consumer controlled by Muslim governments directly.

By 1980 the Western oil consortiums—which once controlled more than 80 percent of all oil sales on the "spot market," that gray trading zone which is the source of last resort for consumers unable to obtain oil elsewhere—controlled less than 40 percent and that figure was continuing to drop. In fact, by 1980 the Western oil companies themselves were forced to obtain 7 percent of their own basic oil needs from that high-priced, desperation market.

By 1980 many of the corporations that had virtually ruled large sections of Africa and Asia from which they extracted their oil had been driven close to collapse by the Muslim governments that cut them off from those crucial supplies. BP by 1980, for instance, had lost 40 percent of its supplies when cut off by Iran, 10 percent more when cut off by Nigeria and 15 percent further when cut off by Kuwait. In 1971, BP had had direct control of 66 billion barrels of oil reserves. In 1980 it controlled only 2 billion barrels of oil reserves.

Another example is Texaco. In 1978 Texaco still had direct control of 3.5 billion barrels of oil reserves. But less than twelve months later its reserves had been cut to 2.1 billion barrels and were dropping further. The company quietly announced a total reorganization.

In similar fashion the Gulf Oil Corporation by 1980 was completely cut off from its remaining Middle East oil reserves and was reorganizing itself as a "North American oil company."

The first beyond-the-well projects undertaken by Muslim governments seeking to expand control across the whole of the global petroleum network was refining. In 1960, for instance, Kuwait controlled neither its oil nor the refined products made from that oil. Those final processes—one of the most profitable parts of the entire petroleum business chain—were largely completed in and around the final destination of the shipped oil: America and Europe. By

1980, however, Kuwait was exporting 30 percent of its prodigious oil pumpings in the form of high-priced, profit-intensive refined products. It was also involved in building programs which would soon allow it to sell 50 percent of all its oil as finished products, totally circumventing the American and European refining and processing centers.

Saudi Arabia, Iraq, Kuwait, Algeria, Libya, Qatar, Bahrain, Syria and the United Arab Emirates during the latter years of the 1970s spent more than $67 billion in the planning and construction of a vast carpet of now refineries, gas-processing facilities and petroleum-based chemical plants. Americans in general have not yet begun to appreciate the extraordinary implications of these programs, which are expanding every year and promise, by the late 1980s, to become a world force in the processed-petroleum products industry.

In 1979, after six years of planning, Saudi Arabia began the two most complex and ambitious construction projects in the history of the industrialized world: two entire cities, both gargantuan sprawls of refineries, processing plants, petrochemical production plants, synthetic rubber factories, manufacturing zones and metallurgy works, aimed at eclipsing America and Europe as the leaders of the world's petrochemical industries.

To say these two projects are mammoth does not capture their full size or implications. Jubail, the site at which construction crews in 1980 had moved more sand than all that moved during the creation of the Suez Canal, is 350 miles square—larger than the 303 square miles covered by the entire five-borough metropolitan region of New York City. Yanbu, the second petrochemical city-in-progress is located on the Red Sea coast and is 60 miles square—the same size as the entire metropolitan region of Washington, D.C.

By 1990 these two Saudi installations, as well as the similarly large installations being built in other Middle Eastern Muslim nations, will constitute the largest collection of petrochemical production complexes in the world. They will provide Middle Eastern governments with controlling influence on price and supply of chemicals throughout the world. They will also be able to put the chemical industries of other nations out of business—because no other nations can compete with the price offered by petrochemical plants sitting atop the largest and cheapest oil supplies in the world.

In late 1980 the *Financial Times* of London was already sounding the alarm about the "savage consequences" such a broad-based Middle Eastern petrochemical industry will have on the entire structure of the globe's chemical markets.

Some further indication of the panic rising throughout the industry can be seen in the crash projects now under way by corporations such as DuPont and Monsanto, which are attempting—without success to date—to find some economically viable method of producing this wide range of petrochemicals from wood pulp or coal instead of oil.

Nor is this an arcane issue likely to affect only industry. There is virtually no product in America which does not involve petrochemicals in its manufacture. One third of all the clothes hanging on the racks in American stores are totally made from petroleum pumped from the ground in the Middle East, processed into viscous chemicals and extruded as synthetic fibers. The 47 million tons of plastics, of which Americans are profligate consumers, are completely made from petroleum chemicals. Over 80 percent of all the world's chemicals are directly made from petroleum, and that percentage is expected to increase to 98 percent in the coming decade.

And, like petroleum, these crucial petroleum chemicals must physically be delivered to the industrial societies which depend upon them to sustain daily industrial operations and economic vitality. The ability to dispatch or hold back the webs of ships which accomplish such deliveries is, perhaps, the single most potent control mechanism within the global petroleum supply networks. In 1967, when Americans and Europeans enjoyed nearly exclusive control of this ship transport system, they were able to use those ships to thwart the first Arab oil-embargo attempt.

But by 1980 that was no longer possible. A new force had burst upon the world of shipping and transoceanic petroleum transportation.

11

THE NEW SEA LORDS

Since the 1940s the sea-lanes have been the primary
avenue of the United States' global power. The
country emerged from World War II as virtual ruler
of the waves in all oceans. But by the 1970s U.S.
naval forces and merchant marine corps had encountered difficulties.

In 1980, for instance, the number of ships being
built at U.S. shipyards was at its lowest since
1953—a year when the sea was glutted with surplus
warships. Much the same as was happening throughout Europe, America had closed the bulk of its
once-booming shipyards, and those remaining experienced increasing waves of layoffs and cutbacks.

On the high seas around the world the U.S.
merchant vessels had become a small and economically unviable presence—a virtual skeletal operation maintained only by the grace of enormous subsidies, loan guarantees and other massive artificial
supports provided by Congress.

Perhaps no other incident so succinctly captures
the state of the American maritime industry as the
fate of the ship *America*—the showpiece and former
pride of the U.S. merchant marine fleet—which,
for reasons of indebtedness, was sold to Liberia.

There, at Monrovia, the *America* is docked as a floating hotel and social center for the Organization of African Unity.

Since the late 1950s the type of ship that has come to dominate virtually every aspect of the world's maritime trade and fortunes has been the crude-oil tanker. By the 1970s half of all the shipbuilding under way in the world involved new tankers—the working shuttle parts of the vastly complex but enormously profitable transoceanic grid of petroleum distribution set up by American and European oil conglomerates. In 1970, 85 percent of all tankers plying the oil routes of the world did so under the direct control of Western oil consortiums. In effect those corporations had annexed the sealanes as another wholly owned part of the global machinery through which they controlled the oil business from the wellheads in Asia and Africa to the pump nozzles in Peoria and Poughkeepsie.

That situation began to change drastically in the 1970s. By 1980 new state-backed consortiums and private firms throughout Asia and Africa had moved to take control of ever-larger chunks of the industries involved in both the building and operation of the world's ships. By the end of the 1970s the Western firms controlled less than 45 percent of the ships carrying oil to Europe and America and that percentage was continuing to drop.

Some of the most active and aggressive of the Asian and African countries in these fields during the last decade have been Kuwait, Saudi Arabia, Bahrain, the United Arab Emirates, Qatar, Iraq, Libya, Syria and Algeria. During the period from 1968 to 1978, for instance, Lloyd's Registry of London indicates that the nations of the free world experienced an increase in the gross tonnage shipped of about 100 percent. During that same period of time the gross tonnage of world cargo being transported on Arab ships increased more than 800 percent. That percentage was continuing to climb throughout the early 1980s.

Much of the Muslim governments' initial advantage in international shipping circles came as a direct result of their new control over that industry's primary international cargo. For instance, Saudi Arabia by the latter half of the 1970s loaded more export cargo than any other country in the world. That cargo provided both the money to fund massive shipbuilding projects and the leverage to demand—successfully—that oil traveling from the Middle East to the West be transported in Arab ships. By 1980 this stipulation had become a standard section of routine oil sales contracts for Middle Eastern oil powers, such as Kuwait.

In 1968 the Arab fleet of ships, many of which were decrepit freighters and fishing dhows, numbered 335 in Lloyd's Registry. In 1978 the Arab fleet numbered 1,550, the bulk of which were state-of-the-art oil tankers, ore carriers, chemical tankers, container cargo ships and liquified natural gas ships.

In 1976, Saudi Arabia, Kuwait, Bahrain, Qatar, Iraq and the United Arab Emirates joined to form the United Arab Shipping Company and the Arab Maritime Petroleum Tanker Company, an affiliate, which, together, operate 270 vessels flying the flag of Kuwait. Also formed have been such companies as the Iraq Oil Tanker Enterprise, the Kuwait Oil Tanker Company, the General National Maritime Transport Company of Libya and Saudi International Petroleum Carriers Limited.

By 1980 these Arab ships were carrying about 10 percent of all the exports leaving the Middle East. And the Muslim governments had launched further billion-dollar programs aimed at taking direct control of 45 percent of all their own exports by 1985. This they accomplished by ultimatum: The Western world could either contract to have its oil, gas and minerals delivered by Arab vessels or do without the oil, gas and minerals in question.

Ahmed Sayyed Omar, senior consultant for the Arab Maritime Petroleum Transport Company, explained, "This is not a commercial venture as such. This is a strategic decision. We must have our own ships to strengthen our hand, to resist pressure from the oil companies or anyone else who seeks to dilute our control of our national assets."

In 1960 the Muslim nations of Africa and Asia had only a handful of ports capable of handling American and European tankers and cargo ships. The rest of their "port" space consisted of little more than open beach front, where smaller dhows were dragged ashore, or crude stone piers for fishing and pearl-diving boats.

In 1980 in the Middle East alone there were 117 major port facilities, all new. Some sense of the extraordinary size of these facilities can be had from looking at a single one—the latest of the fourteen ports built in the United Arab Emirates in the previous ten years. It has seventy berths, providing at that single spot a port cargo capacity larger than that of New York City.

The Muslim countries surrounding the Persian Gulf have collectively become the largest world market for ships, tugboats, floating docks, dredgers, ferries, barges, service craft and luxury yachts. Shipyards throughout the south of Asia have been working around the clock and importing thousands of workers from Europe, Japan and Australia to meet production schedules.

In Bahrain, at Mina Sulman, the $340 million Arab Ship Building and Repair Yards Company—one of thirty-five shipyards and repair facilities erected in the Middle East in the previous fifteen years—opened in 1979. Its launching ways for new ships are the largest available between Rotterdam and Hong Kong and its drydocks are among the largest in the world for supertankers.

In 1980, despite the existing new maritime facilities, Saudi Arabia, Kuwait, Bahrain, the United Arab Emirates, Qatar, Iraq, Libya, Syria, Algeria and Oman all began massive new constructions aimed at adding further cargo zones, harbors, piers, deepwater ports, container complexes and shipbuilding and repair facilities. This at the same time the Conference of the Arab League approved the Saudi Arabian proposal to set up an Arab Organization for Land and Sea Transport, which will consist of both international regulating and investment divisions and will be headquartered in Riyadh. It is planning to establish an organization for world shipping registration in Kuwait—a space-age computer central installation for recording, tracking and controlling oil shipments and delivery patterns around the globe. It is the announced intention of this new enterprise to eventually use its facilities to ensure that all oil shipments headed west travel in ships of Arab registry.

And if there is any one symbolic item that captures the tone and aspirations of this burgeoning maritime trend it is to be found in the fact that, during the five years ending in 1980, Saudi Arabia alone spent $4.5 million to purchase the Steuben glass, Christofle silver and Limoges china upon which its sailors routinely dine as they move their vessels in ever-widening circles around the world's sea-lanes.

12

GOD WILLING, THE BANKS

In 1970 the premiere unit of value on earth—that unit upon which all other aspects of industrial economies were based and calibrated—was the dollar. The dollar was a piece of paper redeemable by other governments for a set quantity of gold held in reserve by the United States Government. In effect, the dollar *was* gold, and all other dimensions of the world financial system reflected this by arranging themselves around dollars in a manner not unlike iron filings forming symmetrical shapes at either end of a magnet. When the magnet moved, the filings moved. When the dollar called, the world responded.

In 1980 the dollar was a piece of paper—nothing more—just green ink pressed into certain designs upon rectangles of processed tree pulp.

America has severed its dollar from the international gold standard because, if it had not, all the gold in America would have been redeemed and removed from the country by foreign oil powers vacuuming up the bulk of United States dollars. In 1980, although there had been no new item of currency printed to physically express the fact, the world had recognized a new premiere unit of value,

the unit of value upon which all other aspects of industrial economies were calibrated: a barrel of oil. When oil called, the world responded.

In 1960 in the territories along the southern shore of the Persian
Gulf—Saudi Arabia, Bahrain, Qatar, the United Arab Emirates,
Oman and Kuwait—there existed fewer than a dozen banks. Banking at that time in these countries was handled largely by *sarrafs,*
money changers operating from *souks,* the marketplaces which have
traditionally been the social and commercial centers in Islamic civilization.

The only United States banking presence was that directly attached to U.S. oil companies in the region. The only major European institutions participating in banking trade were those British
operations left over from the days of the British Empire, when the
Islamic lands along the Persian Gulf had been included as part of
the empire's "India Financial Region."

In 1974, when the tidal wave of petro-dollars from Western industrialized countries began rolling into the Middle East, it brought
with it two separate banking movements. One was the indigenous
banking system established pell-mell through hastily established Arab
central banking institutions. The second was that represented by a
virtual stampede of Western banks clamoring and jockeying for position in what had become the world's most tumultuous—and potentially profitable—financial frontier.

By 1975, when King Faisal died, the lands around the Persian
Gulf and eastern Mediterranean had become the most investment-
intensive zone on earth, sites of the most ambitious, extravagant and
opulently funded construction and development projects in history.
The size and scope of the work dwarfed all other national development or recovery projects of the past—even the Marshall Plan,
which rebuilt Europe.

Muslim governments, awash in sums of money never before available for development, began projects of unprecedented scale: the
most dwelling units ever built at once; the most schools; the most
hospitals; the largest single purchase of computer equipment; the
longest stretches of railroad built in modern times; the most miles of
superhighway laid in a year; the most automobiles, locomotives, jet
planes, trucks, and items of office equipment ever purchased in single transactions.

One of these projects resulted in the construction of both the largest building and largest airport in the world. That airport, at Jedda, in Saudi Arabia, is twice the size of the largest airport in America and, at forty-one square miles, 20 percent larger in land area than the entire metropolitan area of Miami, Florida.

During the period from 1974 to 1979, Saudi Arabia erected a factory every three days, building nine hundred major facilities during those years.

There were, by 1980, more than three dozen completely new cities under way. One was King Khalid Military City. Another was Riyadh Sports City, an entire Olympic urban area where sports were to be played, learned and practiced by athletes living amid facilities of the size and grandeur of Olympiad sites. There was a $2.5 billion University City. And the $15 billion Al Assard City, a completely new urban and industrial community flung up from the sands with housing, factories, airfields, offices, computerized mass transit systems and amenities required for the 100,000 residents who were to man operations in this arms-manufacturing zone making everything from rifles to intercontinental missiles.

In Kuwait construction crews laying out new segments of city and suburbs in a single mistake built 8,000 houses too many. They were also, in 1980, cutting the marble facades for the ultraposh new stock exchange. In less than a decade Kuwait had moved from being a place of coin changers and cart merchants to the site of one of the ten busiest stock market operations in the world.

There were also such projects as ground stations for a new satellite network. In joint ventures Muslim governments of the Middle East were purchasing entire satellite systems as part of what was being installed as the most advanced communications system in the world.

There were a plethora of other capital-intensive purchases and projects under way by the decade's end—such as the largest single weapons purchase ever made, a $24 billion package of French-made tanks, helicopters and other items, including a sophisticated system of radar capable of covering the entire 1,200-mile length of airspace above the Red Sea.

By the mid-1970s the Middle East had become a banker's dream. Never had so much money traveling in so many directions changed hands in such a short period of time.

In 1979 Saudi Arabia, Bahrain, Qatar, the United Arab Emirates, Oman and Kuwait had 273 major banks of their own. The United

Arab Emirates—a small collection of former tribal fiefdoms which in 1979 had the second-highest standard of living in the world—had 430 bank branches, or one bank branch for every 2,000 citizens. This is the densest banking facility per-thousand-residents ratio in the world.

By 1980 Bahrain had more than a hundred major world banks in residence. In less than a decade what had been a backwater society of bazaar merchants had been catapulted into a space-age global banking center trailing only Tokyo, Zurich, London and New York in total volume of transactions and overall importance.

Within two years after Faisal unsheathed the Sword of Oil and seized the global petroleum grids, the world's global matrix of bankers had anchored their operations around the rim of the Persian Gulf. These newly created banking networks, stretching from New York and London and Tokyo to the Middle East, were organized in a manner amazingly similar to the traditional petroleum system.

The new banking conduits provided the international web of "pipelines" along which gushed the daily deluge of money leaving the West and entering the Middle East in the form of oil payments— and then leaving the Middle East to gush back across the world in the form of Arab investments and purchases in the West, that circular flow of wealth which has come to be known as petro-dollar recycling.

Like the original petroleum networks, this new global banking system was originally operated and controlled by Western corporations whose multinational tentacles reached ever deeper into the Middle East.

Each pulse of petro-dollar recycling brought in increasing margins of profits to these Western banks, which often extended themselves further into the Middle East to take even greater advantage of the business and keep one step ahead of their rivals.

Substantial numbers of Western banks extended themselves so far, so fast, that their entire operations became structured in a manner which made them dependent upon continuing large-scale participation in the burgeoning Middle Eastern money market. And just like the petroleum corporations whose overextensions had made them vulnerable to takeover and desperation compromise, the banks' overextensions provided the tools for their takeover by Muslim governments. This trend began in 1977 in Saudi Arabia.

That year the Saudi Arabian Monetary Agency—the central government bank—announced a new program of "Saudiazation" of all foreign banks operating in the country. This was the idea: Foreign banks in Saudi Arabia would be given one of two choices: they could turn over controlling interest of their Middle Eastern operations to the Saudis or they could be immediately barred from doing further financial business of any kind there.

Picture what this meant: Western banks had hastily reorganized themselves like upside-down pyramids, with all the weight of their international structure—from the corner branch office in New York to the Euro-bond market in London—resting upon their petrodollar operations anchored in the Middle East. When those banks turned over control of that crucial Middle Eastern "root" to Muslim governments, they turned over much of the control of their international operations.

By 1980 this Saudiazation had resulted in taking control of the root of some of the West's largest banks. The Bank of the Netherlands became the Al-Bank Al-Saudi Al-Fransi in the Middle East. The British Bank of the Middle East had become Al-Bank Al-Saudi Al-Britani. And the Middle Eastern division of Citibank—the second-largest bank in the United States—had become the Saudi-American Bank.

Thus the Western banking system, which once served as the instrument of American and European power around the world, became the instrument through which Muslim governments extended themselves into the West.

And at the same time they were enveloping the banks of the West, Arab nations' indigenous banks were also exploding outward to encircle the globe. By 1980 twenty-four Arab banks that had not existed in 1970 were among the world's top five hundred banks, and that number was continuing to rise.

Nor were banks the only target of these broad financial campaigns. The Arabs were also moving methodically toward seizing power within the International Monetary Fund, that agency overseeing both the world's banking systems and its international monetary policy.

The International Monetary Fund—the IMF—was created in 1945. It was designed to be the world's first financial superagency.

Set up at the United Nations Monetary and Financial Conference at Bretton Woods, New Hampshire, it has a board of twenty directors and a small group of executive directors who actually run the organization. Since it was started, those executive directors have been chosen by the same procedure: the five countries that put the largest amounts of money into the IMF's operation get to seat their representatives as executive directors.

For more than thirty years that left the executive board—and the global powers of the IMF—in the hands of the same industrial nations: the United States, Britain, France, West Germany and Japan.

Those executive directors have, since the end of World War II, exercised quiet but increasing clout in world affairs. They operate in conjunction with the World Bank, the United Nations Secretariat and the UN Economic Commissioners for Europe, Africa, Asia and Latin America. They fix currency rates against the dollar, regulate trade and fiscal practices and have been the lenders of last resort to the governments of countries temporarily unable to meet their obligations.

This last—the ability to supply or deny the funds necessary to keep a government stable or drastically alter its business climate or political currents—is one of the IMF's most potent and controversial powers.

In 1970, as its largest supplier of funds as well as the leader of the Western industrial alliance, the United States was—both officially and unofficially—the dominating force behind IMF administrative policy. And the dollar was the bedrock around which IMF actions pivoted.

In 1979, when the IMF convened its thirty-fourth annual meeting in Belgrade, a number of things in the world—and in the IMF—had changed. Many of the changes were not well reported in the Western press, which focused on other events that week. The price of gold was climbing in a runaway spiral. In Iran four more pipelines were blasted and the new Ayatollah's firing squads cut down former officials and friends of the Shah. In Israel the Cabinet voted unanimously to expand settlements in the Muslim lands of the seized West Bank. And in the first tentative test of their respective strengths, Jimmy Carter edged out Edward Kennedy in the ballots of the Florida Democratic caucuses.

In Belgrade the joint meeting of the IMF and the World Bank was scheduled to avoid conflict with an annual event to which it had previously paid scant attention: Ramadan, the high Islamic holy days.

And both the official and unofficial international milieu of the IMF had shifted. One of the largest multibillion debtors to the IMF was Britain—a former leading financial power of the organization. The most sought-after, speculated-about and fawned-over officials in and around the gathering were the ministers from the oil-producing countries who, with the snap of a price hike or the turn of a valve, could overturn or completely disrupt any new world monetary proposal with which they did not agree.

At the same time the United States was no longer the largest single supplier of loan funds to the IMF. Saudi Arabia was. The Western industralized bloc no longer held a monopoly on the small executive board of the IMF—the newest member of which was Mahsoun Jalal, representative of the Saudi Arabian Government.

Under the traditional rules, Saudi Arabia took the seat because it was the largest source of funds to the IMF loan pool. Follow this extraordinary cycle of events:

—Saudi Arabia hiked oil prices in a manner which drove dozens of countries beyond the brink of monetary solvency because of staggering petro-debt.

—Then Saudi Arabia lent huge amounts of money to the IMF, which, in turn, lent that money to the countries that needed aid in meeting their burgeoning petro-debts.

—Then those borrowing countries paid that money back to Saudi Arabia for its oil.

In one swoop the Saudis pulled off a coup which netted them petro-profits, increased political clout and real power over international monetary affairs as administered by the IMF.

13

MUSLIM MERCHANT ADVENTURERS

The worldwide campaigns of petro-pressures, global monetary machinations and Islamic diplomacy in the United Nations were only parts of the overall jihad strategy set in motion by King Faisal in 1973. Those moves were aimed at the exterior networks of the Western Alliance—the international political, financial and industrial systems to which each nation is attached, like grapes along a vine.

At the same time, the Muslim oil powers launched another level of programs aimed at using "recycled" petro-dollars as the vehicle penetrating deep into the interior fabric of each of those target nations, each of those separate grapes along the vine.

It was in this second series of moves that the new oil powers began purchasing the corporations, real estate, banks, bonds, brokerage houses and other bedrock domestic institutions which serve as the pillars of each target nation's internal political system.

These broad penetration moves were undertaken by both Middle Eastern governments and individuals, and, although they were directed from no single office or agency, they proceeded in a cooperative spirit. Most often these activities progressed through a sort of financial twilight zone in which the interests of individual entrepreneurs and their sponsoring governments were inseparably intertwined. This technique is the modern-day equivalent of the merchant-cum-government consortiums such as the Dutch East India Company, the Compagnie Française de Indes or the Merchant Adventurers, Inc., of London which led the eighteenth- and nineteenth-century invasions and commercial colonization of societies throughout Africa and Asia.

The Muslim merchant Ghazi who form the cutting edge of this modern thrust into the interior body of each of the West's industrialized nations have more resources at their command than any other similar merchant expansionist group has ever had. No other group of persons anywhere on earth, at any time in history, ever commanded such overwhelming amounts of wealth. Some sense of the potential power this value represents can be had by contemplating the fact that the entire fortunes of both the Rockefeller and Rothschild dynasties do not equal the holdings of a single branch of the current family tree of the House of Saud.

By the end of the 1970s, for instance, the Saudi Arabian Monetary Agency faced the ponderous and enormously complex task of investing $380 million a day—$16 million an hour, every hour of the day and night—all year long, year after year. This represents only the amount of money left over after all the costs of oil production have been paid; after all Saudis have been provided with new housing, free education, free medical care, free professional training; after the costs of running every government department and program had been paid; after foreign aid grants have been dispatched to half the countries of the world; after global diplomatic campaigns have been funded; after the latest generation of students has been shipped out to the elite universities and technical academies of the world; after the year's new banks have been launched; after the year's bills for the largest and most complex construction projects in the history of the world have been covered. After all this, there is *still* $380 million left over *every day* in the Saudi Arabian central bank which has to be "placed" in the West.

"Placed" is a timid word which means that $380 million worth of something is purchased somewhere in the world every day. In a 1980 interview with the *Financial Times* of London, a senior official of the Saudi Arabian Monetary Agency complained, "If I get sick and miss a day's work, that means that I have to place almost $800 million the next day. It is rather difficult."

And consider this: The Saudi Arabian Monetary Agency is only one of a dozen major government central banks, only one among hundreds of Middle Eastern governmental agencies, only one among thousands of government-connected companies and individuals who are also faced with such pressures and who form the body of the overall petro-penetration thrust into the economies of the West. One of the reasons the total scope of this activity—and its ultimate implications—have largely escaped the Western public is because of its mind-boggling spread. The very enormity of the activity renders it incomprehensible. This range also makes the subject a difficult one for the media in any single Western nation. Each country's primary news vehicle—television—largely chooses to note only those elements of Arab global action which immediately affect that country's audience in a manner lending itself to visually intensive representations easily included in any given evening's staccato of news reports.

And another reason for the public's lack of knowledge about this multifaceted force is the institutionalized Arab mania for secrecy. The commercial strategies for entire continents are planned in secrecy; contracts with thousands of Western firms are written in a manner making secrecy one of the aspects of the agreement; entire staffs of multinational corporations are signed to secrecy agreements. In the fall of 1981, for instance, staff members at Citibank headquarters in New York inadvertently made public some details of the institution's substantial dealings with Kuwait. Kuwait immediately withdrew more than $3 billion from that multinational bank and redeposited it in other banks which promised to more carefully protect information concerning Kuwait's investments in the United States. Even governments—such as that of the United States—must pledge themselves to secrecy before Muslim governments will agree to do extensive business or undertake new "recycling" ventures. In 1979 the U. S. Treasury Department confirmed that it had made "special commitments of financial confidentiality to Saudi Arabia" and other OPEC governments in return for their pledge to continue "recycling" investments into America. The Treasury and Commerce departments also agreed not to keep full records or make public the information they did gather concerning the patterns of investments by Arab individuals and governments in the United States. Similar agreements have been made with other governments, such as those of European nations and Japan.

The sum total of this trend is that the few details about Arab investing which do escape to be highlighted by television in the West appear to be disjointed, isolated incidents popping up, as it were, from nowhere to fade back almost immediately into an equally unimportant place in the community memory.

However, if one attempts to assemble the global patterns of just the known Arab investment activities—those aspects of the petro-penetration strategy which have been revealed by accident, political controversy, unavoidable public recording requirements, government intelligence agency investigations, litigations or scoops appearing in various of the world's financial journals—the picture is quite vast. If you stretch an eight-by-eight-foot map of the world across the wall and begin methodically drawing a single line connecting the government agencies, government-backed companies or government-connected individuals of the Middle East to their various known investments, the lines would soon form a net wrapped around huge portions of the world.

By 1982 there was virtually no major industrial nation in the free world in which the Arabs had not successfully inserted themselves as an irresistible mainstream political force, no nation in which the Muslim oil powers had not established themselves as a major presence in the highest circles of government, industry or society.

While these global "recycling" programs ultimately involved tens of thousands of Arab government officials, royal family members, diplomats, bankers, brokers, businessmen, bureaucrats and other assorted functionaries, their basic operational techniques were the same. And at the leading edge of these multipronged continental offensives were four individuals of particular note. Born into the breach of epochal change, these four typified an entire generation: sired as the last sons of a medieval desert era, born first sons to the Arab space age. In their personal deportment and business methodology they would come to epitomize—in a manner not unlike the behavior of the Guggenheims, Rockefellers, Mellons and Rothschilds of an earlier time and place—both the best and the worst of their civilization.

The four are:

—Suliman Olayan, the son of a Bedouin spice merchant who grew up in trading settlements looking out at a horizon dominated by the European gunboats that had ruled the region for more than a century.

—Akram Ojjeh, the son of a Bedouin cloth merchant who grew up in the crooked lanes and brazier-hazed *souks* of European-garrisoned Baghdad.

—Ghaith Pharaon, the son of Saudi Arabia's first ambassador to Paris during the period when France was shipping ever-larger numbers of Legionnaires across the Mediterranean into battles aimed at retaining control of rebellious Muslim colonies.

—Adnan Khashoggi, the son of Bedouin Arabia's first modern physician who grew up in a mud-walled oasis town as it exploded into a city. The far dunes were thrust up with steel towers and the DC-3s dumped off the latest deliveries of gold bars in wooden crates at the end of the new runway.

Suliman Olayan had been one of the daily gaggle of Bedouin teenagers who gathered around the Aramco drilling locations in the 1940s, both to gawk at the foreign strangers and their curious metal contrivances and also in hopes of being picked for a day's labor. Olayan's advantage came after he began memorizing the names of thousands of oil-rig parts in both Arabic and English, thereby making himself a walking encyclopedia whose presence and two-way translations were of immeasurable worth to both Arab workmen and American engineers. Previously, one of the largest problems snarling work at the technologically involved drilling sites was the inability of the American foremen to communicate with laborers unattuned to modern machinery. Olayan's position evolved into that of intermediary and translator between the engineering crews and the court of Ibn Saud. Eventually, the business opportunities this would spawn would see Olayan working in partnership with Saudi family members such as Prince Khaled, the man after whom Olayan named his son. In 1980, Olayan would become a director of the board of Mobil Oil Corporation, one of the companies for whose engineers he had once fetched wrenches and goatskins of water.

Akram Ojjeh, a studious bookworm of a boy in a family that revered learning, had received a scholarship that took him from Baghdad to study philosophy at the Sorbonne in France. After graduation he became a journalist and editor of the anti-Nazi Paris Arab newspaper, *Le Monde Arabe*. When the Germans panzered France, *Le Monde Arabe*'s officers were sacked and its editor fled the country to become an anti-Nazi radio broadcaster in the war zone across Muslim North Africa and Palestine. At war's end, Ojjeh returned to the trades of his father—cloth and dry goods—and simultaneously began dealing in the hottest commodity in that region where Saudi-backed Palestinians, American-backed Zionists and occupational British troops were clashing: guns. By 1950 Ojjeh had set up the first ammunition factory in Saudi Arabia and had become the exclusive procurer of weapons for the Saudi court. His son, Mansour, was named after Saudi Prince Mansour, who was both patron and partner in the weapons business that became the foundation of a commercial Ojjeh empire. Ojjeh, in the 1970s, would become a routine luncheon partner with world leaders such as French President Valéry Giscard d'Estaing.

Ghaith Pharaon had surveyed the surrounding desert landscapes of his youth from an enviable position: the inner windows of the palace of the House of Saud. Pharaon's father, Rashid Pharaon, was the best friend of Prince Faisal, then the Foreign Minister organizing Saudi Arabia's first system of modern diplomatic missions. Faisal provided the choicest new consular spot—Paris—to the elder Pharaon. And so it was that the younger Pharaon began his early education in the "City of Light." His formative college years were spent at the American International University in Beirut, the U.S.-sponsored campus which was the turbulent center of the Harakat al-Qawmiyyin al-Arab, the student activist movement which would change its name several times before assuming its final form: the Palestine Liberation Organization. After obtaining a master's degree in petroleum engineering at Stanford University, Pharaon went on for a doctorate from Harvard Business School. Then, financed by King Faisal's bank, he began the business empire which would eventually provide him entrée to the innermost offices of the Carter White House.

Adnan Khashoggi as a boy enjoyed all the privileges of the son of the man charged with keeping the King of Saudi Arabia alive and well. Mohammed Khashoggi, as the first modern-trained physician in the kingdom, occupied a position of extraordinary intimacy and power within the Saudi ruling family. He was the man who brought the first electricity to the desert—a gas-fired generator whose original purpose was to power the X-ray machine installed in the King's royal clinic. When the X-ray machine was not in use, the elder Khashoggi rented out the generator, thereby founding the King's first utility company. The younger Khashoggi was sent to the British-stiff, ultraproper Victoria College in Alexandria, Egypt. After graduating from that boarding institution, he was sent to major in petroleum engineering at the Colorado School of mines but, of his own volition, entered Chico State College in California and began studying economics and business. Khashoggi quickly earned a reputation for flamboyance as a money flasher and high roller. Out of school, Khashoggi almost immediately began to undertake multimillion-dollar deals purchasing trucks, construction equipment and—the commodity which would become his mainstay—weapons for Saudi Arabia. His empire of enterprises would rapidly propel him into the highest levels of world industry and make him a frequent luncheon partner of President Richard Nixon.

These four men, each in his own inimitable fashion, would play a major role in the Arab campaigns which began changing the face of the world in 1973: Olayan, the natty, conservative oil technocrat who shunned the limelight and worked over his balance sheets; Ojjeh, the journalist-turned-gunrunner who evolved into a collector of Europe's rarest objets d'art; Pharaon, the hard-boiled, cigar-chomping, Harvard-educated financier, and Khashoggi, the Machiavellian industrialist whose unbridled methods and glittering life-style would eventually subject him to the enmity of his original sponsors in the court at Riyadh.

14

MASTERS OF THE
CHAMPS ÉLYSÉES

There are those who would argue that the cross-roads and unofficial capital of Europe isn't Paris but instead—the place where the political, financial, artistic and social movers of the Continent converge in a heady mix of sleek roadsters, cut crystal and libidinous abandon—Cannes. One hundred miles due east of the French industrial hub at Marseilles, it is the central bead on the necklace of resort cities which curve across the Riviera toward the Italian border: Toulon, St. Tropez, Cannes, Antibes, Monaco. The stretch of coast is the place where the Alps take their final turn south, break off in ocher cliffs plunged into turquoise water fringed with eucalyptus and bougainvillea.

It is also the site of the most expensive real estate in the world. The hillsides in all directions are up-holstered with a tapestry of castles, estate houses, grand villas and châteaus: whitewashed walls, foun-tained central courts and red tile roofs fluttered with sea gulls. Below, the yachts glimmer mahogany and brass. Beyond are the two Lerin islands that guard the harbor—their perimeters still studded with the fortifications built in the tenth century to protect against the armadas of Muslim dhows ferrying armies into the jihad for control of southern France.

In the mid-1800s this coast was strung with little more than a few isolated fishing villages. It was "discovered" by England's Lord Brougham, who conceived the idea of establishing a resort for royalty on its shores. Brougham was former Lord Chancellor of England, author of *Colonial Policy of European Powers* and one of the leading aristocrats in Europe's imperial capitals. He was, for instance, the inventor of the "Brougham"—the elegant single-horse carriage which became *de rigueur* for royalty.

In the late 1800s, by the time the British Imperial Armies had slashed their way across half of Asia and Queen Victoria declared herself Empress of India, Cannes had become the wintering spot for all the ruling families and VIPs of Europe. Its sidewalks and docksides ran thick with queens, kings, empresses, grand dukes, princes, counts, ministers to the Kaiser, Hapsburgs, Churchills, Vanderbilts, Astors, Krupps and the like. It was, for instance, a favorite haunt of the Rothschild dynasty. Lionel Walter Rothschild of London and Henri Rothschild of Paris would begin their roadster races in the City of Light near the Champs Élysées and speed south through the wine country onto the twisting mountain roads for the final dash along the coast to Cannes and Monaco and the gay round of parties and celebrations.

By the turn of the century, in both political sinew and architectural grandeur, Cannes had become a tropical Versailles, the unofficial "southern capital" of European government. Its hotel salons were decorated with frescoes depicting famous battles and Greek mythology. Its bathtubs were of black marble. Its faucets of gold. Its dining-room walls were hung with silver-threaded tapestries and patrons lounged in Louis XV chairs of silk and rococo gold. It was here that the decisions which often toppled prime ministers, launched wars, collapsed businesses, boosted the stock exchange or depressed the commodity markets were often made.

One of the individuals instrumental in establishing Cannes as a twentieth-century power center was King Edward VII of England. Long one of Cannes' most renowned residents, Edward laid the foundation stone for new yacht jetties, supervised social events and financed part of the costs of the Promenade de la Croisette—the central boulevard of gardens and grand walks serving as the community's main street and socializing spot. Edward also frequently ran the government of Britain by remote control from Cannes. As his armies were consolidating their conquests in the Muslim lands along the western shores of the Red Sea, directly across from Mecca, and taking up the positions from which they would ultimately sweep into Palestine, Edward was attending high-society festivals in Cannes—often dressing up in a scarlet devil costume, complete with horns and pointed tail, and cavorting down the Promenade.

One of the centers of Edwardian society in Cannes was the Hotel Gray d'Albion, originally erected in 1865 as a showpiece of Victorian opulence. It had six dozen boutiques, two hundred rooms and three hundred luxury suites designed for the comfort of guests and friends of the Continent's royalty. "The Gray" also became a popular winter haven for the upper crust of the British military. Yachting in with their baggage trains of menservants and mustache wax, the gentlemen of the crown's khaki would sit in the cool of the evening fanned by fronds, sipping *pastis* and recounting the jolly good actions against the sword-swinging blighters from Cairo to Kabul.

It was from the patios of such landmarks as the Gray, for instance, that petro-baron Edmond Rothschild laid out the plans for the plantation colonies he was establishing in Palestine in the late 1800s. Those private colonies were to be peopled with impoverished Russian refugees who would be required to work growing delicate attar roses and grapes in the deserts near the Jordan River. The roses Rothschild planned to import into France and sell to the Riviera perfume industries at Grasse, just a few miles from Cannes. The grapes were to be imported and funneled into Rothschild's multimillion-dollar wine-making empire.

But by the late 1970s the Gray d'Albion, like the rest of Cannes, underwent a startlingly swift transformation. The Gray was sold to the Arab Abela Investment Group for $13 million. The new Middle Eastern owners completed $7 million worth of renovations and refurbished the structure in a manner which made its previous grandeur look shabby. It was then reopened and immediately became one of the most popular Arab vacation spots. The famous penthouse of the hotel—a 3,280-square-foot glass-walled apartment which commands a spectacular view—was sold for $10 million. Mazen Pharaon, brother and business partner of Ghaith Pharaon, the Saudi tycoon with the PhD from Harvard, bought it. French real estate authorities reported that the per-square-foot sale price—$3,048 per square foot—was the highest amount ever recorded for the sale of a dwelling space anywhere. Simultaneously, Ghaith Pharaon purchased what real estate sources described as "an extraordinary" property in the ultraposh La Croisette quarter of Cannes for $10 million.

The Arab Abela Investment Group and the Pharaons were in the vanguard of a wave of new buyers who set about changing Cannes from an enclave of European royal privilege to a hub of Middle Eastern financial power. A spokesman for Agence Kapnist, an international real estate service company which specializes in properties in the South of France, reported that, by the end of 1979, Middle Easterners had "bought up enormous chunks" of the Riviera in and around Cannes and were buying larger sections every day. Most of those purchases have been made under the aegis of secrecy agreements—binding the seller and realtor to a pledge not to make the details of the transaction public.

Akram Ojjeh, journalist-turned-munitions-mogul, purchased a $5 million villa at the edge of Cannes and bought 80 percent of the Esteral shipyards along the Cannes waterfront. The shipyard is being converted to produce large numbers of vessels for Middle Eastern governments and, in particular, military patrol craft for countries surrounding the Persian Gulf.

Adnan Khashoggi, the doctor's son who became one of Saudi Arabia's wealthiest entrepreneurs, touched down in Cannes and purchased an entire story of the Marly, another of the fabled grand luxury residences in the resort city. The Villa Bagatelle, a landmark overlooking the bay and harbor from a windswept cliff, was bought by Saudi businessman Muffah al Midani.

The Château de l'Horizon, another famed architectural monument, was purchased by Saudi Prince Fahd—later to become King Fahd. The purchase price is not known, but the amount paid for renovation contracting services was $7.5 million. Fahd also bought the Richmond, the high-rise of luxury suites directly next to the Cannes Palm Beach Casino.

Some further indication of the scope of the new wealth pouring into the area can be had from the police blotter at Cannes. In 1980 a member of Qatar's royal family reported that $20 million in jewels had been taken by burglars from his newly purchased villa. His report indicated that each of his four wives routinely carried $20 million in jewels while traveling.

Mohammed Enany, who is a member of the World Islamic Committee, and also a regular in Cannes, reported in 1980 that burglars took $100,000 in miscellaneous jewels from his Riviera home.

Realtors also indicate that what was once the "California quarter" —that section of Cannes renowned for the multimillion-dollar homes of Hollywood movie stars—has become an almost totally "Iranian enclave." In a neighboring section, the most modest Crenoau area, a flurry of Middle Eastern buying and bidding for homes has driven the price of the cheapest house available—any house in any condition—to $2.5 million. In 1979, in an attempt to alleviate some of the pressure for home buyers, three hundred new apartments were built in a project which offered a pleasant sea view but only small, cubicle-like areas of living space. The price for each was $250,000. They sold "overnight" to Arab buyers.

The service industries throughout the coastal region are also evidencing dramatic changes. One example of this trend is the world-renowned Ambassadeur Restaurant in Cannes. It has been lavishly renovated as the Beyrouth Restaurant, featuring Islamic architectural motifs and chic Middle Eastern cuisine. Nearby is one of the area's newest and most visually stunning landmarks—Byblos. It is a hotel that is a sprawling Islamic palace complex. The "rooms" are entire salons removed from palaces—both contemporary and ancient—throughout the Middle East and reassembled at St. Tropez. The ceilings are covered with hundreds of acres of the finest Persian carpets. The floors are cut-marble mosaics and the wood inlaid work represents samples of most of the major dynasties of Islamic history.

This envelopment of the Riviera—its real estate, its yacht basins, its consumer markets, its street-level cultural institutions and its broader and less visible matrices of international financial and political power by Arab interests—is only a portion of a larger metamorphosis occurring throughout all of France. There are now more than two million Muslims in the country, making Islam the second-largest national religion. Only Catholicism commands a larger following. The central mosque of Paris is one of the largest in the world and one of the busiest.

This rise of Muslim power touching into every level of French society has been greeted with different reactions throughout the country. One of the most troubling of these has been an anti-Arab backlash. In 1980 this became a major issue in the city of Roubaix, a community of 110,000 in the northern part of the country near the German border. During the late 1970s, the Muslim population of that textile city grew to over 15,000. An Islamic congregation purchased a $185,000 mansion in the middle of town and refurbished it as a mosque. Town officials immediately began legal proceedings aimed at evicting the Muslim owners and banning the building's use as a place of worship because, they said, it was "not appropriate" to have such an Islamic facility as the central structure of the French town.

A similar incident occurred along the Isere River town of Romans in central France in 1982. The urban area, renowned for its textile and leather industries, became a particularly popular home for Muslim immigrants and, by the 1980s, they constituted 65 percent of the population. In the summer of 1982, a new mosque was heavily damaged by a bomb blast as elected officials received written death threats which warned "We don't want another Mecca at Romans."

Ironically, at the same time an explosion was tearing through the Romans mosque, Islamic officials from across France were gathering a short distance away at the Rhone River industrial hub of Lyons for a two-day seminar on "Islam in France, Presence and Dialogue."

The Paris Government has placed great emphasis on easing such tensions between native Frenchmen and the tide of incoming Muslims. In 1980, President Valéry Giscard d'Estaing announced with great fanfare that public monies would be used to create a national institute for the study and propagation of Islamic culture in France. Sitting on the board of directors of that new organization were six representatives from Middle Eastern states. In 1982—further evidence of the quickening pace of Arab involvement in French cultural life—the brother of Saudi King Fahd, Prince Talal, was nominated to the board of the prestigious Pasteur Institute. The prince has been a leading public advocate for broad new links between French and Saudi educational and scientific institutes.

In the salons and private dining halls of the Parisian social scene in the early 1980s, one of the newest celebrities and topics of conversation was the pianist and composer Ibrahim Souss, who began performing in concert after an eleven-year hiatus from the musical limelight. Souss is the diplomatic representative of the Palestine Liberation Organization in France.

And the country watched with equal curiosity in 1979 as one of the Arab world's most famous artists and art dealers, Wadah Faris, opened the Galerie Faris along the rue de l'Université. By 1982, the shop's burgeoning trade in paintings and prints from across the Islamic Middle East had established the Galerie Faris as a new Parisian landmark.

Elsewhere in the French capital the Arabs have become a pervasive financial and physical presence. Along the chestnut-shaded Champs Élysées, just a short distance from Élysée Palace, residence of the President, the former offices of Merrill Lynch have been taken over by the National Bank of Abu Dhabi. Next to the Ritz hotel, on Place Vendôme, are the calligraphic brass plaques announcing the Banque Arabe de Internationale d'Investissement, which, along with nearby Union de Banques Arabes et Françaises, has become one of the world's major international banking powers. There were, in 1980, more than thirty different Arab banks registered in the city of Paris.

A bit farther down the Champs Élysées, at two locations—one marked, the other not—are the business offices of Akram Ojjeh. Ojjeh also maintains an apartment on the nearby fashionable Avenue Foch and a more traditional French baron's mansion at Neuilly, an enclave of the ultrarich just over the city line. Ojjeh's offices are hung with Chagalls, backgrounded with Mozart and touched here and there with fresh-cut flowers arranged in bone-china vases. While Ojjeh's primary activities involve weapons—he is agent to the Arab world for Mirage jets, Engins Matra missile systems and other manufacturers—he is also involved in various other fields. He has purchased control of Air Alpes and Touraine Air Transport, which crisscross the Continent. He has also acquired French telephone companies, a portion of France's largest bank, Credit Commercial, and the Paris-St. Germain football franchise. Large portions of his empire and operations are shrouded in secrecy and, with the cooperation of the French Government, leave no public records.

Some sense of the growing magnitude of Arab power—and direct Arab influence throughout all levels of French industry—can be had by surveying the tens of billions of dollars worth of weapons systems and military hardware purchased from France by Saudi Arabia and other Muslim nations in the last decade.

In 1970, for instance, France was a relatively minor exporter of military weapons. That year it sold $620 million worth to other countries. But by 1981, and as a direct result of its massive new sales to Arab nations, France had become the third-largest weapons seller in the world. Only the United States and the Soviet Union sold more. That year France exported almost $7 billion worth and was preparing for ever-larger exports. Saudi Arabia was no longer just a customer but was becoming an integral part of the French military-industrial establishment. The Saudis agreed to underwrite government costs for developing a new generation of Mirage fighter jets similar to the American F-15. In return they sought unlimited access to the technology and the French production lines.

By 1982 the business of building military ships and related equipment for Arab nations had become such an enormous project that the French Government set up a new company which now sells entire navies rather than individual ships. La Société Navale Française de Formation et de Conseil, which is run by four French admirals, has its largest contract with Saudi Arabia, to whom it is supplying a multibillion-dollar fleet complete from anchor chains to guided-missile frigates to coastal support networks to boot camps for training the new Muslim sailors. And, under the direct guidance of weapons-agent Ojjeh, France has also been providing billions of dollars worth of other electronic warfare equipment not only to Saudi Arabia but to other nations such as Kuwait, Iraq, Oman, Qatar and the United Arab Emirates.

One of Ojjeh's more controversial projects was the purchase of the one-time flagship showcase vessel of the now-devastated French merchant marine—the ocean liner *France*. A similar controversy was raised in 1977 when Ojjeh purchased the $15 million Wildenstein collection of furniture. The Wildensteins are an old-line European family of art collectors and were among the Zionist movement's most ardent supporters earlier in the century. Much of their internationally acclaimed furniture collection consisted of rare items from the mansions and palatial estates of the various Rothschild families. As the Rothschild fortunes waned, and many of their homes across the Continent were closed, the Wildensteins bought up the most valuable and unique of their antique, gold rococo furniture. In 1977, as the Wildensteins themselves began closing mansions in New York, Geneva and London, they placed the furniture collection on the block. Ojjeh's purchase was, reportedly, the largest such transaction in history.

At the same time, similarly spectacular deals were being made by Arabs throughout Paris. Kuwait's agents were among the most visible and controversial as they bought up some of the capital's most famous real estate. Moving out of newly established Arab banks in the city, Kuwaitis took over the La Réunion Fronciere, a private bank and real estate firm. They purchased the Manhattan Tower skyscraper, a business landmark. And they purchased Fouquet's restaurant, one of the most prestigious establishments along the Champs Élysées. They also took over the Monqual Company, a firm which owns additional large tracts of shops and eateries along that grand avenue whose sidewalk cafes have been as much a symbol of France as the Eiffel Tower. And many of those famed Champs Élysées properties which were not scooped up by Kuwait—the Café de Paris, the Café de la Paix, the Hotel Prince de Galles, the Hotel Meurice and the Hotel Grand—were bought up by the First Arabian Corporation, another group of Arab investors.

Next on the shopping list were the couturier houses. Adnan Khashoggi arrived in France to buy a home, set up offices to process weapons purchases and began branching out in other directions as well. One Khashoggi venture which raised eyebrows was his move into the fashion world. Khashoggi's salon enterprises include one run by Japanese designer Kenzo Takada, who sells Jungle Jap label jumpsuits, designer jeans and similar items of haute couture.

At the far end of the Champs Élysées—past a mammoth winged horse flanking a grand boulevard; past the towering Egyptian obelisk commemorating the European conquests in the Middle East; past the Jeu de Paume, which houses the works of Cézanne, Degas, Monet, Renoir and van Gogh; past the École Militaire, where Napoleon Bonaparte first entered military training as a teen-age cadet; just through the far walkways of the Tuileries Gardens; at the exact center point of Paris—is the office of Ghaith Pharaon. The building—at 4 Place de la Concorde—is the most exclusive commercial address in all of France. Its windows command a view which, in historical, political or aesthetic terms, is stunning. Below, the garden sprawl of the Tuileries; in one direction, the American Embassy; in the other direction, the Hotel Crillon. Beyond, the arched bridges and fabled banks of the Seine. Pharaon bought the place for $15 million and has renamed it the Saudi Arabian Research and Development Company Building.

Pharaon, with the aid of the French Government and the industrial community, keeps a low profile, and the details of his overall operations in Paris are well concealed. One of his known purchases is a large share of BSN-Gervais Danone, a giant French food conglomerate. After buying part of the firm, Pharaon put it to work on a $100 million cold-food-storage construction project in Saudi Arabia. He has also been using his Paris headquarters for coordinating the work of the international consortium of firms he has assembled to provide the services necessary for the creation of the $15 billion Al Assard Missile City project, the construction site south of Riyadh at which an entire industrial city for the production of weapons systems from pistols to intercontinental missiles is being erected. The French Government and weapons industry are supplying the overall direction and technological consultations. One group of companies assembled by Pharaon to work on various aspects of the project include the French transportation systems consulting firm Sofretu, the French construction company Raymond Camus, the Brazilian Government construction company Odebrecht, the Pharaon-owned Texas construction and systems technology conglomerate Sam P. Wallace Incorporated, the Texas architectural firm closely associated with Pharaon's Houston operations, 3D International, and the American Telephone and Telegraph Corporation. This is just one section of the global consortiums which are undertaking the largest, most expensive and most technologically complex industrial development project in history and which will establish Saudi Arabia as a major world center for weapons research, development, design and production.

And that Al Assard project is only the Saudi centerpiece of a larger regional Islamic arms industry now being organized by the newly formed Arab Organization for Industrialization. The new industry is being funded by petro-billions, built by European, Asian and American construction companies at sites throughout the Middle East, and is technologically guided by the French Ministry of Defense under tentative agreements reached between French President Giscard d'Estaing and Muslim leaders in 1980. The French Minister of Defense had indicated that initial plans call for the first production facilities in the Middle East to begin manufacturing large quantities of a new generation of Mirage jet fighters and antiaircraft Crotale missiles. In control of their own missile production facilities, Muslim governments—which are not constrained by problems of cost—will be able to turn out virtually unlimited numbers of ground-missile systems, enabling Muslim armies to create unprecedentedly large and highly mobile missile "thickets" effective against even such sophisticated battle aircraft as the American-made F-15.

Far south of his Paris operations and west of his base in Cannes, Pharaon has also purchased the Château de Montfort, near the Dordogne River in the southwest of France, that part of the country facing the Atlantic Ocean. The Dordogne River begins upland in the snow melts of the central volcanic plateau of France and tumbles down through picturesque ravines to join with the Gironde River in the middle of the province of Bordeaux, the richest and most famous wine-producing region on earth. These rolling carpets of Cabernet and Sauterne and Sauvignon growths and winding roads and stone bridges are, both physically and emotionally, the heartland of France. The very word "château" was coined in this province and means a wine grower's castle along the Gironde and Dordogne rivers, and the area is filled with famous ones. For instance, just west of Pharaon's château are such famed estates as the Château Mouton-Rothschild, Château Duhart-Milon of Rothschild and Château Lafite-Rothschild, the pillars of the winery empire brought to world preeminence by Baron Edmond Rothschild. It was from the Château Lafite that Rothschild originally sent teams of technicians and overseers to organize the grape-growing, processing and exporting operations in the Rothschild labor colony for Russian refugees in Palestine.

Northeast of Château Lafite-Rothschild is the new château of Akram Ojjeh at Lisle-Adam.

Some indication of the local attitudes encountered by Pharaon and Ojjeh and the other Middle Easterners moving through these French heartlands can be seen in the escapades of André Bercoff, a local newspaper writer in Bordeaux. In 1980, Bercoff embarked on the journalistic equivalent of the famed American FBI's ABSCAM scandal. Calling himself "Mohammed Zakher" and wearing pasted-on facial hair, Bercoff rented a hotel room and ran a one-inch ad in a Bordeaux newspaper announcing he represented Arab Corporated and Company and was seeking regional investment ideas. During the three days before he was discovered a fraud—by another journalist who recognized him—Bercoff held court in a hotel room crammed with more than a hundred Bordeaux businessmen offering to sell him things such as a tract of two hundred luxury homes on the coast, factories, resort hotels, châteaus, manor houses, industrial consulting firms of various kinds, department stores, military hardware, jewelry firms, vineyards and other assorted multimillion-dollar properties and institutions.

Further evidence of French attitudes about the Arab invasion can be found in the actions of French President Giscard d'Estaing, who, shortly before leaving office, inducted Akram Ojjeh into the French Legion of Honor. In 1974, France, under the direction of newly elected Giscard d'Estaing, launched the most aggressive campaign of any industrialized nation to realign its priorities and politics in a manner aimed at forging new alliances of Franco-Muslim interests throughout Africa and Asia. Since 1974, when France became the first member country to openly break with the American-led Western Alliance over the issue of the Israeli occupation of the Old City of Jerusalem and the other territories seized during the 1967 war, it has moved rapidly in new directions throughout the Islamic world. During the latter part of the 1970s, France's willingness to join in unorthodox new commercial and political structures—such as that through which the Arab weapons industry is being developed as a subsidiary of the French Ministry of Defense—has enabled it to become the leading Western nation trading in the Middle East.

France, which imports 75 percent of all its oil needs, has urged Middle Eastern governments to buy into basic French industries—particularly those which are petroleum intensive. One instance of this is the hard-hit petrochemical business. In 1980, President Giscard d'Estaing nationalized the petrochemical industry and put it under the control of the government oil company, Elf-Aquitaine. Then the French Government sold Qatar 40 percent interest in its largest petrochemical facilities, at Dunkirk. At the same time, the Paris Government agreed to join its resources with those of the Qatar General Petroleum Company in the construction of a $467 million petrochemical installation in that Middle Eastern country.

France then entered into long-term government-to-government oil-supply agreements with Qatar.

Such government-to-government arrangements drastically alter the traditional patterns of petroleum sales. The private corporations which previously acted as controlling middlemen are eliminated. Petroleum is removed from the realm of free enterprise and, instead, made a direct part of the day-to-day diplomatic relations between two heads of state.

This crisscross of moves intertwined the supply lines, financial liabilities, engineering corps, planning staffs and administrative organizations of the two countries' petrochemical industries, anchoring the direct interests of both on either side of the Mediterranean. The new arrangement retains the profit-making mechanism but discards other forms common to the free enterprise system for a hybrid structure which, in all but name, is a formal merger between entire ministries of two disparate governments, binding each state inexorably to the other in a manner transcending traditional Western concepts of national sovereignty.

By the end of 1980 more than 50 percent of France's petroleum industries had been linked to Middle Eastern countries in such government-to-government agreements.

In 1980, France, which had previously been the first Western nation to officially meet with representatives of the Palestine Liberation Organization as well as the first to invite that group to open offices in a Western capital, announced that as a matter of national policy it recognized the PLO as a government-level entity representing the four-million-strong Palestinian community. Shortly after that, President Giscard d'Estaing announced his government's unequivocal support for the "right to self-determination of the Palestinian people." And at that year's European Economic Community summit in Venice, Giscard d'Estaing led a vigorous lobbying effort behind the scenes for a public EEC commitment for amending the 1967 United Nations resolution on the Middle East, changing the status of the Palestinians from a "refugee problem" to a national entity entitled to form a state on the lands of their ancestors—the Old City of Jerusalem, the Gaza Strip, the West Bank and the Golan Heights.

Within days of Valéry Giscard d'Estaing's initiating these new policies, the following events occurred:

—The Oil Minister of Iraq issued an announcement that France had been granted most-favored-nation trading status and Iraq was increasing production to ensure that France receive "all the oil supplies it needs."

—The Kuwait National Petroleum Company agreed to eliminate Shell and BP from further oil sales between Kuwait and France and signed a long-term government-to-government supply guarantee with the French Government oil company.

—The Iraqi Government placed a bundle of new construction and service orders with French companies totaling $1.7 billion.

—The United States Boeing Corporation, which had been locked in heated competition with the French Airbus Industrie for Kuwait's orders for the first of a new generation of jumbo jets, suddenly lost its bid. Instead, Kuwait placed orders for the $1.6 billion in French A-310 jumbo jets. Immediately, Airbus Industrie began receiving additional billion-dollar orders from other Muslim governments. One of the companies leading the new sales pattern for jumbos is the Middle Eastern Airlines Corporation, which is 70 percent owned by Middle Eastern governments and 30 percent owned by France.

—France was selected over Britain as the primary supplier for equipment, construction services and technological guidance for the multibillion-dollar projects through which Iraq intends to establish an entire, nationwide electronics industry.

—The Iraq Republic Railway Organization placed a $135 million order for seventy-two locomotives from Francorail, the largest single export order ever received by that stalwart French firm.

—Saudi Arabia placed an order for nearly $4 billion in new military supplies, equipment and construction projects.

—Saudi Arabia, Qatar, Kuwait and the United Arab Emirates announced that France had been picked to be prime supplier and consultant for the military equipment throughout the rest of the 1980s.

—Saudi Arabia announced it was providing the funds needed by the French Minister of Defense to underwrite that ministry's new programs developing a new generation of Mirage jets.

Meanwhile, along the Champs Élysées and the Place de la Concorde, the staffs of the plethora of Arab offices and institutions serving as the direct conduits between France and the Middle East began gearing up for the massive amounts of new work generated by this tidal wave of new contracts, this rushing flood of petro-dollars flowing—like new blood through old veins—down the corridors of virtually every major industrial headquarters and government ministry in Paris. And some of the most frenzied activity was taking place in those offices that dealt in nuclear technology.

In the bitter winter of 1973, as the fountains of the Champs de Mars went dirty with ice and the rooms of the rue Cardinal Lemoine went sullen with chill, and as the radios blared out Christmas carols interrupted with emergency bulletins on the oil embargo strangling Europe, four distinctively marked airliners crisscrossed above the city, circling toward landing and secret, momentous events. Two of the craft were emblazoned with variations of the Eagle of Saladin, symbol of a redeemed Jerusalem. One of the planes displayed a crescent and star in a field of green, the color of the Prophet's first battle flag. The fourth plane was painted with an unsheathed sword and the calligraphic script proclaiming, "There is no God but God and Muhammad is the Messenger of God."

The planes—from Iraq, Libya, Pakistan and Saudi Arabia—carried the emissaries assigned to begin top-secret negotiations with the government of France and with each other concerning the purchase of atomic bombs. Paris was about to become the staging point for the Muslim world's nuclear jihad.

Iraq came to convince other Arab nations to recognize Baghdad as the most likely location to establish an Arab atomic industrial base. Libya came seeking simply to purchase completed atomic bombs—from anyone, at any price, as soon as possible. Saudi Arabia came to explore the creation of a Pan-Islamic atomic weapons development program as proposed by the Muslim nation of Pakistan.[1]

Pakistan, a thirty-five-year-old nation which was previously part of India, is not well known to most Americans. This even as Pakistan and India have come to play a crucial role in the conflict which now directly threatens American access to crucial Middle Eastern oil supplies.

Since the 700s A.D., when a jihad punctured the barrier of the Hindu Kush Mountains and spilled Muslim armies across the Indus Valley at the north of India, India has been a country whose culture and politics have been split between two religions and bitter rivals: Islam and Hinduism. Over the centuries in the south of the subcontinent, Hindus continued to constitute the numerical majority of the country's vast population and maintained control of its general government machinery. But in the northern quarter, toward Agra and Lahore, India became a thoroughly Muslim land and site at which some of Islam's most opulent empires rose and fell. Those empires left behind some of the country's most famous landmarks. One of them is the Islamic mausoleum and mosque which has become the very symbol of India: the Taj Mahal.

In 1947, when the Europeans who had colonized India for more than a century withdrew, the northwestern regions declared themselves a new, independent Muslim nation: Pakistan. The truncated remainder of the subcontinent—which is overwhelmingly Hindu—became the India of today. Neither the ancient cultural animosities nor the border disputes between the two have ever ended. Pakistan did not succeed in taking all the Islamic portions of north India when it seceded. Pakistan and India have fought a vicious series of border battles, and each continues—with good reason—to suspect the other of coveting its territory.

Ever since 1965, when they fought an all-out war, each has sought to best the other in weaponry and preparation for future conflicts at the negotiating table or in the battlefields. At the same time, India was determined to be recognized as a superpower in Asia.

Despite the widespread illiteracy and abject poverty found throughout its vast masses, India has developed an extraordinary system of higher education and now has the third-highest concentration of high-technology professionals of any country in the world except the Soviet Union and the United States. By the late 1960s, India had developed a completely independent nuclear industrial system, including the capacity for mass-producing atomic bombs. It exploded its first bomb and was recognized as a nuclear power in the early 1970s.

Pakistan, which also has substantial numbers of high-technology professionals despite its other social and economic problems, began to investigate the feasibility of developing its own atomic bomb-production facilities in the late 1960s.

In 1972 Pakistani President Zulfikar Ali Bhutto secretly launched Project 706—the program aimed at making Pakistan a nuclear superpower with the independent capacity to mass-produce atomic bombs. Bhutto that year nationalized the country's steel and heavy metals industries, heavy engineering industries, heavy electrical equipment industries, petrochemical industries and all utilities in a move that consolidated his personal power. The move also provided the tight controls necessary to turn all the nation's resources to the secret bomb project. Bhutto sent scientific teams across the country, surveying for uranium deposits. They found large quantities in sandstone formations along the Indus River in central Pakistan, near Dera Ghazi Khan.

That same year Bhutto had scientific teams under the direction of the military begin drawing up the complex plans for two completely separate bomb-development programs. One program would seek to build plutonium bombs, the other enriched uranium bombs.

In order to produce plutonium, Pakistan had to obtain a nuclear reactor and the special facilities for separating plutonium from spent reactor fuel.

In order to produce enriched uranium, Pakistan had to acquire the secret technology of uranium gas centrifugation, the complex process in which uranium gases are spun at high speeds, separating the highly radioactive molecules from the less radioactive molecules, eventually resulting in concentrations of the most radioactive and unstable type of uranium.

Pakistan had already set up an Atomic Energy Commission and purchased a small nuclear reactor from the United States in 1965. It prepared to purchase a larger reactor from Canada. A large reactor was the centerpiece crucial to Project 706's plutonium production.

Pakistan also successfully inserted a spy—Pakistani physicist Dr. Abdul Qadir Khan—inside the uranium enrichment plant operated by a consortium of European countries at Almelo, the Netherlands.

One reason for Pakistan's ambitious moves toward the atomic bomb-building business had to do with the successful bomb project of its archrival, India. But another reason had to do with Islamic Pakistan's growing sense of direct involvement with the jihad for Jerusalem and a desire to financially amalgamate itself with the oil-rich Muslim nations to the south.

Although Pakistan—an impoverished, oil-barren nation sharing a border with China—is not readily associated with the Middle East by most Americans, the country has been one of Saudi Arabia's closest allies. A new nation which forcibly declared, rather than passively inherited, its modern Islamic identity, Pakistan was one of the earliest and most fervent supporters of King Faisal's Pan-Islamic movement—that call for all Muslim nations to join as an international political force coordinated from Mecca.

In 1973 Pakistan adopted a new constitution and became an Islamic republic, a nation whose economic, administrative and judicial systems were guided by Koranic, rather than secular, law. And that same year it gathered the technical expertise needed to begin a nuclear weapons development project. However, the Pakistani Government remained as poor as it was devout and lacked the enormous amounts of capital required to surreptitiously build a nuclear weapons industry from scratch.

Pakistan proposed to the oil nations of the Middle East that the Pakistani capital of Islamabad, near the Chinese border, be designated and developed as the womb of the Muslim world's nuclear weapons development efforts. The Islamabad argument was persuasive because it solved the single largest potential problem facing any Arab effort to acquire full atomic weapons production facilities: physical security in the face of inevitable Israeli aerial attacks. Unlike Arab capitals, Islamabad was beyond the range of Israeli jets. Nuclear facilities established in Pakistan would be virtually untouchable by the Israeli Air Force, which was then striking at will inside surrounding Arab countries.

In 1972 President Bhutto began meeting with Arab heads of state to discuss his idea for a Pan-Islamic atomic weapons program centered in Pakistan and funded by the oil-rich nations of the Middle East. Several Arab nations were then secretly exploring various avenues which could potentially lead to the acquisition of nuclear weapons. There was interest in Bhutto's plan, but no commitment.

But by late 1973 the Arab attitude concerning atomic weapons had suddenly changed from interest to determination. The governments of Saudi Arabia, Libya and Iraq each began actively seeking the technology of atomic bombs.

This was not a cooperative effort. The man who controls the Arab world's first functioning atomic arsenal will be in a position to orchestrate the international political pressures necessary to dismantle Israel's hold on Jerusalem. And he will also become a cultural hero on the level of Saladin and undisputed leader of the entire Muslim world.

The leaders of Saudi Arabia, Libya and Iraq each wanted to be that man.

For this reason the meetings which began in Paris in 1973 were a crisscross of efforts. Pakistan representatives met with representatives from Saudi Arabia and Libya. Pakistanis also began negotiations with French officials and businessmen involved in the sale of nuclear technology and materials. Iraq's representatives arrived to begin their own foray through Parisian government and industrial circles in search of nuclear technology. Iraq had declined to take part in the joint Pakistani proposal and was proceeding on its own plan to become an independent nuclear power.

Meanwhile, the Saudis and Libyans sought to win exclusive control of Pakistan's programs. According to sources at those meetings, the Saudis offered "several billions" of dollars to fund the Islamabad atomic weapons research programs. Libya offered Pakistan $500 million immediately as well as access to uranium. The dual plutonium/uranium enrichment projects Pakistan was planning would require enormous amounts of uranium—far more than Pakistan had the means of extracting from its own deposits.

Libya would initially gain the upper hand by virtue of its willingness to forgo further negotiations or such time-consuming formalities as cooperation pacts or signed contracts. Massive amounts of cash—packed in suitcases and flown in Libyan airliners from Tripoli —began suddenly flowing into Islamabad. Unable to find enough uranium in its own deserts to meet its commitment to Pakistan, Libya would send agents into neighboring Niger, topple the government, support the installation of a new one and immediately become the largest purchaser of Niger's prodigious uranium ore output. And soon, for the same reasons, Libya would march armies south in an effort to seize those parts of the nation of Chad that are also rich in uranium ore deposits.

Saudi Arabia and Pakistan would also continue their more extensive and detailed negotiations concerning long-term nuclear weapons development and a far-reaching military and economic alliance.

At the same time it was undertaking the first stage of these various arrangements with Saudi Arabia and Libya in Paris in 1973, Pakistan was also opening talks with French industrialists and military officials. Soon the same company which had once secretly sold the plans for a plutonium reprocessing plant to Israel—Saint Gobain, the private firm which functions as a direct extension of the French military's atomic weapons facility—sold a similar set of plans to Pakistan.

Iraq, at the same time, was meeting with the same French nuclear officials in Paris and laying the groundwork for its own multibillion-dollar buying spree. One of these purchases would be a plutonium processing reactor crucial to Iraq's atomic plans. Another—incredible in its physical detail and logistical complexity—involved the delivery of an entire French city of nuclear research facilities, including everything from streets and sewers and electrical lines to isotope labs, computer centers and engineering workshops.

Those historic Paris meetings resulted in waves of lucrative contracts for French industry and were one of the reasons that France was provided with special oil deliveries throughout the embargo that disrupted other industrialized nations.

By 1980, as the Saudi-Pakistan nuclear alliance was reportedly preparing to test a nuclear bomb and as Iraq was preparing to start up its French-supplied reactor near Baghdad, the Paris Government's relations with the Arab world became a major political issue in France.

The country's Israel lobby—traditionally a political force as potent as the parallel lobby in America—waged a major campaign to defeat the architect and guiding hand of thickening Franco-Muslim relationships: President Valéry Giscard d'Estaing. The Franco-Israel lobby backed socialist François Mitterrand, who had been an ardent supporter of Israel and one of the most caustic critics of the French drift toward the Muslim powers.

In a surprise upset, Mitterrand defeated Giscard d'Estaing and, in early 1981, assumed the office of President of France. The government of Israel and the Franco-Israel lobby were delighted and predicted major realignments in France's foreign policy priorities.

For more than four months after taking office, Mitterrand remained something of a hermit in the Presidential Palace. He made no major domestic appearances and announced no plans for state visits to foreign countries. It is customary for the new French leader to symbolically set the tone of his foreign policy through his choice of countries to be visited during his first trip abroad as President. The press in France and throughout the other countries of Europe widely speculated that Mitterrand would go to Israel first.

Mitterrand provided no clues of his intentions as he remained ensconced in his office, gathering the reins of power and learning the innermost secret workings of the government, military, industry and economy of France.

Then, on his first trip as President, he flew to Saudi Arabia, where he was greeted at the airport by the late King Khalid—the man who directly controlled 53 percent of the oil France needs every day. Mitterrand met with Arab leaders, assuring them that French industry would continue to be the largest seller of arms in the Middle East. And, in another symbolic gesture, he lifted the embargo on sales of French weapons to Libya, authorizing immediate shipment of Mirage 2000 fighter jets to Tripoli.

Mitterrand's new Foreign Minister, Claude Cheysson, was dispatched to Lebanon. There he met with Yasir Arafat, whom he hailed as "a representative of the Palestinian people." And, in private communications, President Mitterrand informed Israeli Prime Minister Menachem Begin that France had no alternative but to support the international call for the creation of a Palestinian state.

In the summer of 1981, after Israeli planes invaded Iraq and bombed the nuclear reactor which French engineers had just finished erecting near Baghdad, the Mitterrand government issued blistering denouncements of the attack. And, a short time later, the Mitterrand administration announced that the French military and French industry, in return for hundreds of millions of dollars in new contracts, were willing to provide the services and equipment necessary to rebuild that plutonium-producing facility in Iraq. The Franco-Muslim atomic cooperations which began in 1973 were to continue.

In 1982, as Israel launched its invasion into Lebanon, Mitterrand stepped forward as the Western world's leading spokesman against the Jewish state's actions. He called for a mobilization of world opinion against Israel; censure by the UN; and total, unconditional, Israeli withdrawal from the newly conquered territories. At the same time, he led the ten European Economic Community countries in a public condemnation of Israel and an affirmation of their earlier call for the "Palestinian people to exercise duly its right to self-determination."

As a capstone of this campaign, Mitterrand received PLO Foreign Minister Farouk Kaddoumi at the Presidential Palace and, in effect, welcomed him as the representative of an Arab state.

15

THE LAND OF GNOMES AND GHAZI

In Europe's two famed "cities of banks"—Zurich and Geneva in Switzerland—the Muslim oil powers were already a strong force in the late 1970s when a sudden turn of events brought even more Middle Eastern money into the country.

In 1979, when the United States attempted to freeze the assets of Iran throughout the international banking system, the oil nations responded in two ways to what they perceived as a potential threat to their own international deposits. One response was to increase their efforts in setting up their own international financial networks, which would be immune to such exterior influence. Another response was to vastly increase the use of Swiss trustee accounts and of what the *Financial Times* of London described as "faceless intermediaries" in the country renowned for its official system of absolute secrecy in banking.

One high international banking official with direct connections to the Swiss banking community explained, "The influence of the OPEC nations [in Swiss financial matters] is prodigious. In fact, it would not be inaccurate to say that, in many ways, Switzerland has become an economic colony of

OPEC. I don't feel there is anything wrong with this. In fact, both parties have benefited greatly from these new developments."

Geneva, which is crossroads for large portions of the Western world's finances, is also the headquarters of some of its most important associations and agencies. For instance, it is the European headquarters for the United Nations. And in recent years this city, nestled around a broad, Alpine lake, has also become a major social and vacation center for Middle Easterners. In late June the press reports, "The Arab season in Geneva has begun. King Khalid of Saudi Arabia has flown in with his entourage. The left bank of Lake Geneva (Vesenaz, Collonges-Bellerive) is Saudi territory. The right bank, stretching toward Luasanne, is favored by the Kuwaitis, the Qataris and various citizens of the lower Persian Gulf."

One of the community's larger new property owners and power brokers is Akram Ojjeh, who established Geneva as the headquarters of his financial conglomerate, Technique Avante-Garde, better known as TAG Finances. Ojjeh is just one of the flood of Arab entrepreneurs and financiers who have moved into the Swiss economy and caused mixed reactions from the country's government and public. On one hand the government has taken steps to make it easier for Middle Easterners to buy into local industries and financial establishments. On the other hand the same government created new laws recently that halt further land purchases by such foreign investors. Public controversy erupted throughout the 1970s over Arab purchases of some of Switzerland's most cherished historical landmarks. The worst outcry came when former Saudi government official Abdullah Mahdi made a bid to purchase the Grandson Château, one of the most famous Swiss castles. This came at the same time Middle Easterners were virtually scooping up Swiss hotels, Swiss corporations, Swiss hospitals and even Swiss schools. By 1978 the resident and transient population of Muslims in Switzerland had become so significant that the late King Khalid of Saudi Arabia had a cathedral-size mosque and Islamic cultural center built in the center of Geneva to serve them.

In 1980 Switzerland again experienced record property sales to foreigners, and the Swiss Minister of Justice established a complicated system of monitoring and severely limiting further such purchases in Swiss towns. Many Swiss communities—particularly those noted for famous ski facilities—are almost entirely owned by foreign interests. In seventeen towns the Justice Ministry's new rules halted all sales to non-Swiss citizens because those resort areas had become enclaves of foreigners—largely Middle Easterners who had bought up whole mountainsides of cabins, lodges and châteaus.

On the business side no such protectionist sentiments have manifested themselves. Swiss commercial enterprises remain open and enthusiastic to Arab investments. While the bulk of such transactions remain secret, some sense of their direction can be seen in the recent moves of Hentsch and Co.—one of Switzerland's stuffiest and most prestigious banking establishments. Famous for its snobbish refusals to allow "outsiders"—major European institutions across the street —to participate in any of its undertakings, Hentsch and Co. waggled more than a few bushy eyebrows in the cafes of Geneva and Zurich with its announcement of a merger with Arab consortiums. The new Hentsch-Arab ventures are aimed at moving the venerable firm into the mainstream currents of the Middle Eastern money markets.

Arab investors also purchased Total Suisse, a refining and marketing group, and own controlling interest of one of Switzerland's two oil refineries. This provides Middle Eastern businessmen with control of 50 percent of the processed-petroleum products marketed in the nation. A consortium of Arab investors also purchased Gatoil, a Geneva-based petroleum exploration, production and refining firm whose largest international subsidiaries are located in London, Beirut and Texas. It is through such European-based international conglomerates that Middle Eastern groups have often extended themselves invisibly into countries where "Arab" investments receive negative public attention and political pressures. For instance, investments made from Geneva by such firms as Gatoil are recorded in America as "Swiss" investments.

Directly across the border—within yodeling distance of the computer-crammed complex that is the headquarters of Adnan Khashoggi's Triad Holding Company in Liechtenstein—Middle Eastern oil powers have become a major presence in Austria. One of the world's most famous and active addresses is Obere Donaustrasse 93 in Vienna, the headquarters of the Organization of Petroleum Exporting Countries and a facility that has made that city a daily crossroads for the political, financial and cultural commerce between East and West. The Danube city, which is densely strung with universities and technical institutes, has also become a major educational center for students from around the Muslim world.

In Vienna a grand mosque—its broad dome and starkly modern minaret standing out in sharp contrast against the baroque facades of the Catholic cathedrals for which the city is famous—has been completed inside the ancient walls that, for nearly five hundred years, served as the last barrier against the Islamic Empire, which had enveloped all of Balkan Europe. The new $6.2 million mosque was funded by the Keeper of the Holy Cities of Islam—the King of Saudi Arabia—and was needed to minister to the 50,000 Muslims in the immediate environs of the capital. The project, which was directed by the Vienna Islamic Center, is only another of the many evidences of thickening ties between Austria and such Muslim oil nations as Saudi Arabia.

By the end of the 1970s Austria's fiscal condition had been ravaged by year-after-year record trade deficits—wealth sent out of the nation to pay for oil—and by oil shortages which affected every segment of industrial life.

In 1979 Austria and Saudi Arabia negotiated government-to-government agreements under which Austria was guaranteed long-term oil supplies as a part of the two countries' overall diplomatic relationship.

That same year Jewish-born Austrian Chancellor Bruno Kreisky granted the Palestine Liberation Organization diplomatic recognition and publicly urged other industrialized governments to do the same because, Kreisky said, "Western nations need Middle East oil."

16

GERMANY AND
NUCLEAR JIHAD

During the 1970s West Germany quietly evolved as a major cultural center for Europe's rapidly expanding Muslim communities. The Islamic Cultural Center in Cologne grew to the point of needing fifteen imams to tend to the needs of West Germany's 1.5 million Muslims. The institution also serves as an information clearinghouse and primary center of authority for congregations as distant as those in Switzerland and Sweden. Each year it is the Cologne center that imports 160 additional Islamic clergymen who are needed throughout the Continent for the services of Ramadan, the high Islamic holy days. And in 1981 eleven different Muslim nations were donating the funds and supports needed to set up a German Institute of Arabic and Islamic Studies in Frankfurt to further service Germany's Muslims.

A substantial portion of this new Muslim population, now spread across the lands of the Rhine and the Ruhr, were imported into labor-short Germany in the late 1960s. That was at the time the German industrial rebuilding programs hit full speed and propelled the nation into the position of technological and financial leader of the West—rivaled only by Japan in productivity and innovation. Throughout the late 1970s, however, the country's economy slowed and began to decline, many of its most vital internal supports crippled through lack of fuel stocks or price increases, which undercut the fiscal viability of entire segments of industry. In 1979, West Germany—the linchpin economy of Europe's heavy industrial complex and the third-largest importer of oil in the world—lost 19 percent of its petroleum supplies when the Islamic revolution of Iran shut down that nation's wells. In a desperate search for oil, the West German Government was forced into the Rotterdam Spot Market, where the worldwide pressures had driven prices up more than twice the official posted OPEC price. The Organization of Economic Cooperation and Development reported West Germany had a critical problem and that "for the first time since the days of the immediate postwar recovery, there is a real risk that the short- and medium-term growth of living standards and employment will be constrained by the availability of a key industrial input: energy."

The same year West Germany ran its first trading deficit since 1965— $5 billion—and the central bank was forced to begin drastic measures to protect the deutsche mark. Within the next twelve months the deficit—the outpouring of West Germany's economic vitality—tripled. The Bundesbank issued a report calling for further emergency actions and a governmental "reorientation" of West Germany's traditional trading patterns to place fresh emphasis on the Middle East, the only potential source of both the oil and capital needed to stabilize the nation's worsening condition. Struggling to overcome a monetary crisis, West Germany was able to borrow $500 million from the United States. At the same time, Saudi Arabia offered $2.8 billion in funds, which West Germany accepted. At the same time, the Saudi Arabian Monetary Agency began purchasing massive amounts of West German government notes, an action which catapulted the deutsche mark upward in both value and reputation as a new world reserve currency backed by the oil wealth of the Middle East. The West German Government signed a sweeping scientific and technological cooperation pact with Saudi Arabia providing that country direct access to the latest German industrial breakthroughs and resources. The Saudi Government issued a statement saying it would continue to seek ways to develop closer ties with West Germany but that West Germany must publicly endorse the "just political concerns" of the Saudis.

The West German Government took measures removing the previous restrictions which limited investments by foreigners in strategic industries. Kuwait purchased 30 percent of Korf Stahl AG of Baden-Baden, one of the nation's largest steel firms. Kuwait also purchased 10 percent of Metallgesellschaft, a Frankfurt-based metals and engineering conglomerate. Kuwait and Qatar purchased at least 15 percent of the stock of the two giant chemical corporations, Hoechst and BASF. The Arab Banking Corporation took over Richard Daus & Company, a major West German bank. Kuwait purchased 14 percent of Daimler-Benz, the largest manufacturer of cars, trucks and buses in West Germany. Suliman Olayan of Saudi Arabia became a major investor, but the details of his transactions, like those of the bulk of the other Middle Easterners moving into the West German economy, are veiled in secrecy.

In 1979 Juergen Moelleman, leading member of Parliament, opened a new public dialogue when he presented an eight-point position paper calling for government endorsement of a Middle East settlement based upon Israeli withdrawal from the Old City of Jerusalem, the Gaza Strip, the West Bank and the Golan Heights and the formation of a "state organization" to represent the interests of the Palestinian people. At the same time, West German government representatives met in Beirut with officers of the Palestine Liberation Organization. Former West German Chancellor Willy Brandt, in widely publicized ceremonies, met with Yasir Arafat.

In 1980 West German Chancellor Helmut Schmidt was credited, along with French President Valéry Giscard d'Estaing, as being the moving force in the behind-the-scenes efforts which engineered the official tilt of the European Economic Community in favor of the Palestine Liberation Organization.

Two weeks after that, Saudi Arabian King Khalid flew to West Germany for a state visit. At the end of his tour he announced that West Germany had been awarded a $910 million contract for laying water pipeline systems throughout Saudi Arabia and that the country had also been granted favored-nation trading status as it prepared to submit its bids on a wide range of multibillion-dollar electrical generation, desalinization and petrochemical facility construction projects.

Some of the more interesting and important of the Muslim world's industrial dealings in West Germany have occurred in and around the small village of Watchberg-Pech, south of Bonn. Situated in the highlands overlooking the Rhine, Watchberg-Pech is a hamlet as quaint as it is obscure, which is probably why it was chosen.[1]

In 1977 Ikram ul-Haque Khan, a soft-spoken and eminently polite Muslim businessman, moved into a modest town house in the village. On one floor he set up a small apartment residence. On the other he established a tiny office from which hundreds of millions of dollars worth of orders for special metal parts and electrical equipment began flowing.

Khan was an official in the Pakistan Ordinance Service and kingpin in an underground network established by the Arab-Pakistani atomic bomb consortium to secretly purchase nuclear industrial equipment throughout Europe. Khan's primary job was to buy, on a piece-by-piece basis, an entire centrifuge plant needed to concentrate large amounts of uranium gases into bomb-grade enriched uranium.

In Pakistan the administrative headquarters of the Arab-Pakistani bomb project had been established within the Pakistan Institute of Science and Technology. PINSTECH was located in a heavily fortified compound in the northern outskirts of Islamabad. Here Muslim scientists, engineers and architects had laid out plans for several different types of nuclear installations. Located at various sites around Pakistan, these facilities were required for either the plutonium bomb project or the enriched-uranium bomb project. There were nuclear reactors at Chashma and Islamabad, a uranium refinery at Lahore, a fuel assembly plant at Sargodha, a heavy waterworks at Karachi, and a plutonium reprocessing plant and uranium enrichment plant at Islamabad.

Many components of these facilities could be purchased on the world market. They were common—although extraordinarily expensive—items of technology used in the nuclear power generation industries. However, two key items—the plutonium reprocessing plant and the uranium enrichment plant—could not be obtained on the open world market. Both the processes and the machinery of extracting and enriching uranium were tightly controlled by the Western nuclear monopoly, led by the United States. Nonproliferation protocols banned the sale of either to the Third World nations.

Pakistan purchased a plutonium-producing nuclear reactor from

Canada and initially made arrangements to quietly purchase an entire plutonium reprocessing plant from France. But at the last minute the United States discovered this and pressured France to cancel the order. Then, much as Israel had done years before in the same situation, Pakistan secretly purchased the process engineering designs and construction blueprints for a plutonium reprocessing plant from France. Operatives from Pakistan and other Muslim nations then set up a series of dummy companies in Europe and, piece by piece, purchased all the parts and materials necessary to assemble their own plutonium reprocessing plant near Islamabad. That provided the final item needed for the plutonium bomb project.

For the parallel enriched-uranium bomb project, the Arab-Pakistani consortium had to perform a similar feat. First they had to acquire the exact designs for the complicated uranium enrichment process. Then they had to purchase the highly specialized parts secretly. A uranium enrichment plant is like a very large factory in which hundreds or even thousands of centrifugal machines must be operated. Each machine is a complex, space-age item of technology made up of components and special metals produced by only a limited number of companies around the world. Each of those companies purchases its supplies from hundreds of other subcontractors. The list of the hundreds of obscure small companies which produce these critical parts for uranium enrichment equipment is one of the most secret documents in the world, closely guarded by the Western governments that control the uranium enrichment industry.

However, the spy Pakistan had planted in late 1972 in the uranium enrichment center in Holland left his job suddenly in 1975. He took back to Islamabad the precise plans for constructing uranium enrichment centrifuges as well as the list of every company in the world capable of making the unique parts.

In 1977, armed with shopping lists prepared from this intelligence, Ikram ul-Haque Khan traveled to West Germany, rented an unassuming apartment in the quiet village of Watchberg-Pech and began spinning webs of bogus companies across all of Europe. That whitewashed, two-story flat suddenly became the headquarters for dozens of companies ordering hundreds of millions of dollars worth of custom-made items of "industrial equipment." Khan headed a web of operatives stretching across all of Europe, each authorized to spend as much as $1 million with no paper work to overcome any "obstacles" hampering their intended purchases. Moving through the West German industrial centers, which were already inundated with billions of dollars of heavy-equipment orders from Muslim states and eager for more, Khan and his agents performed their jobs unnoticed and unimpeded. Their dozens of "West German" front companies were able to easily place orders with German firms as well as with other firms dealing in nuclear hardware in Britain, Belgium and Switzerland. The bogus companies had their purchases shipped to West German addresses. Once the purchases were received, that particular company was folded and its "inventory" resold to Pakistan. Much of the equipment was then hauled to Switzerland, where it joined the daily skylift of gargantuan amounts of goods shipped to the Middle East. In at least one instance, three C-130s—each with a cargo capacity in excess of fifty tons—were required to carry a single load of "industrial machines" to Pakistan. There entire factories of nuclear parts were unpacked from their West German, Swiss and Belgium crates and assembled into a uranium enrichment plant in Islamabad.

And as Pakistan's agents moved discreetly about West Germany on their missions, Libya's agents were also making the industrial rounds from Düsseldorf to Stuttgart in search of materials for Colonel Muammar el-Qaddafi's increasingly eclectic atomic endeavors. Qaddafi, who continued to provide funds and uranium to the Pakistan project, had nevertheless become impatient with it. For one thing, Islamabad was proceeding slowly and methodically toward the development of an entire, self-contained nuclear industrial base capable of ultimately mass-producing atomic weapons rather than quickly building a few bootleg bombs. For another, Saudi Arabia and Pakistan were coalescing toward a broad military and economic alliance which was squeezing Libya out as a controlling influence in the Islamabad project.

Qaddafi had already attempted to purchase a ready-made bomb, retail, from China. But China declined the offer. Qaddafi then turned to India. India declined to sell Libya a ready-made bomb. Then Libya demanded that India—which imported substantial amounts of Libyan oil—transfer to Libya the technological details necessary for quickly building a bomb from scratch. India refused. Libya cut off India's oil. India turned elsewhere for oil. Libya turned elsewhere for bombs.

In 1975 Libya signed a nuclear cooperation pact with Argentina and the Soviet Union. Qaddafi purchased a nuclear research reactor and nuclear research institute from the Soviets. He continued to supply uranium to Pakistan at the same time he began stockpiling uranium in Libya. And his invasions south into the uranium-rich regions of Chad continued.

Apparently confident that he would eventually, somehow, obtain atomic weapons, Qaddafi, in the late 1970s, sent agents to West Germany to begin shopping for an entire rocket delivery system for carrying atomic warheads. Libya was seeking much the same sort of deal as Israel had arranged with France in the late 1960s when private French firms sold the Tel Aviv Government the parts and technology for making the Jericho rockets necessary for raining atomic warheads on surrounding Muslim capitals.

In West Germany, Qaddafi was looking for a firm capable of building a ballistic missile which could carry an atomic bomb about three to four hundred miles—or about the distance from Libya's eastern border zone to Jerusalem. Qaddafi's agents found what they were looking for in Stuttgart. Situated along a river valley in southwestern Germany and studded with ornate public fountains, opera houses and fifteenth-century castles, Stuttgart is also a center of the German high-technology electronics industry and large-scale factory operations. It has also been a major center of interest to Arab investors. For instance, the headquarters of Daimler-Benz, the automotive firm now partially owned by Kuwait, is there.

Stuttgart is also a center of the rocket research for which Germany has been famed and the home of the West German Orbital Transport and Rocket Company—the only private rocket-making firm in the world. Headed by West German aerospace engineer Lutz T. Kayser, the company, known as Otrag, was formed in an attempt to capitalize on the predicted 1980s boom in communications satellite launching. But it quickly learned that there is even more money to be made by selling missile systems and full-scale rockets to Third World nations, which can't easily obtain such heavy-duty, intercontinental hardware from Western governments.

Libya and Otrag signed a contract and, shrouded in secrecy, the Stuttgart firm began transporting large amounts of equipment to a site three hundred miles deep into the Libyan deserts. Intelligence reports indicated that launching tracks had been constructed and that a small city of engineers and laborers appeared to be testing rocket engines and guidance systems. By 1981 West German engineers continued to ship ever-larger amounts of parts and equipment into the Libyan rocket program at the same time they hauled out ever-larger amounts of petro-dollars. The money was only one of the rivulets joining into torrents of petro-payments splashing into the industrial valleys of West Germany, where unemployment, recession and energy instability made the deluge a welcomed event.

In neighboring Belgium—in whose capital Akram Ojjeh maintains a headquarters for his international construction operations and from which he also makes his twice-weekly flights to Riyadh—economic conditions had also taken a drastic downturn in the late 1970s. By 1979, Belgium's unemployment rate broke 10 percent because of what the government described as "massive industrial shutdowns," and the Chase Econometrics Center issued a report predicting that Belgian national growth would be further damaged by loss of the Iranian oil upon which it was heavily dependent. That same year the government began negotiations that resulted in government-to-government, long-term oil-supply agreements with Saudi Arabia. At the same time, Belgian Foreign Minister Henri Semonet met in Brussels with Palestine Liberation Organization Foreign Minister Farouk Kaddoumi and issued an official statement endorsing "Palestinian autonomy" as the central principle of any Middle East peace settlement.

In Ireland—whose boldly innovative fiscal policies had earned it the reputation as Europe's "miracle economy" by the end of 1975—the nation entered 1979 in the throes of financial disaster: its economy writhing under a zooming inflation rate, a trade deficit of $2.5 billion and a 100 percent dependence on imported oil. The Irish Central Bank that same year issued a report in which it stated that predicted inflation rates would rise by as much as 20 percent in the immediate future at the same time the gross national product—which had increased yearly for two decades—would experience zero growth. Unable to meet its national minimal fuel requirements that year, the government invoked emergency powers and seized control of the privately owned petroleum storage and distribution networks throughout Ireland. At the same time, the government dispatched the Foreign Minister for a round of visits and negotiations throughout the Persian Gulf and announced a major change in its position on the Middle East. It publicly called on the United States to officially recognize the Palestine Liberation Organization in all negotiations involving the Middle East crisis.

In Denmark—a nation noted in continental financial journals for its "diminishing reputation in worldwide financial circles"—the government in 1979 was plagued by critical problems of a crumbling internal economy, an inflation rate of 15 percent, widespread unemployment and a $17 billion trade deficit for imported oil. Despite this record outflow of national wealth, the Danes were still unable to acquire normal amounts of oil needed to fuel their already battered industrial operations.

In early 1980 the Danish Government launched new initiatives, seeking to form closer cooperative ties with Middle Eastern countries. A $99 million loan was granted to the government by Saudi Arabia. Danish oil representatives opened simultaneous negotiations with the countries of Saudi Arabia, Kuwait, Qatar, the United Arab Emirates and Iraq.

In mid-1980 the Danish Government, in return for long-term, government-to-government supply guarantees of oil with Saudi Arabia, signed one of the most unusual contracts ever written for an international trade agreement. As a stipulated section of the contractual agreement which obligates Saudi Arabia to supply oil, Denmark, in return, is obligated to "conduct itself in such a manner as not to bring the kingdom of Saudi Arabia or any of its departments or instrumentalities into disrepute in the international oil community or in any other manner whatsoever." The contract also stipulates that oil and other items of trade between the two countries are to be carried in Arab vessels.

At the same time, Ghaith Pharaon had just purchased control of neighboring Norway's Concordia Shipping Lines and changed their name to Saudi Concordia, and Adnan Khashoggi had purchased control of neighboring Finland's Oy Finnlines, reforming it as the Saudi International Shipping Company, headquartered in Riyadh and specializing in trade between the Middle East and northern Europe.

During the same week these oil contracts were signed, Denmark and Norway led the moves within the Helsinki meeting of Nordic foreign ministers which resulted in that group's international communiqué endorsing the "necessity of realizing the legitimate national rights of the Palestinians."

17

ARABIA-UPON-THE-THAMES

Great Britain's relationship with the Muslim petro-powers has evolved in a somewhat different manner from that of other Western nations: Each year British imports of oil have decreased.

In 1970, in an event which would alter that country's future in about as drastic a manner as possible for an industrial nation of the era, British crews discovered major oil fields in the North Sea.

The development of the fields occurred gradually, but steadily, over ten years time and did not insulate the nation from the impact of the Middle Eastern oil actions in the 1970s. In 1977 Britain was still importing large amounts of oil and recorded the largest yearly outflow of lost national wealth in its history—an event accompanied by a plunging London stock market. The recently nationalized British steel industry reported record losses as that business continued to collapse in spasms of layoffs, shutdowns, demonstrations and spreading chaos. Parliament voted to nationalize the devastated shipbuilding industry and began by immediately laying off tens of thousands of workers. The nation experienced its worst wave of business failures in the postwar period—2,349 in twelve months. And the

British Government was forced to seek $3 billion in emergency monetary aid from the Bank of International Settlements to protect itself against a new internal threat to its fiscal stability. That threat was caused, the British Government said, by "deposits of British currency controlled by foreign interests," and the government further indicated it was worried over the increasing possibility that those "major oil states" would soon make "large withdrawals of sterling balances [that] could depress the value of the pound overnight."

Meanwhile, the British Government and business community both switched into high gear behind a movement which had been gaining momentum through the early 1970s—the establishment of London as the international center for recycling the petro-dollars being exchanged between Western industrialized nations and the Middle East.

In its broadest terms this movement sought to tightly integrate the developing financial systems of the Middle East with that of England and to launch aggressive campaigns aimed at luring both Arab financial institutions and investors to Britain. At the same time, the British government-industrial complex moved out against France and West Germany in competition for the largest share of the financial flows, investment capital and tourist trade pouring out of the Muslim oil countries.

Simultaneously, the Prime Minister's office also confirmed press reports that the British Government had begun "occasional, unofficial" meetings with representatives of the Palestine Liberation Organization.

In 1980 Britain achieved petroleum independence and freedom from the direct oil pressure that is the Arabs' most potent political tool against the rest of the West. Not only did Britain produce all the oil it required that year, but it was able to begin exporting oil for sale to its European allies. Ironically, the price Britain charged for its oil was higher than that charged by OPEC. But oil self-sufficiency did not prove to be an overnight panacea for that nation's considerable problems. Although its derricks and tankers were proceeding at full speed, its mills and production lines were not. The country's industrial heartland was a sooty jumble of hopelessly antiquated, shuttered and padlocked factory sites. At the end of 1979 Britain's was declared the "worst" economy of any member of the European

Economic Community. It is some measure of the national dilemma that all the money collected by the government for all the oil pumped out of the North Sea in a year's time is an amount slightly less than that needed to pay out the year's national unemployment benefits. The British Government, which no longer needed Arabs for oil in 1980, desperately continued to court them for their business and their wealth. By the early 1980s that government-assisted influx of Arabs into London had become substantial enough to have changed the cultural tone and physical texture of the former imperial capital.

The number of Muslim professionals—lawyers, engineers, physicists, financiers, scientists and scholars—had become so unwieldy that the Arab League offices were forced to install a computerized information bank to keep track of them all for the social register.

At the same time, one of the poshest new centers of high society is the London Arab Club. Its six hundred-plus members represent the local Arab upper crust and its inaugural dinner in 1981 was an extravaganza attended by Lord Carrington and other of Britain's social luminaries.

And London has become the only city in Europe boasting its own commercial camel-milk parlor—an emporium catering to those with a taste for dromedarian delights. Out in the oak-shaded, castle-studded suburbs is Europe's only estate dedicated to research projects in camel husbandry and dromo-technology, the site at which, in 1979, the world's first automatic camel-milking apparatus was perfected.

At the famed Goddard and Gibbs stained-glass works—previously renowned for its spectacular work in cathedral and synagogue windows—the crews have now been turned to Islamic motifs. Their primary source of orders are the new mosques and Islamic centers going up across Europe and other continents and the homes and palaces of various Islamic figures and financiers who appreciate the ultimate in British stained glass.

Harley Street—London's famed lane of physicians—by the late 1970s had become the most prestigious medical center frequented by globe-trotting Arabs. The street's British doctors had also come to dubious world prominence for the records they set: the highest fees ever charged, at any time, in any civilization, for the professional services required to sustain life and retard disease.

London's hotels, taxis, banks, restaurants and boutiques had refurbished their signs, vehicle markings, brochures and lobby directional plaques to reflect the latest trend in commercial bilingualism: English and Arabic. And London was pushed to new heights in the pages of the *Financial Times*' "Living Costs Overseas" guide. The guide is a listing of the cost-of-living expenses in the sixty-five largest cities in the world and is used as a planning and budgeting tool by business and government executives around the world. In 1976, London was rated the thirty-eighth most expensive city in the world. In 1978, as the movement of Arabs in and through England became a tide, the city had leaped into the eleventh most-expensive-city position. In 1979, when Arabs had unequivocally established themselves as a major new demographic factor, London had vaulted to the top of the list and become the most expensive city in the world to live in or visit.

Four of the better known of those new capital residents are Ghaith Pharaon, Adnan Khashoggi, Akram Ojjeh and Suliman Olayan, all of whom acquired extensive office space and baronial homes in London. Khashoggi's home has a window wall providing an impressive view of Buckingham Palace, next door. Pharaon's town house is on Berkeley Square, directly adjacent to both Saville Row and Picadilly Circus, once the vortex of London's financial and political establishment and traditional stamping grounds for such local British dynasties as the Rothschilds. It was here, for instance, that Lionel Walter Rothschild used to squire about kings, queens, princes and lords of Parliament in a specially designed royal carriage pulled by zebras.

The details of the multibillion-dollar operations in England are hidden behind government-sanctioned veils of secrecy. But Pharaon is known to have purchased into such major British firms as International Foley and Company and the British Mowlem International Company, both of which have now been extended into Saudi Arabia on various construction projects. Khashoggi has purchased banks, travel agencies, furniture factories and insurance firms. Ojjeh's TAG International is active throughout the upper financial circles. Olayan is involved in extensive real estate acquisition and has formed a partnership with Bland, Payne, Sedgewick Forbes Ltd., creating Arab Commercial Enterprises—now the largest insurance company in the Middle East. Olayan is also chairman of the Saudi-British Bank.

In 1980 Britain's fastest-growing new domestic banking operation was the Arab Bank of Credit and Commerce International, which had forty-five branches throughout the country. It was just one of the thirty-two major Arab banks which had set up headquarters in London, transforming whole sections of the city's most fashionable business districts into enclaves whose most common sight is that of an English servant in maroon livery polishing brass entrance plaques engraved in Arabic.

According to government statistics, the largest institutional investor in London—that agency making more purchases at every level of the economy than any other single foreign or domestic enterprise in Britain—is the Kuwait Investment Office. England has become one of the primary targets for Kuwait, the oil-rich nation which, except for Saudi Arabia, has evidenced the most ambitious worldwide financial designs during the decade. The architect of Kuwait's global investment strategies is Khaled Abu Saoud, chief financial adviser to the Emir of Kuwait. Saoud settled in Kuwait in 1954 after being unable to return to his homeland, Palestine. One of the major instruments through which Saoud extends Kuwait's buying power across various continents is the Kuwait International Investment Company, headed by Hikmat Nashashibi, also a Palestinian, who graduated from the American University in Beirut and was trained for three years in a Wall Street brokerage firm before assuming his duties for Kuwait.

By 1980 a whirlwind of purchases had netted Arabs control of some of the country's most distinguished landmarks, and Kuwait acquired the area known as Hay's Wharf. The thirty-acre property—noted by financial journals as one of the "choicest properties in London"—runs along a curving bank of the Thames. At one end the property is bounded by the Tower Bridge, completed in the 1890s in time for Queen Victoria's Diamond Jubilee. The wharf played a major role in the Victorian period as a center of commerce handling the flood of cargoes and riches pouring into London from the plantations and labor colonies of an empire whose gunpowder grip extended to directly control the lives of a quarter of all the human beings on earth. The new Kuwaiti owners of the wharf area have begun to build a sprawling business city in what will be the largest single-property development project in the history of London. When completed, the skyscrapers of Kuwait will look directly across the Thames at the Tower of London, the British Customs House,

Billingsgate Market and will also command a view up King William Street to the Stock Exchange and the Bank of England.

Another of Kuwait's major landmark acquisitions in 1980 was a substantial portion of the British Savoy Hotel group, purchased from the Rothschild Investment Trust of London. The Kuwait Investment Office has also taken the Londonderry Hotel in the Park Lane section of the city, a major interest in the Eagle Star Insurance Group and St. Martin's Property Corporation, a real estate and investment conglomerate.

Arab consortiums have also purchased the Dorchester Hotel and part of Grindlay Brandts and Edward Bates Ltd. banks.

Another Muslim investment group purchased about 25 percent of Lonrho—one of England's largest multinational conglomerates. The purchase provided the investors with direct interests in such diverse Lonrho subsidiaries overseas as pharmaceutical companies in Canada and carpet-making factories in Denmark. In England, Lonrho enjoys holdings in such enterprises as Brentford Nylons Ltd., Dunford Steel Company, the Scottish and Universal Investments Company and Harrods, the London institution fabled as the most exclusive, most expensive and most elegant department store in the world. Arabs have become so taken with the merchandise and atmosphere of Harrods that, in 1979, they began a $32 million project to erect an exact duplicate of the store on the sands near Riyadh. It will be complete even to the red stone architectural trim, the art deco cutglass windows, the snail-shell awnings and the famous Harrods' motto carved in its face: "Everyone, Everything, Everywhere."

London real estate authorities indicate that Saudis have purchased "large tracts" of properties throughout the city's ultraposh Hampstead district. Other real estate reports indicate that "all variety of castles and estates" have been purchased up and down the length of the country by various Arab individuals and groups.

By 1980 Muslims—both as a local cultural presence and financial factor—had established themselves as a major political force throughout British society. That year the Muslim population was more than 1.5 million and England had more than three hundred mosques serving congregations in all areas of the island. And that Muslim community was continuing to expand rapidly. Major new mosque and Islamic cultural-center constructions were either under way or just completed in London, Birmingham, Cardiff, Newcastle-upon-Tyne, South Shields, Coventry and Glasgow. One of the larger mosques and cultural centers was being erected in Manchester, the commercial hub and industrial port in central England which was also the political and financial base for the Zionist movement during the earlier decades of the century. It was in Manchester that the British Rothschilds began in the 1700s as a dynasty, and the city's Jewish community produced some of the nation's best-known members of Parliament, lords of the press and industrial magnates.

In the East End of London—another area previously synonymous with the Jewish community—Muslims have now become a major factor. In 1982 there were more than 30,000 Muslims living in that one community and their need for additional facilities was so great that the Brick Lane and Christian Street synagogues were purchased and turned into mosques. Muslim workers laboriously removed the Hebrew letters and Judaic symbols, replacing them with Arabic and Koranic verse.[1]

Islam is also filtering out to touch the general English population in several cultural ways. One of the most-written-about plays in recent years in London was *Mahjoob, Mahjoob,* a drama about Palestinians living under the Israeli occupation. And in the area of pop culture, one of the country's best-known rock stars—Cat Stevens—has become a Muslim. After changing his name to Yusuf Islam, the former singer has become a leading public advocate for the rights of Muslims in England.

One of the country's newest grass roots political groups is the Union of Muslim Organizations of the United Kingdom, which represents more than one hundred Muslim organizations around the island. Well funded, well organized, by 1980 it had become one of England's most active political lobbying groups.

Meanwhile, Britain has also evolved into the major center in the Western world for the study of Islamic culture and contemporary issues in and around Islam's Middle Eastern heartland. That position is being constantly strengthened and expanded by such things as grants administered through the University of Baghdad to finance chairs of Islamic studies at English universities that do not yet have them and by outright donations—such as the 1980 $1.8 million gift by Sheikh Rashid bin Sayed al Maktoum to the University at Exeter to underwrite the costs of new library constructions.

While the British Government's move to achieve continuing coalescence of political, cultural and financial ties with the Muslim Middle East has produced substantial results, it has not been without its difficulties and sticky points. The dynamics of this new relationship between the British government-industrial complex and such capitals as Riyadh are not based on partnership but rather on largesse—delicately balanced largesse. Two incidents indicate how easily—and with what disastrous results—that balance is tipped. One event was Saudi Arabia's abrupt move denying British firms access to hundreds of millions of dollars of new construction and service contracts in the Middle East in retaliation for the British Government's refusal to stop the televised screening of a controversial docu-drama. The film depicted the honor-killing of a Saudi Arabian princess by male members of her family who disapproved of her lover.

The other illustrative incident involved the fracas between the Muslim shipping companies of the Persian Gulf and the venerable Lloyd's of London maritime insurance firm. Lloyd's is—and has been since the late 1600s—far more than a mere purveyor of insurance coverage for ships and their cargoes. It is one of the Western world's oldest and most unique commercial institutions, performing the duties of an unofficial international government regulatory agency at the same time it shapes the trading patterns and practices of both the world's merchant marine and shipbuilding industries.

Lloyd's also serves as the nerve center and organizational force of a global intelligence network keeping track of more than 30,000 vessels around the world and providing crucial data required on a daily basis by the military and governments of every industrialized nation. An integral part of the financial and social fabric of aristocratic England, the firm's multibillion-dollar capital base for operation is provided by the yearly investments of more than 17,000 Englishmen gambling portions of their family fortunes in the seafaring insurance trade, a source of vast revenue, as every ship in the world must be covered to protect its owners against the catastrophic consequences of a sinking or other, similar, disaster. This need for protection and potential for profit was never greater than during the last ten years as the maritime cargo routes became dominated by the tanker trade: each ship loaded with a cargo worth tens of millions of dollars, but with the possibility of its draining away through even the tiniest hole or crack in a ship's hull.

By the late 1970s the growing fleets of Arab-owned tankers had become a major factor in the worldwide patterns of maritime oil trade. Arab shipping companies, which were transporting ever-larger amounts of oil, were also purchasing ever-larger amounts of insurance to cover these vessels. Meanwhile, Lloyd's was charging ever-larger amounts of money to provide that coverage. In 1979, in an act that brought the dispute between Arab shipping magnates and Lloyd's to a head, Lloyd's announced that yet another "surcharge" would be added to insurance premiums for ships traversing the Persian Gulf region. Arab governments and companies objected and argued that they were being charged exorbitantly high prices by the London firm.

Lloyd's, in effect, countered by refusing to reconsider the latest price hike and indicated that the Arabs would either accept its judgment that the Persian Gulf was a "war risk" area in which higher rates were justified or they could do without insurance.

Within weeks representatives of six Arab governments and seventeen regional Arab companies met in the United Arab Emirates, threw in $3 billion as seed money and announced the creation of the Arab War Risk Insurance Syndicate, the new Arab global maritime insurance consortium offering multibillion-dollar insurance coverage to the world's tanker fleets.

In response, Lloyd's in London announced that it was rescinding its war-risk surcharge for oil tankers in the Persian Gulf—immediately—and was prepared to offer normal lower rates, suggesting that there was no longer a need for the Arabs to continue with their plans to set up a new, Arab version of Lloyd's backed by oil wealth.

The British insurance industry—the broad bedrock financial establishment of which Lloyd's was a leading member—registered record losses that year, another evidence of the severity of the deteriorating economic foundations not only in Britain but all of Europe. *The Economist* of London published a report indicating that European nations had suffered an unmitigated decline in the rate of financial growth, employment and productivity between 1973 and 1979 as a "major singular response to high oil prices." The European Economic Community in its yearly report indicated that its member nations had experienced a loss of 1.5 million jobs during the previous four years and that the trend promised to continue. The Atlantic Institute—a continental "think tank" and European equivalent of America's prestigious Brookings Institute—brought together government, business and academic leaders from across Europe for a seminar on economic recovery. The meeting issued a call for closer ties between European nations and OPEC countries and declared that the West must "learn to live" with the Muslim-dominated oil cartel because it had become "the motor of Western economic growth." The institute's British, French and West German leaders also charged that the "American talk about smashing the cartel is dangerous, irrelevant rubbish."

It was through this atmosphere that Foreign Secretary Lord Carrington walked in 1979 when he stepped before the microphones and read the prepared statement with which the British Government formally broke with its ally and former patron, the United States. In a move that rent wide the Atlantic flank of the Western Alliance, the British Government officially disassociated itself from the United States Camp David summitry process, which had been boycotted by every Muslim state except Egypt. Lord Carrington declared that the British Government could not be a party to the process or its results because the Washington Middle East initiative "takes no account of the legitimate rights of the Palestinians, which go well beyond their status as refugees, nor does it take account of the Palestinians' belief that they are a separate people with the rights to a homeland."

The drift between London and Washington continued to widen in the 1980s and, by the time Ronald Reagan took office, the British Government had assumed an unabashedly pro-Arab posture in the Middle East. The British position became a particular sore point for Reagan's first Secretary of State, Alexander Haig. Shortly before his ouster in 1982, Haig caused a minor trans-Atlantic scandal when he publicly castigated Carrington as a "duplicitous bastard" for supporting the cause of the Palestinians.

18

LATIN AMERICA'S
NEW PARTNERS

Although most Americans would not immediately
connect Latin America in any significant way with
events in the Middle East, those two regions' interests have been intertwined since World War II, and
in the late 1970s Muslim petro-powers began large-
scale operations throughout Latin America and the
Caribbean. By 1982 a broad new web of connections drew the collected nations of Latin America
and the Muslim Middle East ever closer as military
allies, political friends and trading partners.

Brazil had become a major armorer to the Muslim nations. The Brasília Government is now a
major contributor of military hardware to the arse-
nals of such nations as Iraq, Kuwait, Qatar and
Libya. During its war with Iran, for instance, Iraq
armies moved about in waves of Brazilian-supplied
Cascavel ("Rattlesnake") light tanks. And Brazil's
fourth-highest-ranking military officer, General Samuel Alves Correa, is his country's ambassador to
Iraq, heading up a team of diplomatic "advisers"
stationed in Baghdad.

Muslim nations have begun providing massive
amounts of foreign aid to Latin American countries
and have otherwise moved toward assuming direct

links in the internal politics of the region. Saudi Arabia, for instance, sought and was granted observer status in the Organization of American States in 1979.

Latin American countries are becoming the leading suppliers of foodstuffs and substantial suppliers of industrial goods—such as tanker ships—to the Muslim world.

States such as Saudi Arabia, Kuwait and Iraq have become a primary source of public funding in Latin America, providing several billion dollars a year in loans to a growing number of Latin governments.

The previously invisible community of Arab residents throughout Latin America has suddenly begun widespread political and social organizing activities aimed at solidifying and celebrating their ties to Middle Eastern homelands. In 1981, for instance, Brazil was the site of the annual World Assembly of Islamic Youth and the first Latin American Islamic Olympiad—both funded by Saudi Arabia.

And these growing interconnections between Latin and Islamic governments represent a reversal of the historic trend in which Israel previously enjoyed the status of Latin America's primary Middle Eastern military ally and trading partner.

Brazil, the largest and most heavily industrialized of the nations of the southern hemisphere, has led this movement away from Israel as part of its quest to obtain the massive oil supplies and new capital required to continue the expansion of its industrial base.

Diplomatically, Latin America has played a crucial role in the modern history of Middle Eastern affairs. In the 1940s the region became a major target for activities of the World Zionist Organization's political organizers. Then local Zionist federations were established as lobbying groups in countries throughout the lower hemisphere. In 1947 it was thirteen of those Latin American nations that cast the deciding block of votes providing the single-vote majority in the United Nations General Assembly which carried the resolution creating the new State of Israel.

Historian Edy Kaufman of Hebrew University in Israel has described how, after that successful United Nations vote, Israel sought to maintain strong ties with those nations and "benefited from a solid and well-founded base of intense pro-Zionist activity sustained by Latin American Jewish communities."

Throughout the 1970s those Latin American ties became even

more important to Israel as that nation became increasingly isolated from the mainstream of the world's diplomatic and economic communities. As it was losing the diplomatic support of many countries throughout Africa and Asia, Israel became increasingly dependent on such nations as Guatemala, Venezuela, Ecuador, Brazil, Chile, Argentina, Peru, El Salvador, Costa Rica and other Caribbean powers. Those Latin relationships remained particularly strong into the 1970s. For instance, even as the United States' and Israel's European allies declined in the late 1960s and 1970s to transfer their embassies to Jerusalem—a move sought by the Tel Aviv Government to aid its claim to that city, seized during the 1967 war— twelve Latin American nations did make the move.

At the same time, oil-dry Israel, whose only Middle Eastern source of petroleum had been the Shah's Iran, was also heavily dependent on the oil supplies it received from Ecuador. After the fall of the Shah in 1979, those Latin American oil links took on an even greater importance. And in the 1970s Latin America became the single most important source of revenue for Israel outside of the United States.

By the mid-1970s, Israel—the state originally designed as a nation of communal farmers—had become a country whose single largest and most profitable export commodity was military tools. Weapons were not only Israel's biggest domestic industry but also its main source of income from abroad. In the early 1980s in excess of $2 billion a year was derived from this trade.

By the late 1970s, Israel had become firmly established as the arsenal of South America: the single largest supplier of weapons systems of all sorts to the region—Ouragan bombers to El Salvador, Shafrir infrared missiles to Chile, Kfir attack jets, Arava gunships and troop transports to Ecuador, Nicaragua, Honduras, Bolivia and Mexico. And the Uzi and Galil machine guns had become the standard equipment for almost every army, navy, special forces and secret police force throughout South America. Former Nicaragua dictator Anastasio Somoza, for instance, was one of Israel's largest customers for Galil machine guns.

Argentina is second only to South Africa as the world's largest purchaser of Israeli weapons. The importance and extent of this connection became evident during the 1982 Falkland Islands War when the Argentine Air Force flew squadrons of Israeli-supplied

Dagger and Skyhawk jets while ravaging a British landing flotilla in the South Atlantic. The Buenos Aires Government also maintains a navy of Israeli-built patrol boats and an awesome arsenal of other Tel Aviv exports including high-tech ship-to-ship and air-to-air missiles.

Israel has also evolved as a military surrogate for the United States in Latin America. Unable to completely circumvent congressional resistance to increased military aid to dictatorships in the post-Vietnam era, Washington took to using Israel as an undercover stand-in. This resulted in some unpublicized wars-within-wars in such places as Nicaragua. There Israeli advisers provided massive amounts of Israeli weapons to the Somoza regime, which was battling Sandinista insurgents who were being supplied and aided by Palestinians. There are about 20,000 Arabs living in Nicaragua. Many fought with the Sandinistas. In the end, shipments of arms from the PLO were crucial to the overthrow of Somoza and the ouster of both American and Israeli interests from the country.

In 1981 in El Salvador, the Reagan administration avoided further controversy over its increasing military aid to the ruling regime by having Israel "loan" the right wing dictatorship at least $21 million. The loan was then returned as part of the following year's U.S. aid package to Israel.

In 1982, the American-Israeli connection became an increasingly public subject in Latin America as Guatemalans blew up the Israeli embassy in Guatemala City. The attackers were protesting the flow of Israeli arms to the ruling junta. Such Latin business accounts take up almost three quarters of all the weapons exported annually by Israel and thus are now one of that country's most important staples of international commerce.

Latin America has also played a central theoretical role in every major energy program and foreign policy overview involving oil forwarded by American Presidents, from Nixon to Reagan.

Each administration has pointed out that the untapped petroleum deposits of the lower hemisphere potentially offer America and the West a future respite from Arab-controlled oil supplies. The rapidly developing Mexican oil fields are one of the deposits often pointed to as an example of the region's petro-potential for America's industrial energy needs in the future.

Ironically, although the bulk of the Latin American landmass—from the Rio Grande to Tierra del Fuego—is known to be glutted with rich mineral and oil deposits, with the exception of Venezuela and Ecuador, the only two OPEC members in the Western hemisphere, South American countries have not developed their potential. There are several reasons for this, including difficulties of the general terrain, regional political instabilities, lack of technological skills and, most common, the lack of the massive capital investments required for such large-scale, high-risk development projects.

Nor are the operating wells of Ecuador and Venezuela of comfort to the rest of Latin America. For instance, Brazil—the fourth-largest country in the world, whose territory covers half of the South American continent—shares borders with both countries but gets almost no oil from either. And Brazil, which has only two small petroleum fields, needs oil: enough oil to run more than fifty steel mills operating around the clock at full capacity; enough to run thirty-five shipyards, which are among the busiest in the world; enough to run 1,900 factories and plants, which constitute the tenth-largest petrochemical industrial center in the world; enough to run the blinking, humming, techno-intensive, ultramodern skyscraper complexes, which are the eighth-largest computer centers in the world; enough to run 4,000 textile mills, 1,000 shoe factories and the sprawl of booming plants which constitute the eighth-largest car-manufacturing industry in the world, led by the mammoth operations of Brazil-Volkswagen, which is to the South American economy what General Motors used to be to the North American economy.

Eighty-five percent of all the oil needed to sustain this precariously balanced petro-powered complexity of machineBrazil comes from six nations: Saudi Arabia, Kuwait, Iraq, Libya, the United Arab Emirates and Algeria. Or at least it used to until 1974 when it ceased coming, and what had been for more than a decade the fastest-growing industrial economy in the Western hemisphere began crashing. By 1982 major shifts had occurred in Latin America's political alignments, characterized at one end by the continued souring of relations on all levels with the United States and at the other end by new, expansive alliances with governments of the Muslim Middle East.

These new alliances developed chiefly around four avenues of mutual interests: the foreign aid provided to Latin American nations by

Muslim governments; the multibillion-dollar investments being made throughout the area by Muslim governments and individuals; the government-to-government oil-supply negotiations and agreements through which Latin countries were obliged to obtain their oil from the Middle East, and the growing visibility and influence of the indigenous Arab communities throughout Latin America.

This last is one of the least publicized aspects of the new Arab presence south of the United States. Latin American governments estimate that during the last two decades the immigrant Arab population of the area has swelled to more than two million. Those Latin American Arab communities—consisting mostly of Arab businessmen—are largest in Argentina, Venezuela, Brazil, Chile, El Salvador and Honduras. The last three of these report that substantial portions of their Arab communities are comprised of Palestinians who migrated to the lower Americas to escape the war-torn Middle East. In 1972 these scattered and previously out-of-touch Arab communities came together in an attempt to create a regional entity representing their interests: the Pan American Arab Congress.

In 1974, reacting to the new waves of Arab nationalism sweeping out from the latest Middle Eastern war, the Latin American Arab representatives formed a much better-funded—and pointedly politically oriented—new agency, the Federation of Arab Organizations of Latin America.

At the same time, a broad range of new financial thrusts by Middle Eastern powers into Latin America were organized and launched from offices set up throughout the Caribbean islands—those offshore banking havens which have traditionally served as both tax blinds and sanctuaries of secrecy for governments, corporations and individuals moving large amounts of cash between the Americas and the rest of the world.

One of the main centers for this activity is Curaçao, located in the Netherlands Antilles sixty miles off the coast of Venezuela and renowned for its white beaches, coral reefs, quaint Dutch architecture and two commodities which have made it wealthy: the oil which moves in vast quantities through its sprawl of refineries, and money which moves in equally vast amounts through its free-trade-zone banking centers. It is now the site of such institutions as the Saudi-European Investment Corporation, Alef Investment Corporation, Arinfi Trust, Finarab Trust, Sharjah Group Trust, the Euro-Kuwaiti

Investment Company and Credit and Commerce America Holdings —just some of the more than thirty-three major Arab banking institutions established throughout the Antilles, Cayman Islands, Bermuda and the Bahamas.

These Middle Eastern financial institutions and individual enterprises have become a major source of the loan funds needed by Latin American governments to continue their daily operations as well as their long-term development projects. Some sense of the pervasive nature of these monetary flows through Arab institutions and into the Latin American economy can be had by reviewing just those loans publicly acknowledged. In 1979 alone offshore Arab institutions channeled:

—$50 million to various government agencies in Peru.

—$100 million to various government agencies in Ecuador.

—$330 million to the state oil company, government development departments and the national bank of Chile.

—$356 million to the national housing institute, state electric company and various governmental agencies in Venezuela.

—$600 million to the state electric company of Mexico.

—$1 billion to the state oil company, state electric company, various governmental agencies and the national bank of Argentina.

—$2.1 billion to the state oil company, state electric company, Ministry of Industry, national bank and other various governmental agencies of Brazil.[1]

Such loans also provide the initial footholds on the continent for other ventures. It was in such a manner—with a $250 million loan to the government of Paraguay in 1978—that the legendary Saudi Arabian investor Adnan Khashoggi began his operations in the region.

From loans Khashoggi spread out rapidly in all directions, forming the Alkantara Trading Company, which now oversees a multibillion-dollar Latin American commercial empire that includes meat packing, furniture-making, timber harvesting, real estate development, hospital management, heavy machinery production, interior decorating services for the ultrarich, and shipping concerns involving both oil and other cargo. Khashoggi's headquarters and the largest concentration of his business ventures are in Brazil, the second-largest exporter of foodstuffs in the world. With Khashoggi's companies leading the way, Brazil by 1981 had become one of the main suppliers of food products of all kinds throughout the Middle East.

The government of Kuwait has purchased 25 percent of Araven Finance, a major Latin American financial institution headquartered just off the coast of Venezuela, and has also signed agreements for a joint Kuwait-Brazilian investment bank to underwrite the capital costs of the huge agricultural, industrial, petroleum and mineral development projects to be undertaken by the two nations throughout Brazil. In its most spectacular move, Kuwait purchased 10 percent of the Brazilian Volkswagen Industries—the country's largest company and a bedrock institution directly supporting thousands of ancillary Brazilian shops and factories in the metal crafts, machine tools, plastics and rubber fabrication trades.

One of the Arab world's largest interests in Brazil is weapons. The only Latin country with the established industrial base capable of supporting a full-fledged space-age weapons industry, Brazil in the early 1970s began a rapid expansion of its armaments manufacturing operations. Previously, large portions of Brazil's arms and arms manufacturing direction came from the United States. But in 1977 Brazil canceled a twenty-five-year-old military assistance agreement that was the mainstay of its relationship with the United States and struck out on its own as a major producer and exporter of weapons systems of its own design.

It was also at this time that Brazil broke with the United States over the issue of the Middle East, becoming the first Latin American nation to announce full diplomatic recognition of the Palestine Liberation Organization. Brazil's move was soon followed by Mexico and Venezuela, which also announced full diplomatic recognition of the PLO. The new PLO offices in the capitals of Brasília, Mexico City and Caracas became further sore spots in the worsening relations between Latin America and Washington.

By 1980, according to international armaments industry publications, Brazil had become "unquestionably the largest and most technically advanced arms producer in the third world."[2]

Evidence indicates that some of the nation's most eager arms customers are Muslim Middle Eastern states whose orders have provided the major impetus—and capital—for further expansion of the Brazilian armament production facilities. Libya, for instance, since 1977, has been regularly placing orders—hundreds at a time—for

Brazilian-designed Cascavels. These are armored vehicles slightly smaller than a tank and made specifically for desert warfare. Qatar has also become a major customer for the sand-warfare vehicles. Libya has also been purchasing large quantities of Urutus, specially designed amphibious armored personnel carriers which can operate in deserts and also move across water to land troops. Another Brazilian desert armored vehicle—the missile-launching Sucuri—has been a big seller with Iraq and other Persian Gulf countries.

And, in 1980, Saudi Arabia and Abu Dhabi opened negotiations with Brazil for large, long-term purchases of Embraer gunships, troop transports, radar reconnaissance aircraft and other weapons systems.

As a direct result of the Arab purchases, long-term orders and infusions of massive amounts of funds, Brazil's arms industry has also become a major factor in the arms trade throughout South America. According to military experts, it is fast becoming the "arsenal of South America," taking up increasingly large portions of the continental markets and revenues that previously went to such outside arms producers as Israel.

Many of these weapons transactions are being made as part of the overall government-to-government oil-supply arrangements negotiated annually between Latin American and Muslim countries in the Middle East. Such arrangements are new and have eliminated the middleman participation of the United States oil companies, which previously provided Washington with at least an indirect avenue for influencing the proceedings.

One of the most controversial agreements between governments has been made between Iraq and Brazil's state nuclear industry.[3]

Since it was first invaded and occupied by Europeans in the 1500s, Brazil's southern mountain ranges have been famed for their buried treasures. Gold and silver were so abundant that early invaders often encountered cliffsides glittering with exposed veins. Ravines and donkey trails cut back and forth across gigantic swirls of exposed iron ore bleeding rust down entire mountainsides or swaths of fuzzy asbestos rock carpeting whole valley bottoms. Today the 360,000-square-mile province, which stretches inward from Rio de Janeiro and the Atlantic Ocean in lower Brazil, is still known by the Portuguese term for "General Mines"—Minas Gerais.

One of the more peculiar minerals found in Minas Gerais is thorium, a rare silverish metal which begins to go black even as miners pick it from rock, exposing it to the air. Thorium—named for the Norse god of war—is a radioactive mineral used in fueling reactors and indicates the presence of other radioactive minerals such as uranium. Brazil discovered that it had the third-largest deposits of thorium in the world and took this into account as it began wholesale industrialization in the wake of World War II.

In the 1950s, as it was embarking on the programs that would make it the most technologically advanced of the Third World nations by the 1980s, Brazil laid out plans for a massive nuclear industry. Work on the first Brazilian atomic reactor began in 1957. By 1965 it had three small atomic reactors in operation. Brazil currently has one of the most ambitious national nuclear development programs in the world outside the United States, the Soviet Union and European nations. Three large power-generation reactors are now being built. Six more are being readied for construction. The three functioning research reactors are having their facilities expanded. By the late 1970s Brazil had surveyed a tiny fraction of its mountains and confirmed nearly 300,000 tons of uranium deposits. There are further indications of huge additional amounts throughout the country.

In 1971 Brazil signed a history-making $5 billion agreement with West Germany to purchase the facilities needed for the entire uranium fuel cycle. Included were facilities for uranium prospecting and extraction, uranium refining, uranium enriching, reactor fuel and rod fabrication, plutonium reprocessing, and manufacturing plants able to produce clones of these same systems. This gigantic deal was the final step in Brazil's plans for becoming a completely independent nuclear power on a scale similar to that of the United States: able to supply its own electrical needs with reactors at the same time it can build, maintain and sell all aspects of nuclear technology. It will also be able to produce and sell huge quantities of all types of radioactive fuel materials, including plutonium and enriched uranium.

By 1978 Brazil's nuclear facilities had become the focus of two major international controversies. On one hand the United States wanted to stop them. Washington pressured European nations in an attempt to halt the sale of nuclear equipment or technology to Brazil.

On the other hand Iraq wanted to join them. Baghdad pressured Brazil to open its nuclear development programs to Muslim participation.

Iraq's atomic plans revolved around the plutonium-producing reactor and the city-sized nuclear research center it had purchased from France after the 1973 war. As those constructions were moving toward completion near Baghdad in 1978, Iraq had to address the problem of acquiring the other materials it would need to make bombs. To extract plutonium from the used reactor fuel would require the very special and difficult-to-obtain plutonium reprocessing facilities. To amass enough enriched uranium for bombs, Iraq would either have to purchase that material ready-made or begin experiments on enriching techniques at its research center. The development of sources for massive amounts of uranium was essential. And while Iraq did have uranium deposits in the sands of its western deserts, it did not have the facilities for recovering sufficient amounts of that material.

France was not willing to sell Iraq any uranium beyond that directly required to fuel the reactor. So Iraq began purchasing large quantities of low-grade uranium ore from Niger. But that wasn't enough. Iraq turned to its list of petroleum customers. One of those that had both uranium deposits and a desperate need for Iraqi oil was Portugal. Portugal, which has one of the least viable industrial economies in Europe, struggled throughout the 1970s to stave off national bankruptcy. One of its problems was the price of oil. The other was supply. It already purchased 45 percent of all its daily oil needs from Iraq and needed more. Iraq agreed to increase oil supplies to the Portuguese Government in return for 120 tons of uranium oxide. Portugal agreed and became a uranium supplier to Baghdad.

The second-largest purchaser of all the oil pumped from Iraq's wells each year is Italy. Italy is also one of the industrialized nations hardest hit by the oil shortages and price hikes of the 1970s. In 1978 Prime Minister Giulio Andréotti's government came to power and toppled months later after an attempt to grapple with widespread civil unrest caused by fuel shortages, zooming inflation, unemployment and industrial disintegration failed. Naples had become a virtual city of the unemployed: a sprawl of slum housing, squatters' havens and rampant crime. Rome was repeatedly shut down as police, journalists, civil servants and thirteen million assorted labor unionists staged weekly strikes protesting economic conditions. The new government of Prime Minister Francesco Cossiga announced a new tack—a new program of greatly expanded trade overtures to the Muslim governments of the Middle East, who had been coolly received in Rome in the past. The Italian Government opened new trade negotiations with several Arab countries. Its largest deals were discussed with Iraq, which was seeking mammoth purchases of armaments, nuclear equipment and uranium.

Just one of the transactions that came out of those negotiations was the largest weapons-for-oil swap ever made—a $2.5 billion arrangement through which Iraq exchanged long-term oil supplies in return for a small ready-made navy of Italian-made warships and other equipment.

Italy sold Iraq the special equipment needed to reprocess plutonium from reactor fuel and also opened negotiations aimed at providing Iraq with a multibillion-dollar heavy-water reactor and nuclear research center. And almost immediately Iraqi students and technicians began arriving at the Casaccia Research Center outside Rome, where they began training in plutonium reprocessing and uranium technology. Iraq also demanded that Italy sell it ten tons of uranium. Italy agreed and became a uranium supplier to Baghdad.

However, Iraq's nuclear relationship with European nations came under increasingly close scrutiny in the Western press. Italy's sale of plutonium equipment to the Baghdad Government created a storm of international criticism and controversy. And Iraq began focusing more of its nuclear attentions into Latin America and Brazil—the country which was on the verge of becoming an atomic superpower and which, each day, imported 110,000 barrels of Iraqi oil.

Iraq sought to negotiate an agreement in which Brazil would share its atomic technology freely with Baghdad. Brazil declined to specifically agree to such a full technological partnership with Iraq, even though it continued its program of selling massive amounts of weapons and industrial equipment to the Muslim power.

Iraq threatened to cut off Brazil's oil in 1979 if Brasília did not agree to share its full nuclear technological resources with Iraq.

Other Muslim oil suppliers indicated they would not increase their exports to Brazil to make up for any Iraqi slowdowns or cutoffs of oil.

Brazil capitulated and signed a nuclear cooperation pact with Iraq, agreeing to provide nuclear technology, nuclear equipment, nuclear training for Iraqi scientists and students as well as quantities of low-grade uranium, enriched uranium and plutonium. The Iraqi-Brazilian atomic pact was the keystone to a new era in which the Brazilian Government opted for a near amalgamation of its economic, technological, industrial and military establishments with those of Middle Eastern nations. The country that was already a site of substantial financial activities by Arabs was now inundated with massive new investments, industrial contracts, financial aid programs and cultural exchanges from the Muslim world.

By 1981 the full-scale programs of arms supplies, military advisers, technological assistance and industrial supports being provided by Brazil to Iraq resembled nothing so much as the programs previously established by the United States in support of such nations as Taiwan, South Vietnam and Israel. And the level of sophistication of the equipment being developed and produced by Brazil for the Middle Eastern oil powers such as Iraq appears to be rapidly approaching yet another breakthrough. The respected *Excelsior* newspaper of Mexico City, which closely covers armaments developments in Latin America, has recently reported that Brazil was on the verge of mass-producing ICBMs—intercontinental missiles capable of carrying nuclear warheads. Mexican journalist Fernando Meraz reported that Brazil's government arms industry was taking billions of dollars in orders for soon-to-be-available "aerospace missiles, teledirected ICBMs, missile-launching jet planes, bombers, submarines" and other high-tech items of space-age weaponry previously produced and controlled exclusively by the United States and the other industrialized powers of the northern hemisphere.

Nor has the United States Government watched this increasingly powerful technological alliance between Muslim and Latin nations passively. Washington has attempted to thwart Brazil's decision to become an independent conventional weapons producer capable of providing whole armies worth of modern weapons to Middle Eastern nations. And Washington has pressured Brazil to halt the programs through which it is now supplying nuclear assistance to Iraq through Engesa—the government-supported Brazilian arms conglomerate which is in charge of both conventional weapons sales and nuclear technology transfers to Iraq. Brazil has ignored Washington's objections.

For all their smooth points, the relationships of Muslim and Latin governments have not been without problems or friction. The 1979 showdown between Brazil and Iraq over the question of Brazil's nuclear cooperation was only one of the rougher spots in the developing new alliance. Another dramatic face-off between Muslim and Latin capitals occurred in 1980 over the question of Jerusalem.

Israel's government had, by then, officially declared that the Old City of Jerusalem—an urban area outside the borders of the State of Israel—was to be the capital of the "Land of Israel."

The "State of Israel" is a United Nations-created zone running largely along the industrialized coastal plain of the Mediterranean. The "Land of Israel" is a biblical term describing an expanse of geography including all of the State of Israel, all of the territories seized by that state in 1967 and large additional areas of several other contiguous Muslim states located between the Euphrates and the Nile.

Israel's claim to the Old City of Jerusalem was physically bolstered by two things: the ten-year, wide-scale eviction programs through which Muslim inhabitants had been systematically removed and replaced with Israeli inhabitants, and the existence of thirteen embassies of foreign nations which had previously agreed to move from Tel Aviv to Jerusalem at the request of the Israeli Government. Those embassies included that of the Netherlands and twelve Latin American countries, which were among Israel's largest weapous customers.

Other nations had contemplated acceding to Israeli requests for embassy transfers from Tel Aviv to Jerusalem in the 1970s but had been put off by Muslim pressures. Canada, for instance, under Prime Minister Joe Clark, in 1979 announced it would transfer its embassy from Tel Aviv to Jerusalem. In response, Saudi Arabia and Kuwait announced the cancellation of more than $400 million worth of contracts with Canadian firms and said they would begin immediate withdrawal of billions of dollars in deposits from Canadian banks. Within one hour of that international announcement, the Canadian dollar had plummeted in value and Canada was moving toward the brink of a national monetary emergency. The Canadian Government announced that it was postponing its planned embassy move pending "further review." The embassy was never moved.

In August 1980, following the Israeli Government's declaration of annexation and call for all embassies in Tel Aviv to be transferred to Jerusalem, Saudi Arabia, Kuwait and other Muslim oil powers announced that any country that either moved its embassy to Jerusalem or continued to maintain an embassy established in Jerusalem would be "cut off" from all further relations with Muslim nations of the Middle East.

In October 1980 the last two remaining foreign embassies in Jerusalem—Guatemala and the Dominican Republic—packed their furnishings and began vacating the city.

At the same time, in 1980, the relationship between Muslim Middle Eastern governments and Latin American nations appeared to be broadening both financially and politically. Branching out of the larger industrialized countries, such as Brazil and Argentina, the Muslim oil powers initiated new activities throughout the smaller, underdeveloped countries of the region.

Guyana, for instance, signed new agreements for economic, scientific, cultural and technological exchanges with Libya and Iraq aimed at boosting the development of that country's bauxite industry and linking other aspects of its economy to Middle Eastern markets. Simultaneously, the Guyanese Government issued a statement changing its foreign policy and officially recognizing the Palestine Liberation Organization.

Grenada signed new agreements with Algeria for agricultural, industrial, scientific and cultural exchange programs and received subsidies for the completion of its new national airport. Simultaneously, the government of Grenada issued a statement changing its foreign policy and officially recognizing the Palestine Liberation Organization.

Jamaica, which received $10 million in credits from Kuwait, $10 million in credits from Iraq and $50 million in credits from Libya for development of its fledgling aluminum industry, also announced that year that it was breaking with the United States and officially declared recognition of the Palestine Liberation Organization.

19

THE NEW POWERS
IN FAR ASIA

Indonesia and Malaysia are places not easily visualized by most Americans. Neither are they connected by the average American with the history or future of the United States.

Most Americans, for instance, tend to remember the oriental portion of World War II as a conflagration that began at Pearl Harbor and flashed across the Pacific rather than as a campaign that began at Camranh Bay and was waged for control of the Islamic lands of Indonesia and Malaysia in the southern reaches of the China Sea. The move that assured war occurred as the Japanese invasion fleets steamed into Camranh in lower Vietnam, the staging point from which they pushed out in an arc of attacks aimed at seizing the petroleum, rubber, timber and metal minerals that Japan required to feed its new factories and secure its position as an industrialized world power.

In retaliation for this plunge south into the European-colonized Muslim resource regions of Indonesia and Malaysia, the United States cut off its steel exports to Japan—a move quickly followed by the attacks on Pearl Harbor, the only United States naval station capable of moving against further Japanese operations in the China Sea and lower Pacific.

In the 1970s Arabs began moving in force across these same southern Asian regions, retracing with Lear jets and 707s the criss-cross of routes cut a thousand years before by the dhows that first stitched the Orient together as an integrated trading empire with Africa and Europe. And the focus of these Arab moves was not unlike that of the Japanese in an earlier decade: the securing of the resource-glutted Muslim reaches of southern Asia.

Indonesia and Malaysia form a 5,000-mile barrier crescent of islands whose narrow and easily fortified straits form the only waterborne passage for traffic crossing east and west below China. At the center of the group, sitting astride the single busiest waterway on earth—the Strait of Mallaca—is Singapore, the financial hub of southern Asia and the city from which the British Empire exercised control of a vast area of water and resources east of India.

Today, Indonesia and Malaysia play a major role in the international economy and are the source of several commodities critically important to the industrialized world. On the average, 45 percent of their exports are now consumed by only two nations: Japan and the United States. Between them, Indonesia and Malaysia hold several global records: the most populous Muslim nations; the largest deposits of petroleum in far Asia; the largest exports of tin; site of the largest liquified-gas plant; the site of the third-largest complex of petroleum refineries, and the most perfect soil and climate for growing hardwoods, rubber trees and palms. The two nations are the world's largest exporters of natural rubber, producing more than 50 percent of all supplies of that increasingly precious and industrially critical material. They are also the world's largest producer of palm oil.

While "oil" is a term most frequently associated with underground accumulations of hydrocarbons—petroleum—palm oil is only one of several sources of the various "oils" required in large amounts by a world that runs on machines. The second-largest source of oils used throughout the world each day is palm trees. And the value of palm oil has been increasing as the rising price and scarcity of petroleum oils cause more and more industrial users to seek easily replaceable sources of certain oil products, such as the delicate lubricants, fuels and plasticizing agents from plantations that produce both oil stocks and seeds for new oil trees. In the equatorial tropical climate that is the palm's natural habitat, these oil trees grow much the same as weeds. Like rice paddies in other parts of Asia, they blanket every available acre of flatland, valley floor and hillside across parts of Malaysia and Indonesia. These plantations are important to both the undeveloped and developed worlds. In the undeveloped world, palm oil is the single largest source of cooking oil. It is also a major source of margarine, lamp fuel, candles and animal feed.

And palm oil plays a substantially larger role in the daily life of the United States than is generally appreciated. Automobiles, for instance, depend on it. They can neither be manufactured nor operated without the hydraulic fluid of which palm oil is an essential ingredient. Palm oil is also a major ingredient used in the special plastics required for shatterproof windshields and other auto, bus, truck and tractor parts. One of palm oil's most important uses is as a crucial ingredient in the manufacture of synthetic rubber—the creation from petroleum feed stocks of the tires, belts, gaskets, engine mounts and thousands of other similar parts required by daily operations at every level of machineAmerica.

In 1977, when Ghaith Pharaon's plane landed in Sabah—the far western state of Malaysia, a province plump at the middle with a crisscross of mountains and flat at the edges with broad tropical plains—the first thing he began looking at was oil-palm plantations. Some evidence of the overall direction of his investments can be found in one of his projects in the middle of Sabah's Sandakan area, one of the lushest oil-palm regions in the world—a $12 million palm-oil refinery. Upcountry, the Saudi industrialist picked up timberlands—whole mountain ranges of hardwoods to feed his planned plywood factories along the coast.

In Kota Kinabalu, the port capital of Sabah, which is ringed with rubber tree plantations and looks out on an ocean horizon spiked with drilling platforms tapping into the recently discovered east Malaysian oil fields, Pharaon began his hotel building and land development in 1979. Working through the Hyatt International Corporation, a United States firm of which Pharaon became part owner in 1978, he constructed the complexes with special modular prefab units manufactured by the International Systems Corporation of Mobile, Alabama. Pharaon purchased that United States firm in 1978 and, like Hyatt, immediately plugged it into the global logistical grid he has established to cover every aspect of supply and technical expertise needed throughout his burgeoning worldwide operations.

Pharaon's thrust into the region was only the first of a growing wave of Arab activities there. In early 1980 the Kuwait Investment Office in England quietly purchased part ownership of Harrisons & Crosfield, a London-headquartered conglomerate whose multibillion-dollar tentacles stretch across all sections of Malaysia's developing construction, hardwood harvesting, lumber milling, shipping, chemical, rubber and palm industries. One of Harrisons & Crosfield's most recently publicized accomplishments was an experimental program aimed at perfecting an oil-palm cloning process expected to significantly increase the oil yield of Malaysia's plantations.

Two other Saudi consortiums in 1979 formed SK Timber, a new Malaysian firm spreading out across the state of Sabah and gobbling up both stands of hardwoods and various milling and finishing factories for plywoods and other lumber products. At the same time, Kuwait launched major new initiatives aimed at forming broad new government-to-government relationships on both the diplomatic and commercial levels with Malaysia. One of the first concrete results of this was the formation of the Malaysian-Kuwait Investment Company at Kuala Lampur, the capital of the westernmost of Malaysia's three states, located just a short run up the Strait of Mallaca from Singapore. There is also a newly formed Arab-Malaysian Finance Company and the new Arab-Malaysian Development Bank, set up jointly by Kuwait and Saudi Arabia. Stretching out from Kuala Lampur, the Arab-Malaysian Development Bank was, in 1980, the fastest-growing financial institution in the country and was involved in the funding of massive industrialization projects in the areas of lumber, rubber, mineral extraction, national aviation systems and palm oil.

One of the more extraordinary of nearby Singapore's new banking ventures is the Saudi Commercial Bank. One day it did not exist in Singapore. The next day it was one of the largest and busiest financial institutions in that Asian city of banks. It functions as the hub of Arab financial movements throughout the whole of Southeast Asia, and in 1980 some of the business passing through its offices included a $310 million loan to the government of Indonesia, a

$100 million loan to the government of Malaysia and a $100 million loan to the government of Thailand.

And Saudi Commercial is only one of the twenty-five banks with combined assets of $51 billion that have begun moving toward Singapore—encouraged and assisted by the Monetary Authority of Singapore, which has agreed to maintain total secrecy concerning their local activities. The Bank of Kuwait has moved in. And by late 1981 the National Bank of Abu Dhabi and the Paris-based Union de Banques Arabes et Françaises had been granted licenses for their move. In addition, the Kuwait Asian Bank, the Al Bahrain Arab African Bank, the Arab Banking Corporation and Gulf International Bank were preparing for their licensing and eventual move into the new Arab banking district of Singapore.

Another of that city's overnight wonders is the Arabian Singapore Corporation. Set up by a Saudi consortium in 1980, it became the trading agent for more than three dozen of Singapore's largest companies in less than ten months' time. By the end of 1981 that corporation was so wildly successful that it had begun drawing up plans for the takeover of an entire section of Singapore—to be called Saudi Center and built to house the entire slice of Saudi society: mosques, apartments, office buildings, schools, restaurants, social services, wives, children and servants needed to support the exploding Arab presence in that strategic commercial core of Southeast Asia.

At the northern end of the China Sea, beyond Indonesia and Malaysia, at Hong Kong, the Arabs also touched down in the late 1970s to begin major financial and commercial operations. The island territory, which is administered by Britain but is officially part of China, is a 1,000-square-mile land lined shoulder to shoulder with skyscrapers housing banks, factories, offices and trading companies that have made the territory one of the world's most densely developed. It serves as the major offshore banking center for far Asia and, despite its minor size, is a comparative giant in the industrial world because of its development and export of state-of-the-art electronics, rubber fabrications, high-tech machine tools, textiles and chemical technology. More than 60 percent of all Hong Kong's prodigious yearly exports are consumed by the United States, West Germany, Britain and Japan. It has been, since the time of its development as the British Empire's control point for eastern Asia, a center for the shipping industry and related maritime trades at that end of the continent.

Hong Kong has virtually no resources and no source of revenue other than that generated by its financial institutions and factory production. All raw materials must be imported. Continuous exports are the pivot on which the territory's daily survival depends. Hong Kong, a quasi-independent state tied only casually to China and Britain, takes no official notice of political issues outside those directly involving its national livelihood: trade and finance. Whatever is good for international trade and finance is good for Hong Kong.

In the late 1970s, in a major shift of focus, the Hong Kong Trade and Development Council—the government body overseeing international trading relations of the territory—launched a vigorous new campaign aimed at connecting the territory's industrial and financial bases into the emerging new center of world trade and finance: the Muslim Middle East. One of the lures the island territory has to offer Middle Easterners is touted by the Hong Kong and Shanghai Banking Corporation as a "minimum of government interference" in all aspects of banking, investment and import-export commerce. International financial interests find in Hong Kong a frenzy of flowing cash and passing business opportunities at the same time they are subjected to little or no government oversight and required to disclose virtually nothing about any phase of their operations.

Three of the better-known respondents to Hong Kong's overtures for Arab investments were Olayan, Khashoggi and Pharaon.

Olayan moved into Hong Kong by forming a partnership with Jardine Matheson & Company, the giant trading company that sprawls out from Hong Kong across the whole of southern Asia in shipping, aviation, industrial equipment, construction and transactions in commodities of every kind.

Khashoggi has maintained an unusually low profile, establishing Barrick Investments in Hong Kong to oversee his east Asian operations. A subsidiary, Southern Pacific Properties Corporation, has scooped up land and launched development projects from the China Sea region out into the far reaches of the South Pacific, where Khashoggi has established luxury hotels and other tourist facilities in Tahiti and Fiji.

The most visible Middle Eastern operations in Hong Kong by

1980 were those of Ghaith Pharaon, who had become a major force moving throughout all levels of the territory's financial and industrial milieus. One of his first actions in this center of Asian shipping was to establish the headquarters of his Amar Line Maritime Company, Ltd. Those grandly located offices on Jaffe Road at the base of Victoria Mountain overlook a breathtaking panorama of Victoria Harbor. In the distant haze are the granite mounds of Kowloon Peninsula and its starkly modern port terminals. Everything between is water and a multicolored maritime jumble: tankers, gunwales low to the waves with weight; freighters, chains and bow plates streaked with rust, and junks, chunk-awkward wooden vessels, ribbed sails heavily patched, moving through the channel as if in slow motion toward Macao, sixty miles west at the mouth of the Pearl River, the entrance to the interior of mainland China.

As the junks pass that jut of a city, Macao, they cruise past an architectural landmark—one of the largest urban construction projects ever undertaken outside the Middle East. Working through two of his companies—Saudi Hong Kong Real Estate and Trafalgar Housing—Ghaith Pharaon in 1980 was putting up forty-two skyscrapers at once in what was just part of a larger project in Macao that included new Hyatt Hotel facilities and other business constructions. Pharaon's purchase into Trafalgar Housing, an established Hong Kong corporation, provides him with more than just another large oriental construction firm to add to his string of construction firms. Trafalgar is a huge conglomerate hiding behind an innocuous name. Its multipronged operations stretch from Hong Kong to Singapore and from mainland China into the Pacific and involve lumber mills, mining and drilling operations for mineral extraction, housing, tourism and one of the Orient's largest experiments in marine agriculture. Back across the water from Macao, in Hong Kong, another of Pharaon's Hyatts, overlooking the same harbor as his shipping company, pushes into the sky and caters to the trade in the city which, outside of London, has become one of the most expensive in the world to live in or visit.

And up the Pearl River, deep inside mainland China, Pharaon has also begun operations—shrimp farming projects undertaken in cooperation with the Chinese Government aimed at ultimately taking advantage of the mainland's insatiable appetite. Nor is Pharaon the only Middle Easterner to have moved into China. In 1980 the

Union de Banques Arabes et Françaises provided the Bank of China with a $300 million loan and sought to further penetrate the newly progressive economy of the vast People's Republic. Meanwhile, Total Suiss and Gatoil, two "Swiss" companies taken over by Arab consortiums in Geneva, were expanding their oil exploration, drilling and development programs in China.

And the Chinese Government was making other serious moves toward a new era of financial and technological exchange and political harmony with the Muslim world.

By 1981 senior Deputy Prime Minister Deng Xiaoping had afforded diplomatic recognition to Yasir Arafat and invited the leader of the Palestine Liberation Organization to Peking for talks, and the Chinese military was preparing the special shipment which sealed its new relationship with Iraq: 120 pounds of bomb-grade enriched uranium for Baghdad's atomic project.

20

PETRO-YEN AND PALESTINIANS

During the postwar decades, as Japan was rising from the ashes to become a functioning nation again, its world view could be illustrated by a simple diagram of a lopsided barbell. The small end: Japan. The large end: the United States. The connecting bar: the sum total of Japanese international political initiatives—a straight, unwavering line between Tokyo and Washington.

Washington pronounced decisions. Japan followed orders. Japan's association with the United States during the whole of the postwar era was that of a vassal state. This attitude of total subservience represented the forced acquiescence of a conquered people as well as the voluntary compliance of a devastated nation seeking a brighter future.

Immediately after the war Japan became the recipient of unbridled American generosity. American taxpayers provided the funds, the technological expertise, the physical resources and the raft of logistical supports required to rebuild Japan as the fortified farther flank of the Western Industrial Alliance. The country's industrial facilities were not merely re-erected but its social and industrial base re-engineered and structured from the ground up as the most modern national machine complex ever, employing state-of-the-art techniques and equipment not available when America's own industrial base was established in earlier decades.

In many ways Japan's rebuilding was like a bell-jar experiment in which optimum results were guaranteed by the exclusion of influences which might normally impinge on such a project. For instance, Japan did not have to divert enormous portions of its gross national product or its manpower energies into nonproductive weapons systems and standing armies. For thirty-five years the United States provided virtually all of Japan's national defense needs.

In the 1960s, when Japan regained its domestic economic balance as well as its status as a world industrial power, its relationship with the United States remained essentially unchanged from earlier years. That relationship was epitomized by a tradition which began immediately after the war when Japan returned to self-government: the first major action taken by every newly elected Japanese Prime Minister was a flight to Washington, to introduce himself to the President of the United States and affirm his administration's continuing gratitude for all the things America provided the Japanese people.

By 1970 Japan had hit full industrial stride and had become a technological superstate sweeping to positions of world supremacy in many of those fields formerly dominated by its patron. During that decade, as the physical quality and overall reputation of American products and engineering tumbled down the scale, such names as Toyota and Datsun zoomed to the top. Japan became the world's largest manufacturer and exporter of cars. The names Sony and Panasonic rose to lead the world's consumer electronics market; Nikon and Canon to take over the world's camera and advanced optics market. Fujitsu, Ltd., replaced IBM as the leading merchant of computer equipment in Japan, and Japan itself became the second-largest computer purchaser in the world next to the United States—an event whose extraordinary implications are best seen when the two nations are compared in size and population. Japan is the most extensively computerized civilization on earth. Its cities are webbed with the most advanced transportation systems in the world. Its people enjoy the world's highest life expectancy and lowest infant mortality rates. Its factories and research centers are now legendary as the most innovative and efficient. Its workers are renowned as the most dedicated and measurably productive. It has the lowest unemployment rate of any industrialized society. It has the highest national rate of functional literacy and the lowest rate of crime of any industrialized nation. Its steel mills and metallurgy works are the bench marks against which all other nations measure their own. It is the world's largest shipbuilder and maintains the world's largest and most modern merchant marine.

Japan also became the world's second-leading producer of petrochemicals. Only the petrochemical complexes of the United States have greater capacity. This fact is another that can be fully appreciated only when seen in light of the extraordinary inventive genius and technological sophistication required to establish a petroleum-barren island state with very little available ground as the world's second-largest center for processing petroleum into the critical chemicals needed by every other industrialized nation.

During the postwar period in which Japan was organizing and building toward these remarkable achievements, the United States, along with the various other supports it provided, also provided Japan with the majority of its oil needs. And Japan had exceptional oil needs.

Japan, a hydrocarbon-free deposit of volcanic rock, has virtually no resources outside its scenic mountains, quaintly twisted trees, fish-rich waters and industrious people. Unlike America, whose factories can often feed themselves from the mines, wells, forests and agricultural tracts of the nearby landscape, Japan can provide itself with almost nothing. Every day everything it requires to be a modern machine civilization—from food to lumber to iron ore to oil—must be transported from somewhere else. To get a simplistic picture of this situation, imagine Japan as one giant assembly line sitting on a single lump of rock in the middle of the ocean. At one end a daily clog of ships dumps a cornucopia of raw materials. At the other end another clog of ships loads the shining cars, radios, computers, musical instruments, television sets and other products that are the nation's lifeblood.

And Japan has a desperate need for daily oil shipments. In the event of an oil embargo or other disruption, Japan does not merely dim and slow down as does America. It does not have the thorny political problem of setting priorities for allocation of insufficient supplies of domestically produced oil. Japan simply stops. Dark and cold. Completely. That stark fact in the 1970s darkened every door-step, conference table and election in "The Land of the Rising Sun."

Throughout the first half of the 1970s, Japan weathered the oil crisis better than other industrial powers. Almost immediately following the Arab oil embargo, the Tokyo Government designed and imposed the most stringent and all-encompassing national energy-conservation measures of any country. Simultaneously, government and industry turned the full focus of their inventive genius to a countrywide program to find more efficient ways to perform the same machine functions with less fuel. And the government established the largest strategic oil reserves of any nation in the world —lining entire harbors with previously mothballed tankers and cargo vessels transformed into floating oil-storage depots.

However, by 1977, Japan was no longer able to manage the storm of financial shocks and fuel shortages sweeping across the country and affecting every segment of a crumbling national economy.

In 1978, after Japan suddenly lost its daily oil supplies from riot-ripped Iran, the Ministry of Home Affairs invoked emergency powers and took administrative control of the bankrupt city of Tokyo. Tokyo had become the eleventh major Japanese city taken over by the central government in an effort to avoid social collapse and upheaval as the municipal machinery caved in under the weight of overwhelming fuel shortages and catastrophic economic dislocations. Japan that year reported a record number of business bankruptcies. More than $1 billion in assets of failed firms were going on the liquidation block each month. That country also recorded its highest rate of unemployment since the 1950s—a period when it was still rebuilding from the war.

At the peak of this crisis, Prime Minister Takeo Fukuda announced that the government was moving in new directions in its foreign policy as well as its international commercial planning and would be taking actions aimed at "expanding Japan's regional ties" with its "Asian friends" and "natural trading partners."

It was during this period that a virtual parade of government emissaries and businessmen's missions began moving across the skies between Tokyo and the capital cities of Saudi Arabia, Kuwait, the United Arab Emirates and other Middle Eastern countries. Some feeling for the topsy-turvy changes which were occurring in Japan's trading patterns and political outlook can be had by contemplating the following two turnabouts:

—In 1970 Japan obtained more than 80 percent of its daily oil supplies from American multinational oil companies. By 1980 those oil companies had been toppled from international power and no longer controlled the global petroleum distribution grids. Japan that year was getting 93.7 percent of all its daily oil supplies through direct government-to-government agreements with eight Muslim countries. The largest single supplier was Saudi Arabia.

—In 1979 Toyota, the corporate titan that, for a decade, had been the largest single money-maker in Japan and a symbol of that nation's industrial independence, was knocked out of first place. The new company that had become Japan's largest corporate money-maker was the Arabian Oil Company, an enterprise co-owned by Japanese and Arab interests.

In public communiqués issued during that turbulent pivotal year of 1978 in Japan, the government emphasized repeatedly that its traditional ties with America would remain "strong" but that it had no alternative but to "readjust to the realities of the new world energy and economic situation." Prime Minister Fukuda departed Tokyo for the first-ever visit by a Japanese head of state to the Muslim Middle East for a round of oil and economic negotiations, which ended in ceremonies in Riyadh. There Saudi Arabian King Khalid announced that Japan was to receive an increase in oil supplies and that Japanese firms would be heavily involved in all phases of the multibillion-dollar petrochemical construction projects throughout the kingdom.

Simultaneously, Prime Minister Fukuda issued a statement in Riyadh affirming Japan's desire to become "politically and diplomatically" closer to the Arab states. In his statement Fukuda asked that "Israel withdraw from lands occupied in 1967, including Jerusalem, and recognize the rights of the Palestinians to self-determination."

That year a dramatic change also occurred in the previously cool relationship between the Japanese Government and the Palestine Liberation Organization. After a series of talks, these two things happened:

—The Japanese Government publicly issued an invitation to the

PLO to open an "information office" in Tokyo. At the same time, the government denied that the action represented a break with the United States because, it said, the PLO had not been granted diplomatic recognition.

—The Palestine Liberation Organization dispatched an ambassador-level representative to Tokyo and, secretly, opened formal diplomatic relations with Japan. The diplomatic representatives did not receive Japanese officials at the PLO information office but rather in another special office located inside the embassy of the United Arab Emirates in Tokyo.[1]

That year also saw the beginning of a rush of investment by Arab states in Japan.

The government of Kuwait, moving out through its Kuwait Investment Office, showed a particular interest in petroleum and mineral-development companies and bought up substantial portions of the Teikoku Oil Company, the Nippon Mining Company and the Maruzen Oil Company. In addition, Kuwait moved quickly into Japan's heavy industry, making headlines and sparking controversy as it purchased up entire annual bond issues by such firms as Nippon Miniature Bearing, Okuma Machinery Works, Uny Supermarket Company, Clarion Electronics Company and Kitazawa Valve.

In 1979 Kuwait began its buying spree by grabbing up at least $1 billion in corporate stocks. During the next two years it was reported to have reached more than $5 billion in stock holdings in Japanese companies and was preparing for further massive purchases. By 1982 the Kuwait Insurance Company had joined Japan's second-largest securities company—Yamaichi—to establish the Kuwait-Japan Investment Company to handle additional billions worth of transactions planned into the mid-1980s.

In Tokyo there also opened the new Saudi-Japanese Investment Corporation, which simultaneously set up offices in Riyadh. The new enterprise initially described itself as a bank, but later Japanese press reports detailed it as a new quasi-governmental agency directly linking the Riyadh and Tokyo governments and providing the channel through which tens of billions of dollars in secret transactions began passing between the two countries. The Saudis reportedly sought the arrangement in order to purchase huge additional amounts of Japanese government securities outside normal banking channels, thereby keeping all details of those purchases secret. The Japanese Government reportedly sought the arrangement in order to transact large secret oil purchases and conduct other matters of business and diplomacy they wished to shield from media attention. For instance, the new arrangement proved helpful to the government's continuing buildup of a strategic oil stockpile. In previous years Japan had incurred the wrath of the rest of the industrialized world because of its frenzy of buying for the strategic stockpile and its willingness to pay any price for the oil—driving up spot market prices and otherwise increasing the upward pressures across the petroleum purchasing board. Now Japan's continuing massive purchases of oil for storage occur directly with Saudi Arabia as part of the two nations' larger diplomatic relations and are not recorded or known outside of those few top Japanese and Saudi officials in the Saudi-Japanese Investment Corporation, who complete the details in secrecy.

Those secret undertakings are in addition to other publicly announced agreements reached between Saudi Arabia and Japan in 1980, such as the program in which the Saudis began purchasing at least $2.4 billion a year in Japanese government bonds—a move which had an electric effect on the yen. In return, Saudi government agencies were granted direct access to the Japanese Government's highest-classified institutional centers for technological research, development and design.

In 1980 the Japanese daily newspaper *Nikei* published an investigative report which detailed how, during the preceding three years, Saudi Arabia, Kuwait, Qatar and the United Arab Emirates had made massive stock purchases in at least ninety-six of Japan's largest corporations.

During the summer of 1980, as Middle Eastern newspapers confirmed that Arab monetary leaders planned a "slight shift" in investment patterns to place new emphasis on Japan, the Tokyo Stock Exchange was inundated with the largest amounts of capital ever entering the market at a single time. Press reports indicated that Tokyo residents were flocking to the stock market and gawking because they had "never seen an Arab in person before."[2]

Within two months both the level of trading and the prices of stocks across the board had been driven to the highest levels ever recorded in the history of the exchange. Throughout 1981 those records were repeatedly broken as Muslim oil powers became the most potent financial force in the domestic economy. In late 1981 decisions made in the executive suites of two government offices—the Central Bank of Kuwait and the Saudi Arabian Monetary Agency—were solely responsible for the multibillion-dollar maneuver which overnight lifted the Japanese yen from a fifteen-month slump and transformed it into one of the most desired and valuable currencies in the world.

European financial authorities reported that some of the largest purchases of Japanese corporate stocks were being made by Crédit Suisse—the Swiss investment firm through which Kuwait makes investments around the world. By 1981 that single Swiss bank had become the fifth-largest stockholder in the giant Hitachi Ltd., a leader of the world's electronics industry. Crédit Suisse also bought up large chunks of Asahi Glass, Kubota (Iron Works), Toshiba, Fujitsu Ltd., Matsushita Electric, Nissan Motor and Mitsubishi Chemical. And by year's end two other Swiss banks which function as Arab investment vehicles—Swiss Union Bank and Capital Investment International Bank—had positioned themselves to make similarly massive purchases of stock in Japanese corporations.

Mitsubishi, which has attracted huge investments from several Middle Eastern investment vehicles, is one of Japan's largest corporations, involved in everything from construction to chemical plants to electronics to weapons systems such as aircraft and missiles. It was one of the major corporate powers responsible for the design and management of the massive petrochemical complexes which rocketed Japan to world leadership in the chemical industry in less than a decade and a half. By the end of the 1970s Mitsubishi, now partially owned by Arabs, had virtually exploded across the whole Middle East. Its level of activities became so hectic that a new corporate headquarters had to be established on Bahrain to coordinate the firm's multibillion-dollar projects in eleven Muslim nations. One of its largest undertakings involves the technological guidance and construction engineering for the rising cities of petrochemical factories which, when completed, will be the largest such facilities on earth and are expected to make Saudi Arabia a world power in the chemical industry by the 1990s.

By decade's end more than 80 percent of all the construction and service contracts held by Japanese firms for all projects outside the country involved projects in the Middle East.

And the flow of financial transactions between Japan and the Middle East had become so overwhelming that Japan was forced to open ten new banks on Bahrain to relieve the administrative pressures.

According to the Japanese Ministry of Finance, the nation's total trade with Middle Eastern nations in 1972 was about $1 billion. By 1980 the total amount of goods and services being exchanged between Tokyo and Muslim capitals had increased by 5,000 percent—to $50 billion annually.

Saudi Arabia in 1981 had become the largest single customer for Japanese goods and services in the world. It was the second-largest importer of Japanese cars and trucks—only the United States imported more. It was negotiating the largest purchase of industrial robots and automated factories in history from Japan—an entire network of high-tech facilities capable of eventually turning out goods of the quality and complexity of Japan's but without having to pay Japan's high fuel costs.

Iraq was the second-largest purchaser of Japanese high technology and nearly 50 percent of Baghdad's countrywide construction projects were being raised by Japanese firms. Tokyo has also become one of the largest suppliers of industrial technology and equipment to Libya. It was also building steel plants, ports, electronic works, cement works, petrochemical complexes, schools, hospitals, factories and other such installations throughout the Muslim countries of North Africa. In Algeria alone, 2,000 Japanese technological supervisors were needed in residence to direct the sprawls of industrial construction.

Japanese manufacturing methods and technologies, which have already devastated the United States' industrial hold on world markets, are now being cloned in billion-dollar lots at hundreds of locations across the Middle East. These transfers are not random transactions. Rather, they represent the early stages of a broad merger between civilizations which possess the resources for raising a new industrial colossus across the whole of southern Asia. Funded and fueled by Muslim oil, designed and built by Japanese genius and staffed from the region's vast pools of cheap labor, this evolving alliance in the southern hemisphere could result in a new era of near total Asian dominance of the world's industrial economy by the year 2000.

During this same period of the late 1970s, as this relationship between Japan and the Muslim world was solidifying, Japan's relationship with the United States was beginning to fray at about the same rate.

This deterioration in the Pacific quadrant of the Western Industrial Alliance manifested itself in several areas, one of the most obvious of which was the mounting discord in basic trade relations between Japan and the United States. American industry and unions, unable any longer to compete with the superior factories and dizzying productivity of the Japanese, increasingly pressured Congress and the White House to raise stiffer barriers against the flow of low-priced, high-quality Japanese cars, electronics, heavy industrial machinery, plastics, televisions, computers and other consumer goods that had captured the American market. Those sanctions and threats of sanctions against Japanese goods by the American Government sent waves of bitter reaction throughout Japan, where the press characterized the United States' actions as an unfair punishment of Japanese efficiency, dedication and productivity.

In 1981, with its new $12 billion budget for weapons development, Japan became the largest military spender in all of Asia, outside of China. The United States has expressed mixed reactions to this. On one hand the move helped ease the financial burden of Asian defense borne by the United States for the last thirty-five years. But on the other hand it caused increasing concern in the Pentagon. There military authorities demanded that Japan agree to share its advanced weapons research secrets with the United States.[8] The Japanese politely declined. Japan, now the world's center of advanced electronics and other high technology, has the potential for making the world's most advanced space-age weapons systems—systems easily able to outperform those of the United States. For instance, Japan is now moving forward so fast in computer development that American industrial and military officials have publicly warned that the United States is less than a decade away from becoming as dependent on Japanese computer technology as it is on Arab oil.

Diplomatically, the relationship between Tokyo and Washington took a major downturn in 1979 as Japan refused to heed a United States' call for a boycott of Iran. During the first six months of that boycott period, Japan's overall trade with the revolutionary Islamic Government in Tehran increased by 481 percent. Japan also refused to cooperate with the United States' embargo of the Soviet Union following Soviet moves in Afghanistan. And the Japanese Government launched an uncharacteristically aggressive new campaign of independent international diplomacy aimed at weaving closer ties with the nations throughout southern Asia. Some sense of the new importance of this diplomacy in Japan's future plans was evident when the Japanese broke one of their traditions at the turn of the decade. Instead of boarding a plane for Washington, the newly elected Prime Minister boarded a plane in the opposite direction— flying to the Muslim OPEC nation of Indonesia on a tour throughout the southern Asian region which Tokyo is now helping to industrialize in the same manner that it was once helped by the United States. It is from this area—for which Japan once waged a disastrous war—that the country gets 97.5 percent of its rubber, 99 percent of its tin, 95 percent of its palm oil and 94 percent of the hardwood supplies crucial to its home industries.

In 1981 Japan's normally reticent national spokesmen began, for the first time, to openly confirm the government's decision to loosen its ties with the United States. Naohiro Amaya, a former senior government official, pointed out to reporters that the United States' oil production would last only into the early 1990s and that even the Soviet Union's would dwindle by 1995 or so. However, Amaya explained, Muslim nations would maintain their current overall levels of oil production until at least 2040 or longer. For this reason, he said, the government had no choice but to "establish closer ties with those nations through economic and technological cooperations and cultural exchanges, to say nothing of diplomatic efforts."[4]

Government economist Masao Sakisaka explained, "Japan today depends on the Middle East for 70 percent of its total energy consumption. The present 'affluent society' can be likened to a castle built on Middle East oil."

And late in 1981 the Japanese Government ended three years of diplomatic subterfuge and public vacillation and announced its formal recognition of the Palestine Liberation Organization as "the representative of the Palestinian people." In a move which he explained was part of the government's desire to "make the difference between American and Japanese Middle East policy even clearer," Prime Minister Zenko Suzuki met with Yasir Arafat for diplomatic talks.

Afterward, Suzuki told reporters that "Japan considers the question of Palestine is at the heart of the Middle East conflict" and endorsed a proposal for the creation of a separate Palestinian state on Arab lands seized by Israel in 1967. Suzuki's endorsement called for the new capital of the Palestinian state to be located in the Old City of Jerusalem.

21

COMING HOME
TO HOUSTON

Passengers aboard a plane leaving Kuwait and flying due west around the world could put down on any continent along that route and feel reasonably at home. The sights and sounds and smells are much the same throughout that corridor of latitude taking in the upper reaches of the Persian Gulf in Asia, the lower Nile in Africa and Galveston Bay in North America. Generally, territories along this zone tend to be as insufferably hot as they are flat. And they are also largely arid, managing to fringe themselves with luxuriant subtropical growth only where their edges touch large bodies of water. The other common feature they enjoy is oil. Along this same meridian—from Saudi Arabia and Kuwait in Asia, to Libya and Algeria in North Africa, to Louisiana and southeastern Texas in North America—lie the world's largest deposits of oil.

This last feature provides for further man-made similarities in the regions on all three continents. Pipe tends to be laid so thickly across the ground in these places that from the air it resembles broad sections of riveted rug. Derricks are so dense across both land and water that all horizons appear to be hung with low-slung curtains of steel lace. And at the water's edge are herds of tanker ships—awkward, hulking vessels lowering ever deeper as they feed.

The southeastern part of Texas, where such sights abound, is not the Texas familiar to most Americans, whose image of the state has been forever colored by popular Westerns. That Texas—the Texas of cactus stands and gulch buzzards, sagebrush and canyon burros, mountains and mesas—does exist, but it is located some five hundred miles northwest of here. This southeastern Texas is quite different. It is the Texas of bogs and bayous and desert land gone lush with irrigation. It is the Texas of the date palm and crimson hibiscus, melon vines and sprawling cypress roots, Spanish moss and magnolia blossoms and the ubiquitous machinery of the oil trades.

Just south of Galveston Bay begins a city-sized tangle of pipelines, towers, tanks, vats and steaming chemical works which are the world's largest collection of petroleum processing facilities. This center is dubbed "The Golden Triangle" by bankers and businessmen on the ground. It is also called "The Spaghetti Bowl" by the pilots who use it as a major landmark when dropping from the stratosphere to begin their approach into the Gulf Coast region.

And for the Middle Easterners who have been making this approach into Texas in ever-larger numbers since the early 1970s, the landscapes below offer a soothingly familiar panorama of palm fronds and pumping stations, flatlands and flare pipes, sulfur fumes and searing sun. And this physical atmosphere is only one of several reasons why Arabs have come to think of a flight from the Persian Gulf to the Galveston Bay area as something other than a trip to a foreign country. Indeed, it is now more like a pleasant passage to another corner of their own realm.

During the first forty years of the world's petroleum industry, Texas played no part. The business began and originally took root 1,200 miles to the northeast—in the mountains of western Pennsylvania. There Civil War veterans seeking quick fortunes began using water-well drills to search for rock oil, the new and highly profitable lantern fuel. So close to the surface were those Pennsylvania deposits that they could be located by the seepage pools they left around the mountain valleys here and there. The main body of oil below was accessible to anyone able to drill a hole a few dozen feet through the soft shale.

It was these shallow deposits upon which the Rockefeller oil empire fed and flourished. In Europe the Rothschild oil empire evolved from similar pool deposits at Baku, on the Caspian Sea.

And by the late 1800s both the Rockefellers and Rothschilds had hooked these deposits to webs of petroleum transportation, processing and marketing machinery across two continents. The machinery in those days—leather-thonged, wooden-staved and iron-wheeled—was crude but relatively effective. Like the industrial revolution it fed, it also was rapidly evolving. The technology of pipeline design, railroad and nautical tanker construction and refining and processing chemistry became increasingly more sophisticated. However, the techniques of drilling did not. By 1900 the supply of shallow-pool deposits dwindled as the demand for petroleum skyrocketed. Yet prospecting and drilling remained largely the province of saddle tramps, drifters and roustabouts, who frequently poked hundreds of random holes about the countryside before happening on another shallow deposit.

In 1901 Anthony Lucas, an Austrian engineer recently retired from the Navy, tried a new approach to locating and tapping oil deposits. An engineer by trade with a broad knowledge of geology, he was convinced that the swamps of southeastern Texas sat atop petroleum deposits as vast as they were deep. Surveying the crescent of flatlands running from New Orleans past Galveston Bay, Lucas picked a spot near Beaumont, Texas. There he found promising rock formations and a man-high plateau of dry ground offering a working site safe from flood. Locally, this landmark became known as "Spindletop."

There, amid the mud and mosquitoes, Lucas and his machinist crew turned the craft of hole punching into a high-tech art. Using the latest knowledge in iron construction, cutting-bit metallurgy and machine physics, they raised rigs designed to bore through solid rock to depths never before attempted—or even imagined—by traditional rock-oil prospectors. Local Cajuns thought Lucas and company mad.

But one afternoon the Lucas drill pierced the top of a salt dome, releasing a geyser of slivered stone, spewing brine and venting primordial forces strong enough to twist steel as they blasted up the shaft and rained oil, turning the surrounding swamps black. Almost overnight both the technology and the geography of the American oil business were revolutionized. Scientists and engineers became the new leaders of the trade. The process of prospecting and drilling for oil became its own major industry, dependent on increasingly ponderous and powerful machinery. And the center of the petroleum industry, which had originally been anchored in the Allegheny Mountains near Lake Erie, rapidly shifted south toward the Gulf of Mexico. Lucas's deep well had opened up what would soon be recognized as one of the largest reservoirs of oil on the planet.

That strike ultimately led to the creation of the Texas Oil Company, a firm originally set up in a three-room squatter's shack on the outskirts of Beaumont. In less than a decade the company had been backed by the Mellon fortune, flung up forests of derricks across the plain and was shipping petroleum products from coast to coast, the first independent firm to successfully dent Rockefeller's Standard Oil monopoly.

In 1913 the Texas Oil Company—Texaco—erected what was hailed as an awesome landmark in a region still largely a frontier outback of horsemen and hitching posts. The new Texaco headquarters building shot thirteen stories into the air and was visible, like a lone mountain, to cowboys herding longhorns out on the distant range. The foundations of this architectural monolith took up the entire center of a sleepy settlement on the Buffalo Bayou. Originally, this trading-post settlement had been named for the white man raised as a Cherokee who had led the rebellion establishing the state of Texas: Sam Houston.

And Houston has been an oil-company town ever since.

Within a few years, Gulf, Humble, Shell and others moved in, throwing up their own skyscrapers next to Texaco's and creating the architectural as well as the financial and political core around which all other aspects of the region's life evolved. In 1982 thirty-four of the nation's thirty-five largest petroleum corporations had their principle divisions headquartered here in Houston, the oil capital of the United States.

Houston is also the hub of the world's oil technology, the city that designs, produces and controls the complex machinery with which other nations locate, drill, pump, transport, process and market their oil. The new era of twentieth-century petroleum engineering begun in 1901 by Anthony Lucas became a mainstay around which the rest of the Galveston Bay's industry grew. By the 1930s Houston's factories, foundries, tool shops and assembly plants had become to the world's oil fields what Detroit had become to the world's highways.

By the 1940s the regional webs of oil machinery established in the previous century by the Rockefellers and Rothschilds had merged into a single gargantuan apparatus which encircled the globe and was firmly anchored in only two places: the Persian Gulf fields, which had become its main supply source, and Houston, which functioned as its mechanical heart. Today most of the oil rigs, pumps, pipes and associated petrochemical equipment found throughout the Middle East, the North Sea and other regions of intensive petroleum production are shipped from Houston. That city now conducts an amount of foreign trade larger than most of the countries of the world: $50 billion a year. Half of that entire amount of business is with a single country: Saudi Arabia.

In the 1940s, when the United States began to fully extend its oil-supply grids into the Middle East, it did so from Houston. Entire cities of petroleum engineers and technicians and their families departed from Galveston Bay to set up shop on the sands and salt flats northeast of Riyadh. Bedouins coming off the desert often sat transfixed on their camels—gaping in disbelief at the patches of split-level homes, hairdresser shops, barbecue pits and Oldsmobiles which had suddenly materialized along the shore of the gulf.

Thousands of native Muslims became involved, in one way or another, with those American oil-company communities. Both groups became intimately familiar with each other's cultural peculiarities and histories. Intermarriages occurred. Strong personal bonds of finance and friendship evolved at all levels. Physically, a heavy two-way exchange of personnel began to flow between Houston and the Muslim lands around the Persian Gulf. By the 1950s Texas, like an island separated from the rest of the United States, became intimately linked to that part of the world which would remain an unknown, alien place for the rest of America for decades to come.

The University of Texas and dozens of other schools in the region began enrolling thousands of Arabs being sent to America for educations in high-technology fields under the programs established by then-Crown Prince Faisal. By the 1950s this led to an increasing cultural cross-pollination in southeastern Texas and some unusual sights: clusters of somewhat timid young men, with slide rules in their pockets, speaking Arabic and gobbling chili and tacos at road-side stands where oil truckers in Stetsons and rodeo buckles wished them a hardy "Howdy-do," complete with the obligatory back slap. Those Arab alumni—large numbers of whom are now major government officials and business executives in the Middle East—provide Texas with further unique connections throughout the Muslim world. It was one such alumnus—Abdullah Tariki of Saudi Arabia—who led the Arab move to greatly boost its investments in the United States. Tariki, a graduate of the University of Texas who went on to become both an executive in the Arabian-American Oil Company and Saudi oil minister before becoming an investment representative, stumped through the Houston banking and business community meeting old friends and explaining that Arab nations were planning to increase their spending on U.S. high-technology goods and services to $140 billion annually by the end of the 1970s. Tariki intended that Texans have first opportunity to take advantage of this potential industrial bonanza.

Ironically, the 1974 oil embargo, which devastated much of the rest of the country's industrial base, proved a godsend to Houston. The drastic oil-price increases decreed by Arab nations automatically quadrupled the value of the oil being pumped from Houston's fields each day and brought a tidal wave of new wealth into the city. And the frenzy of new oil drilling throughout America and the world in the wake of the embargo generated unprecedented numbers of new orders for Houston's petroleum machinery industry. At the same time, Houston was being inundated with "recycled" petro-dollars as Arab nations placed multibillion-dollar orders for entire petrochemical processing cities, sprawling new refineries and related construction projects of unparalleled size.

By 1978, as most of the rest of America was sinking into a morass of financial stagnation, industrial bankruptcy and staggering unemployment, Houston's factories were roaring. More than a thousand new workers were being hired every week—and that still fell short of the demand. Between 1970 and 1980 Houston's population increased by 16 percent. During that same period the city recorded two other statistical peaks: the lowest overall rate of unemployment of any urban area in the nation and the highest per capita rate of Cadillac and Mercedes purchases.

More than eight thousand companies in southeast Texas are di-

rectly involved in energy-related industries. The majority of those
are also directly involved in Middle Eastern business. At least two
thousand other Houston-area corporations—ranging from architectural and construction firms to medical equipment and computer
companies—are also heavily dependent upon Middle Eastern clients.
Daily traffic of all sorts between Houston and the Persian Gulf region
is prodigious. Satellite systems facilitate the instantaneous transfer of
billions of dollars between the two areas each day. The United States'
busiest port is Houston, and the bulk of that ocean commerce is either coming from or going to Red Sea and Persian Gulf ports. Substantial amounts of that cargo travel both ways in Arab ships. Arab
shipping firms such as Saudi International Shipping and Export
Company, Arabian National Shipping and the Houston Overseas
Shipping Corporation are among the busiest maritime companies
along the Houston waterfront. Direct daily airline service by such
firms as Saudi Arabian Airlines, Inc., Kuwait Airways and others
puts downtown Houston and Middle Eastern capitals within hours
of each other. And droves of Arab and American engineers, technicians and scientists are in daily motion between Houston's Golden
Triangle of petro-processing plants and the vast construction sites in
Saudi Arabia and other Muslim nations where similar facilities are
being raised. Large numbers of bankers, builders and businessmen
of all types are also in constant transit between the two regions.
Some measure of this traffic can be found in the fact that the Saudi
Arabian Consulate in Houston alone processes more than 300,000
visas a year for Texans traveling to the desert kingdom. After de-
cades of such intense personal and professional exchanges, the city of
Riyadh is as friendly and familiar a place for many Houstonians as
Tel Aviv is for many New Yorkers.

Arab periodicals routinely cover events in and around southeast
Texas and routinely report to their Middle Eastern readers that
"Texans are conservative in politics and religion. They are serious
and straightforward. They keep their promises. As back home, often
a handshake is enough. Like us, they're hospitable. Moreover,
Texans are very pro-Arab."[1]

This access to the business and social centers of the Middle East
has made Houston somewhat different from most of the rest of the
United States. Houston does not accept Arab business ventures but
courts them. It does not tolerate Arab visitors but celebrates them.

For instance, one of the major cultural events of 1982 was the opening of the spectacular "Heritage of Islam" exhibit at the city's sprawling Museum of Natural Science. Focused on a survey of Islamic art works gathered from five dozen museums and archives around the world, the program included a twenty-minute film, *The Peoples of Islam,* and weekly evening lectures that became major social events. Another similar feature is the Houston Planetarium's "Arabian Nights" show, providing an evening under the star patterns as seen from the deserts near Mecca. Other institutions such as the renowned Rothko Chapel in Houston have also hosted gatherings of Islamic lecturers and literary figures from around the world for heavily attended colloquiums with such themes as "Islam: Spiritual Message and Quest for Justice."

The Islamic Society of Greater Houston has more than 6,000 active members. Officials there perform more than two hundred Islamic marriages a year and preside over a community permanent enough to have recently opened an Islamic cemetery.[2] The society also operates summer camps for Muslim children in the Texas countryside beyond Houston and provides experts for a growing number of neighborhood stores that specialize in selling meats from animals slaughtered and dressed in accordance with Islamic dietary laws. There is now a Houston *Voice of Islam* magazine as well as a monthly *Muslim Community News.* And the Institute for Islamic Studies makes a special effort to accommodate the Houston business executives seeking tutoring in Arabic and Islamic business practices.

The local government and business communities of Houston, much like those of Tokyo, London, Paris and Rio de Janeiro, have waged an aggressive ten-year campaign aimed at corralling ever-larger amounts of Middle Eastern business and investments. Its success in effecting a virtual merger between its business community and that of such nations as Saudi Arabia has been one of the primary factors allowing Houston to evolve in the 1980s as an island of boom times and prosperity amid an ocean of American industrial decline and despair.

In 1980 John B. Nicholas of the Houston Chamber of Commerce explained to Houston businessmen that "People don't realize the importance of foreign capital in Houston. We need to make the public aware of the fact that foreign firms provide a large number of jobs here, besides contributing to new development."

James C. Suttles, Jr., president of Suttles International Properties in Houston, explained to the same audience that "Saudis are increasingly getting into real estate here. They are more interested in the physical value of the land than its income-producing properties. Currently, most foreigners are content to remain behind the scenes, primarily interested in the financing required from them and the bottom line of their return. In the future, they will be more concerned about control, but Americans will still be the ones to benefit from foreign dollars because they will be the ones hired to manage, contract, engineer, design and run the developments."

Suttles said that "Foreign investment has provided needed equity for developers without access to conventional money sources. This means there is a new, solid source of capital for development in a period requiring very creative real estate financing. Without foreign investors, the projects going up now in Houston couldn't be built."[3]

Peter J. Tannous, who is chairman of the Petra Capital Corporation, which represents Saudi, Kuwaiti and United Arab Emirate investors, began large-scale operations in Houston in 1978. He told reporters that "whenever you discuss investments today, Houston is almost always the first town on everybody's lips." He said his company was seeking major American firms located in Houston "that seek a friendly, silent investor."[4]

Meanwhile, the Sharjah Group of London—comprised of Saudi, Kuwaiti and United Arab Emirate individual investors and government officials—also went public in Houston in 1978. Dr. David H. Sambar, the executive vice-president of the global investment consortium, confirmed that "We have a continuing interest in Houston and this state."

In 1979 Prince Abdel Aziz Bin Salman Mohamed al Saud arrived in Houston and set up quarters in a spacious suite of offices in the Western Bank building. The new company was called the United Saudi American Commerce Company. Then Prince Abdel Aziz, who had just turned twenty-seven, called a press conference to announce that "The future is here in Houston."[5] He also told reporters that he had $400 million in cash and was seeking to acquire part interest in local oil refineries. And he said his representatives would soon be scouring the Houston, Dallas and southern Louisiana area looking for "developed or developable commercial properties." The dapper prince, who peppered his speech with nonchalant references to his various Lamborghinis and Ferraris, cut a high profile across the pages of the local papers. It was perhaps the biggest such splash since a few years earlier when Adnan Khashoggi touched down, limousined into the city and purchased 21.8 acres of downtown Houston before jetting off toward Brazil for the next day's investments.

Such approaches are not characteristic of the overwhelming number of Middle Easterners putting their money into Texas. While their financial power is a crucial current running through every sector of the Houston region's economic matrix, the actual investors often remain as invisible as they are rich. Despite the open and friendly atmosphere of Houston, many investment officials of the Muslim world follow the circuitous procedures through which they have discreetly placed billions of dollars in investments around the world. Explained one top Houston investment counselor, "The Saudis frequently work through Lebanese or Pakistani advisers. That person will contact a British bank, and the Briton will contact the investment source in the United States." The resulting purchase —be it a factory or a fancy restaurant—is then logged as a "British" investment, in the same manner that tens of billions of dollars worth of Middle Eastern purchases in North America and other parts of the world have been recorded as "Swiss" or "French" purchases because they were carried out through Arab-controlled financial institutions in those countries.

In international banking and diplomatic circles, Houston's preeminent position as the hub of Arab financial activity in North America is celebrated in nicknames: "Mecca West" and "Baghdad on the Bayou," this latter being a reference to the Buffalo Bayou, which snakes through the heart of town to become a deep-dredged canal and, finally, the city's superport.

Authoritative real estate sources report that at least 20 percent of the city of Houston is now owned by foreign interests. If all foreign-owned skyscrapers, condominiums, factories, housing tracts and other properties within the city limits were gathered together in one place, they would create a territory as large as the island of Manhattan.

Authorities indicate that during the last ten years Arab investors have moved across all of southeast Texas, purchasing nearly 14,000 square miles of various properties in cities, suburbs and rural lands.

If all those holdings were put in a single place, they would create a territory about twice as large as the state of New Jersey.

During the first century of its existence, Houston remained a humble and somewhat dingy place, off the beaten track from the rest of the country. Originally laid out as a jumble of huts and tents at the spot where two alligator-infested bayous intersected, it had evolved by 1940 into a city seventy-three miles square. That was a place of gritty streets and soot-belching smokestacks arranged around a central cluster of squarish buildings housing banks and oil companies. Much of the rest of the town, despite the derricks that sprouted willy-nilly from side yards and cow pastures, retained an air of pre-Civil War somnolence. A reporter of the era detailed Houston's port as a place where "Drab, unpainted rooming houses, canoes rotting in front yards, and the shacks of Negro dock workers are fringed by the dusty green of salt cedars and the pastel tints of oleanders."

Forty years later, in 1980, Houston had become a place synonymous with ultramodern design and industrial triumph. It was a magnet for all America, the fastest-growing urban area in the post-World War II years. The city boundaries had continued to heave themselves outward until they took in 450 square miles. The contours of the city sprawled. Like Los Angeles, it had not one but three separate "downtown" districts. Each looked something like a picture from the cover of a science fiction paperback. Buildings did not so much rise, as burst, toward the sky, blades of smoked glass and chrome and mirrors and polished brass and marble. Even many of the sidewalks were tunneled off in Plexiglas, like the walkways of a moon colony.

During the years between 1970 and 1980, when most of this building explosion was going on, Houston was renting out entire skyscrapers before the structures' footings had been excavated. More than three hundred of the largest corporations in America— previously located in such northern centers as Boston, New York, Philadelphia and Chicago—abandoned those deteriorating cities and moved their headquarters to Houston. In 1970 Houston housed about 180 foreign companies and was already established as a major international trading center. But by 1980 it hosted more than 550 major foreign corporations.

And Houston had become *the* banker's paradise in America. Internationally, its reputation as a site of economic vitality and near limitless growth potential was unmatched outside the boom-town banking centers in Bahrain.

New York banks, which had previously been the leaders of the American industry, lost their places as the fastest-growing, most profitable institutions. In the ten years from 1970 to 1980 the two fastest-growing and most profitable banks in the United States were Houston banks—First City Bancorporation and Texas Commerce Bancshares. The third- and fourth-ranked banks were Dallas banks.

In 1970 First City Bancorporation of Houston had assets of just over $1 billion and was the largest bank in the city. In 1980 its assets had grown to $9.5 billion and it was still the largest bank, but dozens of new institutions, including fifty-seven foreign banks, were competing with it.

First City is one of the core institutions of Houston, inhabiting one of its most spectacular skyscrapers and exerting extraordinary influence over every aspect of the city and the region's political and financial affairs. First City, aside from being the largest, is also one of the oldest banks. It was founded in 1928 by a flinty frontier judge and entrepreneur, James Elkins, Sr. He also started the city's oldest and largest law firm, Vinson & Elkins. Together that bank and law firm make Elkins' son and namesake, James Elkins, Jr., the most powerful man in Houston. The younger Elkins, who is chairman of both institutions, is now often described as being to Houston what David Rockefeller of Chase Manhattan is to New York.

Aside from being a czar of the banking community and a titan in legal circles, Elkins is also a pivotal figure in the region's cultural life, being chairman of Houston's Business Committee for the Arts. The president of his banking corporation is the chairman of the Houston Chamber of Commerce, an organization whose power in southeastern Texas resembles that of a shadow government. And Elkins has also employed some of the best-connected and most powerful political figures, the best known of which was John Connally. Connally, the former governor of Texas, former U. S. Secretary of the Treasury and unsuccessful 1980 presidential candidate, has been both a partner in Vinson & Elkins and a director of the board of First City Bancorporation.

And the bank, the law firm and Connally have been some of the most visible partners of the Arab individuals, consortiums and front companies seeking to make massive investments throughout Texas and the rest of the United States.

When Ghaith Pharaon set down in Houston to begin his United States operations, Vinson & Elkins was the first place he went. For starters, Pharaon was interested in buying up banks. John Connally, former top executive of the United States Treasury, and more familiar than most with the intricacies of banking and banking laws, was only too glad to help. In 1975 Connally steered Pharaon toward the $1 billion Bank of the Commonwealth of Detroit. Shortly after Pharaon took over, the bank named a new chairman of the board, Merlyn N. Trued, who, like Connally, was also a former top U. S. Treasury official.

Because the Detroit bank takeover was one of the most visible Arab actions in America in the wake of the oil embargo and the Rabat, Morocco, summit at which King Faisal had announced that the Muslim oil powers intended to begin large-scale takeovers of world industries, it caused a substantial amount of critical comment in the American press. One of the government's chief spokesmen on the matter at that time was Assistant Secretary of the U. S. Treasury Gerald Parsky. Parsky defended the Detroit bank's decision to sell to Pharaon and said that the government found nothing legally wrong with the move. Parsky, deflecting criticism of the event, publicly lauded the sale as "a friendly purchase, a nice, open deal in a well-regulated industry."

Shortly after that Parsky left the U. S. Treasury Department and opened a private practice in Washington, D.C. His firm offered legal and financial consulting services to Muslim oil investors seeking to make large purchases in the United States. One of Parsky's first private commissions was to provide middleman services for Saudi and Kuwaiti investors interested in purchasing large blocks of real estate in downtown Manhattan.

Meanwhile, Pharaon purchased a building in Houston, opened offices and continued expanding under the direction of Connally, whose own offices were in the nearby First City Bank building. Pharaon also joined with another Houston-based Arab investor, Khalid bin Mahfouz. Mahfouz is a banking magnate who shuns publicity and has set up headquarters in a sprawling waterfront villa in River Oaks, the ultraposh enclave of the super-rich that hugs the western reaches of the Buffalo Bayou. River Oaks is a place of estates so large that their stretches of cypress and oak and jasmine and azalea, often running with flocks of quail or stately peacock, seem like nature preserves. There are also driveways longer than many city streets, heliports concealed by sculpted hedges, barbecue pits capable of handling several steers, limousines with tinted and bullet-proofed glass and miles of high walls ending in ornate iron gates attended by armed guards—private armies of the wealthy.

Pharaon and Mahfouz joined with John Connally, who brought in a fourth partner, Frederick Erck, chairman of the board of the Bank of South Texas. The four pooled their money and took over the $70 million Main Bank of Houston. Shortly after the deal was completed, the bank's board received a new chairman—Erck—and a new member—John B. Connally III, son of the former Treasury Secretary.

Connally then directed Pharaon into Georgia. There, in an incident that would propel the Saudi entrepreneur into the headlines, Pharaon began arranging the complex maneuvers through which he would take control of the National Bank of Georgia, then owned by Bert Lance, U. S. Budget Director and best friend of then-President Jimmy Carter.

In September 1977 U. S. Budget Director Bert Lance was forced out of his government post in the wake of two investigations that turned up evidence of wide-ranging criminal activities centered around the bank he owned, the National Bank of Georgia. The Justice Department presented evidence indicating that Lance's bank had been the hub of a loan-pyramiding scheme in which he and other banking associates created bogus collateral which they then used to take out loans from each other. Lance would use some of the loan money to live on and to finance such things as the upkeep of his new fifty-room mansion in Atlanta.

The pyramid—along with Lance's career—began to crumble in the summer of 1977 when the Office of the Comptroller of the Currency and the Senate Governmental Affairs Committee lifted the first corner of the rug on Lance's finances. A federal grand jury laid out a picture in which it portrayed Lance as the kingpin in an international conspiracy involving 383 separate loans for more than $20 million arranged through forty-one different banks stretching from Atlanta to Hong Kong.

In the summer of 1977, before the investigative details unraveled publicly, Lance's personal and business fortunes took a very sudden, very inauspicious turn for the worse. One of his most serious problems was a sharp drop in public confidence in the Bank of Georgia and, hence, an equally sharp drop in the value of its public stock. And Lance—now under scrutiny and prohibited from arranging further interbank loans—was at least $5 million in personal debt.

In September, Lance was forced out of office and, in the space of a few days, the man who had been one of the most powerful in the world was on the verge of becoming a pauper, with no source of income, no assets and debts in the multiple millions.

And then, suddenly, miraculously, Bert Lance's angel appeared out of nowhere. The angel was an Arab. His name was Ghaith Pharaon.

Within two months Pharaon announced that he would buy Bert Lance's badly devalued stock in the National Bank of Georgia for double its market value. When it was over, Pharaon controlled the $380 million bank and a portion of Lance's enormous personal debts had been eradicated.

One month later—January 1978—Lance suddenly received a loan of $3.5 million that allowed him to pay off the rest of his outstanding debts. That loan came from a Muslim banking consortium incorporated in Luxembourg, headquartered in London and operated as a wholly owned subsidiary of another Muslim financial conglomerate in the Cayman Islands in the Caribbean.

Throughout the rest of the Carter presidency, Lance continued to be both the best friend of the President and a financial consultant and agent for various of Houston's Arab investors. Pharaon's linkup with Lance also coincided with the beginning of massive Middle Eastern investments in Atlanta. Arabs purchased a large number of properties in Lance's hometown, including a $100 million Hilton Hotel complex, a 1,700-acre housing development site just outside the city and a variety of banking interests.

Middle East Business magazine at the time reported from the Middle East that "Atlanta is making a big investment play for global money managers and private investors . . . so billions in foreign cash are now being readied for quick entry into the United States."

While Middle Eastern investors would begin to show up in considerable numbers in Atlanta and other cities across the South and Southwest, the logistical center of their national activities remained

Houston. The Texas city's friendly industrial and financial community provided Arab entrepreneurs with an inside view across the entire American economic spectrum. Houston, for instance, is the center of the country's power industry and a crossroads for intelligence of all sorts concerning that industry. By 1980, according to Wall Street and banking authorities, Arab investors had reached out to take up large blocks of stock in dozens of American power and utility companies. Some of the institutions they are known to own a part of are Texas Utilities, Houston Natural Gas, Oklahoma Gas & Electric, Middle South Utilities, Utah Power & Light, Kansas Power & Light, Public Service Company of Colorado, Public Service Company of New Mexico, Arizona Public Service, Pacific Gas & Electric, South Carolina Electric, Southern California Edison, Illinois Power Company, Florida Power & Light, Detroit Edison and Cleveland Electric.

In the 1970s Houston also became the center for the Arab world's new approach to acquiring the billions of dollars for goods and services needed to support the building and development boom in the Middle East. Up until the 1970s it had been customary for Muslim oil nations to merely purchase the goods and services they wanted from U.S. companies. But by the mid-1970s they had begun to purchase the companies instead of the companies' products and services. For one thing, this provided for new levels of direct control over quality and price of the needed items. For another, it further extended the profit potential, allowing Arab powers not only to build what they needed but also to profit from supplying themselves with the materials needed for that building. This was another of the myriad ways the original rush of petro-dollars began to compound itself in value as well as power as the money was put to work around the world.

In 1975 Kutaybah Al-Ghanim, a young Kuwaiti not long graduated from the University of California, came to Houston in the first wave of post-oil-embargo investors and purchased the giant Kirby Building Systems Corporation. The Houston firm specialized in manufacturing prefabricated steel buildings—those erector-set-like constructions which can be trucked to an industrial site and thrown up on a concrete slab, creating instant warehouse and factory space. Al-Ghanim, whose family is one of the wealthiest and most powerful clans in the Persian Gulf region, had his new Houston company build a clone of its complete facilities in Kuwait. Kirby-Houston and Kirby-Kuwait, overnight, became the largest suppliers of steel prefabs not only to the boom-time building industry of the Middle East but to Kuwait's expanding industrial operations around the world.

Ghaith Pharaon was moving in similar ways to purchase Texas-area architectural, engineering and construction firms to service his projects throughout the world. By the late 1970s Pharaon's North American headquarters office in Houston had become so busy it required a full-time executive director. Pharaon hired his counsel from Vinson & Elkins, John Connally's law partner, Frank Van Court.

One company Pharaon purchased a controlling interest in was the CRS Group, Inc. The Houston architectural, design and engineering firm had frequently had contracts for work in the Middle East since the 1960s. For instance, in 1964 it designed the Saudi University of Petroleum and Minerals at Dhahran. At the time Pharaon took an interest in it, CRS was doing about $20 million a year in sales. After purchasing part of the company in 1978, Pharaon chose to remain invisible and installed Frank Van Court on the corporate board of directors. CRS immediately began reaching out to purchase other engineering and design firms and became a self-contained conglomerate capable of designing and managing the construction of city-sized projects. It also leapfrogged out around the world, becoming a major designer of Pharaon's sprawling construction projects in Saudi Arabia and joined Saudi industrial developments as they sprang up on various continents. In 1980, two years after Pharaon became its guiding light, the Houston company was doing $65 million a year in sales.

The full details of Pharaon's North American activities are not known because his Houston headquarters undertakes its business in a manner designed to avoid publicity. However, several other deals have left public trails and provide some indication of the scope of Pharaon's interests across the continent.

In Pasadena, California, Pharaon has formed a new joint-venture company with the giant Ralph M. Parsons Corporation called Saudi Parsons, Ltd. Immediately after its formation the new company received a $500 million contract from the government of Saudi Arabia to erect steam-generation plants throughout the kingdom.

In Chicago, Pharaon arranged for another joint venture with Esmark Corporation, a chemical conglomerate. Immediately after the new company was formed it received a $150 million contract to build a phosphate-based fertilizer plant in Saudi Arabia.

In Canada, Pharaon and the Costeel Corporation formed a joint-venture company to build steel mills and processing facilities in Saudi Arabia.

In New York the Saudi business magnate formed another joint venture with Alexander and Alexander, the insurance firm. Pharaon is chairman of United Commercial Agencies, the largest insurance consortium in the Middle East. His new venture with Alexander and Alexander provided him with further access to the multibillion-dollar insurance industry which must provide coverage on the massive construction projects throughout the Persian Gulf region. Pharaon also formed the International Pharmaceutical Products Company in partnership with the Sterling Drug Company of New York. International Pharmaceutical is located in Saudi Arabia, where it is the largest manufacturer of drugs and medical supplies in the region.

In Peoria, Illinois, Pharaon touched down to arrange purchases of the enormous amounts of heavy equipment needed by his various construction and manufacturing firms around the world. He buys tractors, forklifts, heavy earth-moving equipment and other such machinery in $20 million lots from the Caterpillar Tractor Company.

In Mobile, Alabama, Pharaon purchased controlling interest in the International Systems Corporation, a manufacturer of prefab concrete buildings, including modular hotels. Hotel rooms ready for stacking are shipped out to Jedda, Jordan, Tunisia, Malaysia and other sites where Pharaon has construction projects in progress and needs instant housing for thousands of workers. Shipping is not a problem. Pharaon, who owns three different shipping lines, formed a fourth—International Maritime Carriers, USA—to service the vast flows of cargo he sends from Houston and other points along the American coast.

Pharaon, who owns the Arabian Pipeline Construction Company of Saudi Arabia, and is involved in building two vast petrochemical complexes in the kingdom, is also one of the largest purchasers of every manner of petroleum-related machinery, equipment and supplies from hundreds of Houston's firms and factories.

The largest single project Pharaon is involved in is so complex that it is being coordinated by his Houston, Paris and Brazil headquarters: construction contracts for Al Assard city. Al Assard is a space-age city of armaments research, development and production facilities being raised on the sands south of Riyadh in Saudi Arabia. Designed as an urban population center larger than Trenton, New Jersey, Al Assard will consist of normal housing, shopping, transportation, educational and cultural facilities as well as university-like research laboratories, computer and electronics centers, high-tech metallurgy and machine shops and other special institutions and production plants all devoted exclusively to weapons work. The ultramodern city is to be the centerpiece of an independent regional armaments industry that will allow Muslim nations to equip themselves with state-of-the-art electro-weapons. Pharaon has been intricately involved with coordinating the massive $15 billion construction package, which requires supplies and services from around the world. American firms such as Fluor, Bechtel and Ralph M. Parsons are heavily involved, as is 3D International, the Houston architectural firm. Pharaon has also reached out to put French and Brazilian firms into a broad consortium task force of builders and has sought to heavily involve the Sam Wallace Corporation of Dallas, Texas, in the project. Pharaon purchased controlling interest in the Wallace Corporation in the late 1970s.

Despite its innocuous name, the Wallace Corporation—begun as a small construction business more than twenty years ago—is now a corporate colossus with nearly two dozen subsidiary companies in ten states of America, Puerto Rico, England, Costa Rica, Venezuela, Egypt and Saudi Arabia. And while it is best known as a construction and mechanical contracting conglomerate, in the late 1970s Wallace diversified heavily into high-technology fields such as nuclear power. In 1977, for instance, the corporation formed the Wallace Power Company in Atlanta, Georgia. This new subsidiary specializes in installing the massive systems of piping, shielding, instrumentation and other complex equipment used inside nuclear reactors, the special machinery which must contain and control the extraordinary processes through which uranium becomes sun-hot and decays into plutonium.

Ghaith Pharaon has become an American nuclear equipment magnate.

Since the 1940s the American headquarters of the Arabian-American Oil Company (Aramco) was located on Park Avenue in New York City. Aramco was the entity formed by Exxon, Texaco, Mobil and Standard Oil of California as a vehicle for developing the oil fields of Saudi Arabia. By the 1950s Aramco had become the largest and richest industrial consortium in the world and the linch pin of American dominance in the global petroleum business. The Aramco building in New York, the urban heart of the American business community, was both a landmark and a symbol of that dominance. In the mid-1970s, however, both the geography of the American business community and Aramco had changed drastically. Following the 1973 Middle East war, the Saudi Government had taken over 60 percent controlling interest in Aramco. One of the first decisions made after that takeover was to move the American headquarters of the corporation to the "more philosophically agreeable atmosphere of Houston." Today Aramco takes up four skyscrapers in downtown Houston, which has become the headquarters for much of the Saudi Arabian oil operations, which now encircle the globe. The cluster of Aramco buildings serves as the symbolic hub of much of the rest of the Muslim world's political and cultural activities in the United States. In 1977 the Saudi Consulate also moved its headquarters from New York City to Houston.

Houston is now the North American headquarters of the Saudi Research and Marketing Company, the Jedda-based media conglomerate that publishes several of the Arab world's most respected newspapers. Its Houston offices house the operations of *Arab News,* an English-language paper printed in Saudi Arabia each day and circulated throughout the world; *Asharq A-Awsat,* a new Arabic-language newspaper printed in Houston and circulated throughout the United States, and *Saudi Business* and *Saudi Report,* two publications covering events in and around the Saudis' global business and financial empire. Houston is also the headquarters for the Arab-North American Chamber of Commerce and the Arab-United States Chamber of Commerce.

"I feel welcome here," explained Dr. Talal Hafiz, director of

Saudi Research and Marketing to the *Houston Business Journal* in 1981. "You don't see people wearing anti-Arab T-shirts, or see anti-Arab bumper stickers, posters or greeting cards like are seen in other U.S. cities."[6]

Just a quick walk from the Saudi Research and Marketing building on the West Loop in Houston are the offices of the Saudi Arabian Educational Mission to the United States. Previously located in New York City, the mission quietly relocated to Houston in the mid-1970s. It is the headquarters from which the Saudi Government oversees the details of the more than 13,000 students it has enrolled in schools across the United States studying everything from marine biology to nuclear physics. The Saudi Educational office also serves as a low-profile center for the missionary activities of the American Muslim movement and supplies large amounts of books and educational materials used in the growing number of Muslim schools established in black ghetto neighborhoods of America's larger cities.

The Arab offices and agencies in Houston also serve as the major clearinghouse in the United States for the intelligence-gathering activities of the Arab Boycott Office. Although the Arab world originally declared an economic boycott against Israel even as Europeans were setting up the new state in 1948, the boycott remained a largely symbolic effort until 1973. Then the global economic revolution wrought by King Faisal's oil jihad provided Arab authorities with pivotal control of much of the world's financial systems and industrial commerce.

Muslim governments, following the patterns established by the U. S. Government's boycott of such nations as Cuba and China, set up a bureaucracy with worldwide offices and the goal of isolating Israel from the international economic community. Although codified in lengthy legal form, the boycott's principles are simple: Any company or individual who does business with Israel or companies doing business with Israel is immediately disqualified from doing business of any sort in the Muslim Middle East. Companies have to choose between Israel and access to the largest and most lucrative new market for construction and industrial goods in the world.

The boycott is not airtight. Exceptions are made in the interest of military expediency. For instance, despite the fact that Chrysler, Lockheed, Hughes, Raytheon and McDonnell Douglas sell American military equipment to Israel, all are allowed to make billion-dollar sales throughout the Muslim world. Arab governments purchase enormous amounts of Chrysler tanks, Hughes antitank missiles, Lockheed army cargo planes, McDonnell Douglas attack jets and Raytheon antiaircraft missiles. And such exceptions have other benefits. In 1981, for instance, Raytheon was fined by the U. S. Commerce Department for using its market contacts inside of Israel to gather information which it then passed on to the Arab Boycott Office.

Twenty-one Arab countries cooperate to fund and operate the global boycott mechanisms. World headquarters of the Boycott Office are located in Damascus, Syria, where a staff of more than seventy works to collect and collate industrial and financial data from several continents. Information supplied through Arab agencies in Houston, Washington, Paris, London, Madrid, Athens, Geneva, Tokyo, Hong Kong, Brussels and Bonn is used to pinpoint and monitor firms which directly or indirectly are doing business with Israel.

U.S. companies are required to report to the U. S. Commerce Department any contacts they have with the Arab Boycott Office. The department's files on boycott activities are among its most sensitive and confidential. But it has released partial listings of companies that have received requests from Muslim governments to comply with the boycott or lose corporation business access in the Middle East. The Commerce Department has reported that 94 percent of the companies that receive such requests comply with them.

The department has listed such corporations as General Electric, John Deere & Company, General Tire and banks such as the Bank of America, Citibank, Bankers Trust, First National Bank of Maryland, United California Bank, First Wisconsin Bank and the First City Bank of Houston.

By 1975, even as the surrounding Middle East was exploding in an unprecedented frenzy of building and business opportunities, Israel's economy was shriveling and convulsing. Financial journals reported a "sharp decline" in foreign investments in Israel. Such financial institutions as Chase Manhattan publicly refused to open even a small branch office in Israel despite guarantees of large amounts of business and other incentives. American petroleum companies scrupulously observed the boycott, leaving Israel virtually cut off from the technology of the oil exploration, drilling and processing trades —greatly hindering Israel's desperate but ultimately fruitless search for major oil deposits beneath its own sands. The New York *Times* reported that "Israeli manufacturers are beginning to feel the effects of Arab economic warfare." Israeli businessmen began removing the "Made in Israel" labels from their goods and sought other ways to disguise the origin of the products.

The Anti-Defamation League of B'nai B'rith, which began functioning as an antiboycott intelligence-gathering and lobbying network throughout America reported that "banks, freight forwarders, insurers" as well as airlines, shipping and other transportation companies were refusing to do business with Israel or Israeli-connected firms.

More than 3,000 corporations throughout the world are disqualified to do business in the Arab world because of their dealings with Israel. The list of qualified corporations is constantly updated. Companies that cease their Israeli activities are removed from the disqualified list; others found to have established Israeli links are added. Such disqualification can have a devastating effect on a corporation. For instance, the Coca-Cola Company was found to be doing business in Israel at the same time it was attempting to penetrate the exploding soft-drink market in the Muslim Middle East. The firm was disqualified and prohibited from any business contacts in Muslim nations. The Pepsi-Cola company, which refrains from doing business with Israel, leaped into the breach and established its product as one of the major sellers throughout the Arab world.

Most of the companies that cut off Israel in order to qualify for business in the Muslim Middle East do so in a manner aimed at avoiding public attention. One of those few that publicly announced its decision to break off all dealings with Israel was Sea Containers, Inc., a leading world shipping firm handling containerized freight. In 1976 the firm was about to begin joint operations with Israel's fruit exporting industry but suddenly severed all connections with the country and the venture. The president of Sea Containers, Inc., explained to the London press, "Containerization is sweeping through Arab ports like wild fire and Sea Containers is extensively involved. . . . It would be imprudent for us to provoke ill-feeling [there]."

Even the U. S. Army Corps of Engineers, which manages all of

Saudi Arabia's vast multibillion-dollar military construction and training programs was reported to be carefully maintaining a list of qualified American construction contractors for use on such projects.

In 1976—a presidential and congressional election year—the American Israel lobby in Washington cranked up an intense national campaign to pressure the Congress to pass measures making it illegal for a U.S. firm to cooperate in any manner with the Arab boycott. The law enacted at the behest of the Israel lobby imposed fines on companies that complied with the boycott or supplied information to the Boycott Office. But in late 1981 the New York *Times* reported that "American companies that do business with the Middle East are complying with an Arab economic boycott of Israel even though federal law specifically forbids it."

Earlier, banks such as Chase Manhattan, First National City, Bankers Trust and Chemical Bank publicly admitted that they routinely cooperated with the boycott, processing billions of dollars in letters of credit containing boycott restrictive clauses. At hearings in New York the banks' spokesmen held that the Arab boycott was a political issue between two foreign groups which could not be governed by domestic legislation in America. The U. S. Justice Department voiced a similar sentiment as Assistant Attorney General Atonin Scalia went before the House Judiciary Subcommittee and testified that the law interfered with the rights of Americans to express their political views via their business dealings.

Despite the fines which are now levied on American companies cooperating with the Arab boycott, the Commerce Department reports that the number of companies honoring the boycott "has risen each year." Other financial sources have also reported widely that the antiboycott law of the United States is ignored by large portions of the firms doing business in such places as Saudi Arabia and Kuwait. Explained one executive directly involved in such business, "Do you think $120,000 in annual fines really present a problem to a corporation doing $120 million in annual sales in Riyadh or Bahrain? It's just another of the incidental costs of doing business."

Most of the information concerning the Commerce Department's antiboycott files and fines is confidential, but occasional reports are issued on larger violators. For instance, during the twelve months ending June 30, 1981, the 3M Corporation, which is headquartered in St. Paul, Minnesota, and does more than $5 billion in annual sales, was fined $137,000 for 230 instances in which it cooperated with the Arab Boycott regulations. The Rockwell International Corporation, which is headquartered in Pittsburgh, Pennsylvania, and does more than $6 billion in annual sales was fined $71,000 for its 127 instances of cooperation with the Arab Boycott Office during the same period. And ITT, which is headquartered in New York and does more than $22 billion in annual sales, was fined $50,500 for 101 instances in which it was found to have aided the Arab Boycott Office during the year.

The Bechtel Corporation, headquartered in San Francisco, has been an unabashed supporter of the boycott throughout the last decade. The largest construction company in the United States and the largest single contractor in the Muslim Middle East, Bechtel in 1981 charged that the U.S. antiboycott law had become a serious "inhibiting factor" that was keeping many American firms out of the lucrative Middle East builders market, which was being taken over by foreign firms that supported the boycott.

In 1975, before Congress passed the antiboycott law, American firms were receiving more than 10 percent of all construction contracts in the Muslim Middle East. By 1978, after two years of antiboycott enforcement, American firms had only 6 percent of the Muslim Middle East construction market. By 1979 that had dropped to 3 percent and by late 1980 to 1.2 percent. This is no small loss in a $218 billion annual construction market. Meanwhile, Japanese, South Korean, Pakistani, Brazilian and European firms have become the primary contractors in the region. The exact loss to the American domestic economy is not known, but in 1978 the Commerce Department confirmed that every $1 billion in goods and services exported to the Middle East from America supported 90,000 jobs throughout America. The loss of $1 billion would exert the opposite effect on domestic employment patterns.

President Reagan, who came into office in 1981 after a campaign emphasizing restoration of America's economic vitality, has not been a public advocate of the antiboycott law. Commerce Department officials in 1981 confirmed that the overall antiboycott effort was "not a top priority" with the Reagan administration.

However, both the Commerce Department and the Arab Boycott Office continue their operations. U.S. companies that do not accurately report their dealings with Israel are often surprised to find that the Boycott Office carries on continuing investigations of the corporate connections between Israel and the rest of the world. The governments of Saudi Arabia and other Muslim countries provide the Boycott Office with the bulk of its information and directly assist in its intelligence gathering. The Saudi Education Office in Houston, for instance, is renowned as one of the strictest supporters of the boycott.

The legal ground for American companies seeking to do business in the wildly profitable Arab world is a maze: Both the complicated regulations of the Muslim world and the U. S. Commerce Department must be adhered to and this has created what amounts to a new school of law. Immediately after the U.S. antiboycott law was passed, U.S. firms harnessed their extensive legal departments to the task of finding ways around the federal regulations. For instance, one part of the U.S. law forbids a U.S. company to affirm to Arab authorities that its products contain no parts or materials from Israel. The Arab Boycott regulations, on the other hand, require a company to stipulate in writing that no parts or materials in its products come from Israel.

To get around this, corporate attorneys now have their firms list the origin of *all* materials and parts in all products offered to the Arab market. The listing shows, for example, that an item contains parts and materials from Japan, Taiwan, France, South Korea and Mexico. In this manner the letter of the U.S. law is followed at the same time the boycott regulations are accommodated in a back-door fashion.

Meanwhile, the systematic isolation of Israel and the stagnation and decline of the Israeli economy continues. Finding ways to circumvent the boycott's investigators has become a major priority for the Israeli Government. By 1981 the situation had become so serious that the Israeli secret service, the Mossad, was reported to have begun setting up webs of bogus companies on the island of Cyprus in an effort to "launder" the financial and commercial traffic coming in and out of Israel.

At the same time, Houston had become the center of the new industry of legal professionals providing guidance to American firms wishing to navigate the legal complexities of the antiboycott law. The city is now headquarters for the national *Boycott Law Bulletin,* a publication which provides lawyers and other interested parties with up-to-date information on both the U.S. regulations and the Boycott Office regulations.[7]

The *Boycott Law Bulletin* also supplies the names of at least fifteen attorneys in the United States who now specialize in advising companies how to violate neither the Boycott Office regulations nor federal law as they seek business opportunities in the Muslim Middle East. Because both the primary Arab information-gathering sources and the largest concentration of companies doing business in the Middle East are located in southeastern Texas, the *Boycott Law Bulletin* enjoys a growing readership and reputation there.

And Houston has also played a crucial role in other Arab political initiatives in the United States. It was, for instance, the major staging point from which the 1978 national lobbying campaign on the F-15 issue was launched. That lobbying effort resulted in a watershed Senate vote allowing the Saudis to purchase five dozen of America's most advanced fighter planes and ending Israel's thirty years of exclusive access to the Pentagon's most sophisticated weapons systems.

From headquarters in Houston such agencies as the Arab-American Chamber of Commerce reached out across the fifty states to organize seminars in every major American city, seeking to directly enlist the participation of local corporations in the F-15 battle. One of the persons who was a frequent participant in those sessions, lending the weight of his office to the proceedings, was then-U. S. Treasury Secretary Michael Blumenthal. Blumenthal later left government and became chairman of Crescent Diversified, Ltd., and Gentrol, Inc.—two of the larger American investment companies set up by Suliman Olayan.

The Fluor Corporation, whose operational headquarters are in Houston, launched a 1978 program seeking to enlist all its employees and stockholders in the national pro-Arab lobbying effort. Fluor is one of the largest corporations of its kind in the world and employs 23,500 people. It earns $3.6 billion a year and builds factories for extracting, transporting, refining and processing oil, gas, coal and synthethic fuels. Its largest single project is a $5 billion construction in Saudi Arabia.

Other Houston giants, such as the Bechtel Corporation, the Computer Sciences Corporation, Mobil and other similarly large and powerful firms, directly participated in that 1978 effort and then, with an even larger cast of supporting companies, returned to provide national support for the Arab lobby's 1981 AWACS effort. That AWACS campaign was even more successful than the F-15 campaign and established the Arab lobby as an inescapable new force on the domestic American political scene.

In 1979, in yet another political watershed, Houston produced postwar America's first unabashedly pro-Arab presidential candidate. And from the very start Republican John Connally's campaign for the White House was marked with unique milestones. It was, for instance, the first time any major candidate had refused to accept the federal matching funds which carry with them restrictions on the amount of personal donations a candidate may funnel into his own campaign. Instead, Connally announced he would run only on the funds he raised himself. By summer of 1979, as the Connally/Reagan/Carter/Kennedy primary battles rolled on, Connally had raised $4.3 million, largely from corporations in and around his home-base operations in Houston. Another milestone of the campaign is that it was the first to win the open and enthusiastic support of the Arab world. In Kuwait, newspaper front pages announced the formation of Kuwaitis for Connally organizations to back the Texan in his bid for the presidency.

And Connally's was the first campaign which neither accommodated nor attempted to mollify the Jewish voting blocs, which have been a pivotal force in every election since Truman's. In the climax of his run, Connally went before the Washington Press Club for the first major foreign policy speech of his campaign. He called for a reversal of U.S. policy in the Middle East, the pull-back of Israeli occupational forces from all lands seized in 1967, the internationalization of the city of Jerusalem, placing it under sovereignty of Muslim, Jewish and Christian religious authorities, and the creation of an autonomous government body of Palestinians to oversee the formation of a homeland for that displaced people.

Connally said, "The oil of the Middle East is and will continue to be the lifeblood of western civilization for decades to come. The endless wars, threats of wars and economic disruptions coming from the Middle East are, in a very real sense, poisoning the well from which the people of the entire world must drink."

Newsweek reported that "The speech angered American Jews and made U.S.-Israeli relations a divisive presidential campaign issue for the first time. American Jewish leaders were dismayed that the traditional bipartisan support for Israel in presidential campaigns had been shattered."[8]

Less than a week later Connally's appearance at the World Affairs Council luncheon in Philadelphia—a city that is the key to Pennsylvania's electoral votes—was torpedoed by Republican mayoral candidate David Marston. Marston generated national headlines by refusing to appear with Connally at the same time he attacked the Texan's Middle East policy. The Philadelphia *Bulletin* reported that Marston had no choice because "In Philadelphia, the Jewish vote is extremely important to any mayoral candidate."

At the same time, New York Republican leader Vincent Albano released the letter with which he "disinvited" Connally from the party's New York Lincoln Day dinner.

It was downhill from there. In a four-column headline the New York *Times* announced that Connally received a "Chilly Reception in New Hampshire." *Time* magazine, covering the end of Connally's rapidly disintegrating campaign, announced, "$11 million won him nothing." In March of 1980, five months after he gave his Middle East speech in Washington, Connally took to the podium in Houston to announce his campaign had ended. Then he and his wife left. *Time* reported, "Connally and Nellie drove to Houston's River Oaks Country Club for a late supper. As they entered the dark grill room, the home folks' heads turned in recognition. And suddenly, as a group, they stood at their seats and applauded."[9]

Connally, whose pro-Arab presidential bid was savaged by mediaAmerica, which is headquartered in New York, was lionized by corporateAmerica, which is now headquartered in Houston. His campaign reports indicate that the largest contributors to his unorthodox campaign were top executives from 114 of America's 500 largest corporations, including Occidental Petroleum, Mobil, Exxon, Getty Oil, Gulf Oil, Phillips Petroleum, Shell Oil, Standard Oil of California, Superior Oil, Ashland Oil, Cities Service, Kerr-McGee, Rockwell International, Lockheed and Dow Chemical.

22

AMERICA'S ARAB ENERGY CZARS

From the air the three-hundred-mile flight from Houston to New Orleans is a monotonous one. Below, with hardly a change, the scenery of Galveston Bay gently curves along the Gulf Coast to the east to become the Mississippi Delta. To seaward—out at the far line where the gray waters meet the sky—are floating corn rows of oil rigs. Thousands of them. Louisiana is the second-largest producer of petroleum in the nation, its output topped only by that of neighboring Texas. To landward—running north and west as far as the eye can see across the delta regions—is a murky green tapestry of swamps, bogs, bayous and silt basins whose foreboding surface features belie their real worth. And that value goes beyond oil. Thousands of feet down—past a million centuries of black loam, fossil-laden marl and sticky yellow clay—lies a rock encasement containing one of the largest natural gas deposits on earth. And if an airline passenger had X-ray vision, he might be able to see this natural gas cavity outlined as a pinkish-red blob along the land's surface. Called the Tuscaloosa Trend, it stretches across southern Louisiana like some gigantic, elongated muscle, eventually crossing over into Texas, bending south past Galveston Bay and plunging farther into Mexico.

In 1982 Louisiana natural gas deposits such as this one provided more than one third of all the natural gas used in the United States. The reserves here are counted in the millions of trillions of cubic feet of fuel and are among those crucial domestic energy deposits touted by every President from Nixon to Reagan as the means by which the country can attain national energy independence. President Jimmy Carter, for instance, spoke of such domestic deposits when he said, "Americans are just now beginning to realize, with simple common sense, that there are only two ways to guarantee [energy] supply. One is obviously to control our demand. And the other is to develop our own sources of energy to replace foreign imports so that we can have control over our own destiny."[1]

One aspect of this Tuscaloosa Trend deposit is of particular interest. It is partially owned by Saudi Arabian Ghaith Pharaon. Fifty square miles—or an area larger than the city of Boston—of the prime drilling land sitting directly atop these Louisiana gas caverns have been purchased by a company controlled by Pharaon.

Pharaon's reach out of his Houston headquarters and into the adjacent Cajun swamp country north of New Orleans was one of the first moves by an Arab investor into domestic energy properties in the United States. And while making those purchases in Louisiana, Pharaon appears to have gone to great lengths to conceal the fact that he was to be the ultimate owner of the fifty-mile-square parcel of gas fields.[2]

The complex maneuver involved a New Orleans real estate developer, John Connally's law partner, Frank Van Court, two of Pharaon's companies and two other front companies set up to accommodate the sale's cloak of secrecy.

This is how it worked, according to local documents and real estate reports: New Orleans real estate developer Sam Recile used various members of his family to set up a company called Brian Investments.

Brian Investments purchased the fifty square miles of natural gas drilling land in four counties north of New Orleans and then turned it over to another company, which had been set up by Recile, Ascantia, Inc. Recile was president of Ascantia but had a number of other partners who owned at least 50 percent of the firm. One of those partners was Frank Van Court, Pharaon's attorney and investment counselor. Another partner in Ascantia was an investment firm, Iman Investments, Inc. Iman Investments is one of the several companies Pharaon has established in the Netherland Antilles. And still another partner in Ascantia was the Arabian Services Corporation. Arabian Services is one of the companies Pharaon has set up in his Houston headquarters. In a statement to local Louisiana authorities, a spokesman for the Arabian Services Company explained that the fifty-square-mile tract had been purchased for its mineral rights and that Ascantia was arranging with local wildcat drilling firms for the development of its natural gas deposits to feed into the lucrative domestic American market.

Soon after obtaining control of these natural gas deposits, Pharaon moved from his Houston headquarters in a northerly direction, toward Dallas. There he began preparing for the takeover of the OKC Company of Dallas. OKC had begun as a cement company years before but grew into an international conglomerate heavily involved in all phases of petroleum exploration, recovery, transportation and processing. Some of the operations Pharaon hoped to take control of included:

—OKC Refining, Inc., a crude-oil refinery in Texas.

—OKC Petroleum International, which operates oil wells in Latin America and the North Sea fields off Europe.

—OKC Pipeline Corporation, operating crude-oil pipelines in the southwest.

—Compania Humboldt, a Latin American oil and natural gas exploration subsidiary.

—OKC Transport Company, which operates fleets of tanker trucks for petroleum product delivery in the United States.

At the last minute Pharaon's plans to take the company were thwarted as OKC came under scrutiny by the Securities and Exchange Commission. Pharaon's spokesman, Frank Van Court, confirmed that Pharaon had been forced to withdraw his purchase offer at the eleventh hour because of the SEC probe of the firm's past business practices.

However, that temporary defeat was only a minor obstacle for Pharaon, who continued exploring the fifty states for energy companies and properties for sale. Nor was he the only newly arrived Middle Eastern investor evidencing an unusually keen interest in domestic American energy properties. During that same period in the late 1970s representatives of Muslim oil governments:

—opened negotiations with the Council of Energy Resources Tribes headquartered in Colorado. The group consists of twenty-three American Indian tribes whose reservations in ten western states sit atop 80 percent of America's known uranium deposits as well as about one third of the easily strip-minable low-sulfur coal. The negotiations were started by Saudi Arabian emissaries and were aimed at exploring the possibility of "joint ventures" in resource development.

—opened negotiations with twelve regional corporations composed of 3,400 Eskimos and other native Alaskans involved in the mineral rights of various North Slope and offshore oil deposits. The negotiations are aimed at exploring the possibility of "joint ventures" in Alaskan oil and gas development.

By 1982, after several years of methodical investments, Arab powers—individuals as well as governments—had established a pervasive presence throughout America's domestic energy industries. Moving from their Houston headquarters in the center of the continent's energy matrix, they had gained substantial influence with their holdings in oil shale, coal, geothermal and biomass fuel projects; uranium technology, power plants and alternative energy research and development laboratories and engineering firms, and other companies involved in widespread exploration, drilling, production, processing and marketing of petroleum products throughout North America.

In Riyadh in March of 1980, when Saudi Arabia's state oil company purchased all remaining shares of the Arabian-American Oil Company from Exxon, Mobil, Socal (Standard Oil of California) and Texaco, an era which had begun to wane in 1974 ended. The age of the "Seven Sisters" was over. In a flourish of ink and legal papers, the American oil companies relinquished the final strands of their power in Aramco, becoming humble customers to the entity they had originally built into the most powerful petroleum organization in the world. In 1974 Saudi Arabia had given its American partners the option either to sell out their shares in Aramco or lose all their oil supplies. Before the year was over, Petromin, the Saudi state oil company, owned 60 percent of Aramco. In 1980, with a final payment of $1.5 billion, Petromin became sole owner of that company.

The move, which was not publicized at the time it occurred, was largely a symbolic act finalizing on paper what had already become a fact in the field. In Saudi Arabia, as well as the rest of the Muslim oil-producing world, the Western companies had been rolled out of their former position of power. By 1980 they had not only lost their grip on the wells and production facilities but, increasingly, on the refining, petrochemical and tanker-transport industries as well.

Throughout the late 1970s the oil companies retreated back into North America and began a frantic series of moves aimed at finding new sources of income to replace those they were losing in and around the Middle East. One of their new areas of interest was gas stations. Street-corner gas stations had long been the domain of individual neighborhood businessmen. Oil companies traditionally hung their names on the building and supplied the products at wholesale prices but otherwise maintained a detached distance from these independently operated facilities. But once the companies started losing control of the far reaches of their empire—the wellheads and production facilities in Africa and Asia—they suddenly took notice of the profit potential in retail marketing in the United States. According to statistics gathered during congressional hearings on the subject, between 1974 and 1980 more than 100,000 independent gas-station operators were driven out of business as the oil majors reached out to make street-corner marketing facilities direct extensions of daily corporate operations.

At the same time, the oil majors began drastic internal reorganization aimed at transforming themselves from "oil companies" into "energy companies." Seeking to anchor their corporate operations and futures in areas other than petroleum, they reached out to grasp multibillion-dollar chunks of the nation's coal fields, uranium deposits, tar sands and oil shale sites and synthetic fuel development projects.

The most expansive of their new investments involved coal. During the last decade, coal—the substance which originally fueled the industrial revolution—has experienced a resurgence of popularity. In 1980, at their summer summit on energy issues in Venice, the leaders of the Western world—addressing the dual problems of the continuing envelopment of all sectors of the petroleum networks by the Arab world and the inevitable end of major petroleum resources within four decades—called for the opening of a "new age of coal."

New technologies have potentially made coal an extraordinarily versatile commodity. The procedures for mining and moving coal have been revolutionized on the drawing board by advances in industrial robots and new generations of space-age heavy digging equipment. One of the new approaches to coal involves the once cumbersome problem of transportation. New techniques now allow coal to be pulverized, mixed with water and transported through pipelines, like oil. Further new technologies allow for the use of coal dust as an engine fuel similar to vaporized gasoline. For instance, diesel trucks have already been successfully converted to using a fuel of finely powdered coal dust and air. A carburetor-like device provides for an explosive mixture of dust and air to be delivered to the cylinders, where it burns as hot and as powerfully as liquid fuel. Similar new technologies provide the potential for totally new sorts of high-efficiency, low-pollution coal-burning power plants and home-heating units.

The largest deposits of coal on earth are laced back and forth throughout the rocky folds of the North American continent. So vast are these reserves that the United States is now being described in many industrial circles as "The Saudi Arabia of Coal." And one of the major reasons that coal has taken on a new glamour in the West is that, much the same as oil shale, tar sands, uranium deposits and synthetic fuel projects, it appears to be a potential energy source beyond the physical control of the Asian and African governments that now control the world's oil systems.

By 1980 the oil companies had made coal one of the pillars of their new master plans. That year the National Coal Association reported that, in a frenzy of purchases around the United States, oil companies had taken control of at least 25 percent of all producing American mines and owned at least 25 percent of all known coal reserves in the country. The association reported that the rate of continuing purchases and negotiations indicated that by 1985 oil companies would control nearly 50 percent of all coal reserves and mining operations in the nation. In March of 1981, for instance, the Gulf Oil Corporation purchased the Kemmerer Coal Company, which owned coal mines throughout the West. That $325 million purchase immediately made the Gulf Oil Corporation the tenth-largest coal producer in America.

And, at the same time, Exxon, Shell, Mobil, Texaco, Occidental, Phillips and other oil majors were moving with equal speed into uranium mining and processing, nuclear power companies, tar sands and oil shale projects and other such alternate energy ventures. Exxon, for instance, anticipating the advent of a coal-fired society running on electric rather than petroleum vehicles, spent $1.2 billion to purchase Cleveland's Reliance Electric Company, a conglomerate that is one of the largest manufacturers of electric motors in the world.

However, Arab oil powers were not idle observers of this new trend. Much the same as the Seven Sisters had once started with operations centered around wells in southeastern Texas and reached out into Asia, the new Muslim oil powers first consolidated their operations around their Asian wells and then began reaching out into North America. The U.S. oil companies that had been rolled back from Asia in the 1970s were in the 1980s being absorbed into the Muslim oil energy empire.

Reaching out of their American and Bahamian and Swiss and British financial organs, Arab investors began buying up the stock of American oil companies. In one of the largest transactions in the U.S. stock market in 1980, for instance, the Kuwait Investment Office acquired 1.1 million shares of the Gulf Oil Corporation. In September of 1980 John C. Walker, general manager of the Euro-Kuwaiti Investment Company, which is one of several handling Arab investments around the world, confirmed to the Chicago *Tribune* that Arab investors had taken up large blocks of stock even in such lesser-known American oil companies as Southland Royalty, Mesa Petroleum and Sabine. Walker said his clients had "developed a great fascination for oil and gas companies, primarily U.S. domestic companies. We want the guys who have it and the guys who are finding it. We want it all."[3]

Although the bulk of such investments are shrouded in secrecy, by 1982 various financial and corporate authorities had publicly confirmed that Arab investors had acquired huge blocks of stock in other oil companies such as Atlantic Richfield, Phillips, Exxon, Getty, Texaco, Standard Oil of California, Standard Oil of Ohio,

Standard Oil of Indiana, Amerada Hess, Superior Oil Corporation, General American Oil and the Union Oil Corporation.

Wall Street authorities also report that by 1982 substantial amounts of Saudi and Kuwaiti money had been invested in such companies as:

—the Halliburton Company of Dallas, Texas, which does $8 billion in annual sales. The firm is one of the key manufacturers of the special explosives required for well drilling and mining and is also involved in exploring, drilling, producing and processing petroleum throughout the United States, Latin America, Europe and the Middle East.

—Schlumberger, Ltd., of New York City, which does $4 billion in annual sales, specializing in computers, specialized instrumentation, gauges and meters and other electronic equipment required in every stage of petroleum prospecting and production.

—the Smith International Corporation of Newport Beach, California, which does $800 million in annual sales of tools and technologies for oil, gas and geothermal drilling, coal and mineral mining, and other equipment and technical services needed by energy companies in North America, Latin America, Europe and Australia.

—the Parker Drilling Company of Tulsa, Oklahoma, which does $400 million in annual sales of drilling equipment and engineering services for oil and gas exploration on land. The firm specializes in deep-well natural gas drilling throughout the United States, Canada, Latin America and Indonesia.

—the Sedco Corporation of Dallas, Texas, which does $400 million in annual sales of equipment and engineering services for offshore drilling for gas and oil, explores for oil, gas, coal, uranium and other resources, and specializes in cross-country pipeline construction in North America, Latin America, Australia, the Middle East and Africa.

Arab investors have also taken substantial portions of petroleum and energy equipment firms such as Pennzoil, Hughes Tool Company, Transco Companies, Panhandle Eastern Pipeline Company, Cooper Industries, Texas Eastern and United Energy Resources.

Suliman Olayan, according to Wall Street financial authorities, has focused a major portion of all his multibillion-dollar investments in America on "utilities and companies involved in coal and other resources." Olayan is known to own substantial chunks of Conoco,

Standard Oil of California, Standard Oil of Indiana, Mobil, the Washington Light Gas Company and others. He has also taken a strong interest in energy technology companies such as United Technologies, Westinghouse and the Thermo Electron Corporation. In 1980 Olayan, who worked as a day laborer for Mobil Oil drilling crews in the Saudi Arabian desert forty years earlier, became a director of the board of that international corporation. In Houston a corporate spokesman for Mobil explained the addition of Olayan to the board as an attempt to "pioneer new ways to get along with these governments."

In a similar move the Gulf Oil Corporation appointed Ahmed Hijazi as chief executive for Middle East Affairs, the man in charge of obtaining Gulf's crude-oil supplies from Middle Eastern governments. The Palestinian-born petroleum expert left his homeland in 1946 and went on to become an executive in the Kuwait Oil Company for twenty-five years before moving to Houston in 1977 to assume his position as a top officer in Gulf headquarters.

Ghaith Pharaon has also taken an active interest in American oil corporations and owns at least one million shares of Occidental, the oil company which is legally represented by Vinson & Elkins, John Connally's Houston law firm. Like the rest of the newly evolved petroleum firms, Occidental is not merely an "oil company." Rather, it is an energy empire reaching across the United States and the Western hemisphere, with fifty-one subsidiaries involved in everything from Alaskan oil production to Colorado oil shale, to California geothermal deposits, to Pennsylvania coal mines.

When Ghaith Pharaon began buying into Occidental, these are some of the operations of which he gained a piece:

—The Occidental Petroleum Corporation, which obtains crude oil from Libya, the North Sea fields off Great Britain, and Peru in Latin America and distributes it throughout Europe, North America and Japan. It is one of the leaders in the move to locate and develop new oil fields in Latin America and has purchased rights to oil lands in Bolivia, Colombia, Nicaragua and Trinidad. Occidental is also one of the largest domestic producers of oil and gas, with active fields in nine states and reserve fields in fourteen other states. It holds a total of sixty-six federal and state gas and oil tracts in offshore Texas and Louisiana, five federal tracts in offshore southern California and six offshore tracts in various sites throughout Alaska.

—The Occidental Oil Shale Company, which is the largest holder of federally controlled oil shale deposits in America. Its $1 billion oil shale plant in Colorado is slated to begin providing commercial quantities of oil by 1986.

—Occidental Geothermal Properties, which now owns extensive geothermal deposits in four western states, primarily Idaho and the geyser area of northern California.

—Permian Corporation, which is one of America's major crude-oil pipeline companies. Along with the tankers it owns to carry crude oil across the sea-lanes, it also operates fourteen large terminals for deepwater tanker off-loading operations at Brownsville and Corpus Christi, Texas. Its 5,400 miles of pipeline is one of the main conduits of oil transportation throughout the south, southwest and northwestern United States.

—Coal companies, including the Island Creek Coal Company, Coal Properties Company, Coal Ventures Company, Hammer Coal Company, Birch Coal Company, Bird Coal Company, Cherry River Coal and Coke Company, Gauley Coal and Coke Company and the Potomac Coal Company. Island Creek Coal is one of America's largest domestic producers of coal for home, municipal and utility use.

Middle East financial journals in 1981 reported that Muslim oil governments were shifting toward massive investments in coal fields and coal technology companies because they wanted to be "in a position to play a pivotal role in the world resurgence of coal, the only energy source currently capable of making a real dent in oil sales."[4]

North American coal fields, in fact, were among the first items of interest listed in 1974 as Arab consortiums began reaching out of the Middle East to begin their new global investment campaigns. Several Arab interests were represented by Pathlite Corporation in America that year as they sought to locate coal mines and coal fields for sale throughout the United States. Pathlite was a firm organized by former Vice President Spiro Agnew shortly after he was driven from office by the Justice Department's corruption investigation. The full details of Agnew's middleman dealings are not known, but industry authorities have indicated that Pathlite eventually lined up at least sixteen coal mines for sale in Oklahoma, Kentucky, West Virginia and Tennessee for prospective Arab buyers to consider.

In 1981 coal industry authorities confirmed that the Kuwait Foreign Trading, Contracting and Investment Company "has been buying shares in a Pennsylvania coal mining company for several years." However, because the Kuwait coal investments are being handled in secrecy by Merrill Lynch and Company's brokers, no further details of this Appalachian coal offensive are known.

Another group of Arab investors has formed Carbonnera Mining Company and has purchased a number of coal mines throughout the West. According to Mario Araktingi, a consultant for the group, the bulk of its purchases up to 1982 had occurred in Utah.

In 1974 Adnan Khashoggi bought controlling interest in the Arizona-Colorado Land and Cattle Company of Phoenix, Arizona. At the time, the firm was a major producer of cattle and agricultural products. But by 1980 the company had been totally reorganized and vastly expanded to become the AZL Resources Corporation. While it still dealt in cattle and agribusiness, the bulk of its new operations involved domestic American energy projects. In 1980 AZL bought out the Solar Petroleum Company of Denver, thus becoming a domestic American oil company. And in late 1981 AZL embarked on a joint venture with the Kuwait Petroleum Company, forming a $100 million company which set out to locate and purchase leases to oil, gas, coal, uranium and other mineral and energy rights throughout the United States.

In 1979 Adnan Khashoggi's brother, Essam Khashoggi, purchased 50 percent of the stock of the $1 billion Oasis Petroleum Corporation of Los Angeles and immediately began expanding its facilities. Khashoggi controls strings of gas stations in twenty-three western states and has opened up fifty Oasis stations in Saudi Arabia. The company has recently purchased a 30,000-ton oil tanker ship. The control of a major American retail marketing network and the access to the petroleum supplies of his homeland provide Khashoggi with the potential for a company that could undercut all competitors. The key to finishing this corporation's plan for wellhead-to-retail control is a refinery. Oasis attempted to purchase the Gulf Oil Corporation's West Coast refinery operations for $275 million but was turned down. The firm's search for suitably large American refinery facilities was continuing in the early 1980s.

At the same time, Khashoggi's Oasis is moving rapidly into the synthetic fuel business. It is building a $40 million syn-fuel plant in Louisiana that will process wastes from sugar refineries into ethanol.

Ethanol is what is used to make gasohol—the part-gasoline, part-alcohol mixture originally designed to ease the American dependence on Saudi Arabian oil.

Oasis' move toward refinery operation in the United States is only one of a growing number of similar moves by Arab investors. The Arab governments, which have spent $67 billion on building ultramodern oil refineries and petrochemical plants throughout the Middle East, continue to accelerate their purchases of older facilities throughout America and the rest of the world.

In 1980 the Arabian Seaoil Corporation, representing a consortium of Middle Eastern investors, began negotiating for the Commonwealth Oil Refining Company of Puerto Rico. Commonwealth is one of the country's largest refining complexes and turns out heating oil, jet fuel, gasoline and other petrochemical products for the American domestic market.

In May of 1981 the Kuwait Petroleum Company bought 50 percent in Hawaii's largest oil refinery—the Hawaiian Independent Refinery. Kuwait also purchased half of the refinery's parent company—Pacific Resources Corporation of Honolulu. Pacific Resources is a sprawling conglomerate which has exploration and drilling, production and processing facilities throughout the Pacific. It also has broad marketing networks throughout the Pacific and the northwestern portions of the United States. The refinery is the major supplier of jet fuel and other fuels and lubricants to the U.S. military in the eastern reaches of the Pacific.

And in southeastern Texas in 1981, Saudi and Kuwaiti investors took over at least four refineries in Corpus Christi, Port Neches, Winnie and Port Arthur along the Gulf Coast.[5] A spokesman for the American Petroleum Refiners' Association confirmed that at least four refineries had been sold to Middle Easterners. However, the exact details of those transactions are being kept confidential as part of the agreement between the refinery owners and the Arab buyers. The purchases are said to have been arranged through Arab financial organs located in Houston, the Bahamas and Switzerland.

In late 1981, in the largest takeover ever attempted in the American energy industry by Arab interests, the government of Kuwait purchased the Santa Fe International Corporation. It is one of the largest energy companies in not only the United States but in the world. Since its formation as a drilling company in 1946, Santa Fe

International has been heavily involved in all aspects of energy technology, engineering and construction. Headquartered in California, its corporate tentacles are thickly woven through the petroleum machinery matrix of Houston and, from there, stretch out around the world. The company is, for instance, a major holder of drilling leases in the new North Sea fields of Britain and is also involved in large-scale exploration and development of oil and gas deposits along the coasts of China. Its construction, engineering and oil production crews have been a mainstay of the Persian Gulf area oil operations for decades.

In the 1970s, as Arab nations began taking over all branches of the petroleum industry in the Middle East, their moves were largely governed by a general master plan laid out by the Organization of Arab Petroleum Exporting Countries (OAPEC). Throughout the decade, as the better-known, thirteen-member Organization of Petroleum Exporting Countries (OPEC) has made headlines with its price hikes, the lesser-known, nine-member OAPEC has made history with its broad corporate strategy. OAPEC is comprised of government representatives of Saudi Arabia, Kuwait, Iraq, the United Arab Emirates, Bahrain, Qatar, Libya, Syria and Algeria. In terms of the region's oil systems, OAPEC has quietly functioned as something of an invisible government, coordinating information gathering, technical services and overall strategies as various of its member governments took over their wellheads and production facilities and began systematically to reach out toward other sections of the petroleum grids.

OAPEC's methodical moves and broad planning in this area have not been comprehensively chronicled by the general American press and their extraordinary implications are not appreciated by the broad American public. That public still thinks of the Seven Sisters as rulers of the oil world when, in fact, those and the other Western petroleum firms have been severely cut back in the roles they now play in the world of oil. At the same time, under OAPEC's direction, Arab nations have been moving toward the establishment of their own global, integrated oil companies, which will take the place —and power—once held exclusively by the Western multinational oil firms. What is evolving may be similar to the Seven Sisters but more accurately referred to as the "Seven Sheikhs."

The Santa Fe International Corporation has come to play a crucial role in the first full-scale Arab attempt to set up a new, world-wide, integrated oil company on the scale of the Seven Sisters of old. That program was made by the government of Kuwait through its state oil company. The process involved the merging of Kuwait's massive oil reserves and revenues with the "skeleton" of Santa Fe's technological expertise and global reach to all portions of the world. Together they form a new entity that has wells in all major oil-producing regions of the world: exploration and drilling companies, land- and sea-rig construction companies, pipeline companies, tanker ship fleets, petrochemical-plant designing and engineering companies, refinery construction and management companies, marketing apparatuses in place on several continents and solid financial and political anchors in the petroleum capital of the world: Houston.

In 1964, when Kuwait first began moving toward increasing daily involvement with its own petroleum resources, it formed the Kuwait Drilling Company. This firm was somewhat unique: an Arab-controlled company which took charge of exploration and drilling in its own territory. The company consisted of Kuwaiti money and engineers, expertise and equipment provided by Santa Fe International Corporation. Kuwait owned 51 percent of the new Kuwait Drilling Company. Santa Fe held 49 percent of the firm. That relationship between Santa Fe International and the government of Kuwait became a wildly profitable one for both sides and led to a long and prosperous relationship that culminated in the 1981 buy-out that made Santa Fe International an integral and wholly owned part of the Kuwaiti Government.

In the mid-1970s OAPEC sought to form a regional Arab-controlled petroleum industry patterned after the drilling-company success in Kuwait. The goal was to build the organization that would allow the Arab national oil companies to control their moves outward into other, extremely complex portions of the petroleum processing, transportation and marketing matrix in the Middle East. OAPEC formed the Arab Petroleum Services Company, the firm that was to oversee the methodical expansion of Arab oil companies into world oil companies. One of the first actions taken by the Arab Petroleum Services Company in 1979 was the establishment of the Arab Drilling and Workover Company—the working arm of

OAPEC that was to take charge of exploration, drilling and production at new oil sites. That new Arab Drilling and Workover Company was owned 60 percent by OAPEC. The other 40 percent was owned by Santa Fe International, which became to OAPEC in 1979 what it had originally become to Kuwait in 1964.

By that time Santa Fe had also become a sprawling international company involved in everything from oil drilling to power plant construction to synthetic fuel projects to uranium processing.

In January of 1980, as the Kuwaiti Government was negotiating with its long-time friends in Santa Fe International for a total buy-out of the company, those same Santa Fe executives were reaching out to quietly purchase another American firm called the C. F. Braun Company for $296 million. At the time, Santa Fe issued a statement saying it was acquiring the Braun engineering firm "to complement Santa Fe's talents in assembling underwater pipelines, offshore platforms and harbor facilities."

Aside from its work on such large but relatively routine construction projects, Braun is also involved in designing, building and customizing nuclear reactors. Not only does the company build nuclear power plants, but its engineers are also heavily involved in the farther, exotic ends of the nuclear energy process. For instance, the firm is one of the handful of American firms that designs the special plutonium reprocessing facilities required by the Pentagon. Braun also revamps existing nuclear reactors, modifying them to enhance their plutonium-producing capabilities. This is also done under contract for the Pentagon.

Less than a year after Santa Fe International took over the highly specialized nuclear engineering firm, its board of directors and stockholders voted to sell out their company and all its holdings to the government of Kuwait. Kuwait was offering double the market value of all outstanding Santa Fe stock.

In December of 1981 Kuwait completed its purchase of all Santa Fe International's holdings for $2.5 billion in cash. It was the largest single investment made by Arab interests in America.

For its money the government of Kuwait got what it needed to build a multinational oil company potentially as large as Exxon. And, in the same move, the government of Kuwait also became the sole owner of the C. F. Braun Company, one of the crucial corporate components in the U.S. military's atomic programs and a firm which, according to a report by the Congressional Office of Technology Assessments, "would be of use to any nation that wishes to produce nuclear weapons."

23

"WE LOVE ARAB MONEY AS MUCH AS ANYBODY ELSE'S"

In 1982 former President Gerald R. Ford was director of a company solely owned and operated by the government of Kuwait. Perhaps no other fact so succinctly illustrates the extent of the revolution in relationships that has occurred between the Muslim world and America in the last ten years.

Ford, who joined the growing list of top U.S. government executives to leave office and become privately involved in the entrepreneurial efforts of the world's new financial powers, was a director of the board of Santa Fe International Corporation when that firm began courting a Kuwaiti takeover. When the vote came, Ford was in favor of selling the company and its nuclear weapons engineering departments to the government of Kuwait. Ford's spokesman said that his participation in the vote was affirmative but "passive."

The end result was that the former President whose administration institutionalized the extraordinary procedures which help hide the full extent of Arab investments in America now is employed by those same investors.

This is a point which has been well documented but which is not well understood by the general public: During the last ten years the White House, under four presidents, has not suffered Arab initiatives but solicited them.

Casual agreements which evolved during the Nixon administration in this regard were formalized as executive branch policy by Ford. The same measures—which offer Muslim oil nations guarantees of secrecy in return for their investments throughout America—have been adhered to by both the Carter and Reagan administrations. These policies have been part of the executive branch's quiet but vicious competition against the governments of such countries as England, France and Japan, which are also aggressively seeking to corral the largest share of the Muslim world's financial surpluses.

The exact amount of investments placed in America by various Muslim oil nations is not known and can only be estimated. Estimates provided by the U. S. Treasury and Commerce Department have been acknowledged by American, Middle Eastern and European financial authorities to be grossly distorted on the low side. This has apparently been a direct result of the presidential agreements to obscure the full details and scope of Arab financial activities in the United States. In September 1981 the Treasury Department reported that at least $62 million in OPEC investments had been made in America. That same month David T. Mizrahi, editor and publisher of the authoritative *Mideast Report,* reported that the total amount was nearly $200 billion. Such arguments are largely academic, given that sums of money ranging several tens of billions this way or that of a hundred billion are beyond the practical comprehension of most Americans.

Virtually all world financial authorities now agree that the daily flows of money between the Islamic oil world and the United States are vast to the point of having inseparably intertwined the domestic economies and daily fiscal stability of both regions. A crash of the American economy or banking system would wreak similar havoc throughout the economies of such Middle Eastern nations as Kuwait, Saudi Arabia, the United Arab Emirates and Qatar. Cataclysmic disruptions in the financial or industrial systems of those Muslim countries would, likewise, trigger a financial and industrial catastrophe across America.

In 1974 the Nixon administration first began to seek Arab investments in U.S. government securities—the various interest-bearing certificates the government sells to raise money for its daily operations. At certain times the Treasury offers a certain number of these certificates, which in the past were largely bought up by American banks, corporations and institutional investors like insurance companies. Shortly after the oil embargo, King Faisal's money managers began seeking places to reinvest the nation's new oil profits. Then-Treasury Secretary William E. Simon set up the system which provided Saudi Arabia and other Muslim oil nations with preferential treatment of their security buying requests. Those requests were so enormous that the Treasury Department soon established new facilities for issuing large numbers of securities just for the Saudis. The regular purchase of such U.S. securities became one of the staples of the Saudi Arabian Monetary Agency's (SAMA) broad investment strategies. In 1981 the U. S. Treasury Department—which has systematically underestimated all aspects of Arab investment in the U.S.—reported that the Saudis alone held $30 billion in U.S. securities. The same certificates are reported to be equally popular with Kuwaiti, Qatari and other Muslim oil government investment ministries.

As the new Arab investors were reaching out of the Middle East into the North American government securities market, they also began to reach toward those institutions which would become the vehicles for the rest of their global financial dealings: banks. In the immediate post-embargo period, Ghaith Pharaon, Adnan Khashoggi and Khalid bin Mahfouz led the Arab move into the American banking system. Pharaon teamed up with Mahfouz and John Connally in Houston to buy the Main Bank of Houston. Pharaon went on to purchase controlling interest in the Bank of the Commonwealth of Detroit and the National Bank of Georgia. He later sold his interest in the Detroit facility to Roger Tamraz, who heads an Arab investment consortium, and his interest in the Houston bank to Mahfouz.

Khalid bin Mahfouz's family owns the National Commercial Bank of Saudi Arabia—the bank which originally backed Pharaon's world ventures and which is integrally involved in every facet of Saudi Arabia's financial revolution. In Houston, when Mahfouz took control of the Main Bank, he began reorganizing it in a manner which would become typical of the Arab entrepreneurial efforts in U.S. banking circles. Mahfouz immediately expanded the mediocre bank's tiny international division. The Main Bank began receiving massive amounts of business from the Middle East. Nearly 75 percent of all that business came from a single Saudi Arabian institution: Mahfouz's National Commercial Bank. The Main Bank of Houston had been made an extension of Saudi Arabia's burgeoning and wildly profitable banking empire. The lure of such transformation began to send ripples across America's banking community, whose members actively began seeking liaisons to the Muslim world's financial systems.

However, such moves were often neither smooth in their execution nor lacking in public controversy. This is nowhere better illustrated than in San Jose, California. San Jose—which bills itself as the "Dried Prune Capital of the World"—is not a chic, trendy spot like its northern neighbor, San Francisco. Nor is it a glittery media hot spot like Los Angeles to the south. Physically, it is not even a "city" in the traditional sense of the word. Viewed from one of the mountains which surround it, San Jose is a loose cluster of farmland and suburbs which meander southward across the broad valley from the lower tip of San Francisco Bay. Carpeted with some of the most fertile soil in America, this valley has prospered on its agriculture for more than two centuries. Today San Jose is the largest frozen vegetable processing and packaging center in the country.

During the last decade large portions of farmland have been converted into unusually attractive industrial parks. Laid out like college campuses, many simulate the gardens and Spanish architecture of the sixteenth-century missions that still dot the area. But inside the graceful buildings, modern technology holds sway: The parks are fast becoming a national center for the electronics and computer software industries.

Here in an area of agribusiness empires, high-tech industrial centers, up-scale shopping malls and boutiques and hundred-year-old banks, the politics, general economy and social milieu can be summed up in six words: very solid, very conservative, very rich. Adnan Khashoggi first came to this part of California as a young man to attend Chico State College, north of San Francisco. Later, in the early 1970s, he returned and began his wide-ranging investment activities. One of his first purchases was a small bank in Walnut Creek—an ultraaffluent community on the outskirts of San Jose. There newly elected Democratic Congressman Fortney Stark sold Khashoggi majority control of the $100 million Security National

Bank, which runs five offices throughout the Alameda and Contra Costa county areas. Then Khashoggi began his move against the First National Bank of San Jose. His attempt to buy the First National was to prove unsuccessful—one of the few times Khashoggi was thwarted in what would become a multibillion-dollar buying spree in the United States. Left behind were the bankers, municipal officials and documents generated by that attempt that revealed an inside picture of the Arab entrepreneur's operational techniques.

Khashoggi's contacts began with members of the bank's board of directors interested in exploring the possibility of a link-up with the new Arab financial powers. At first, Khashoggi's approach was low-key. He arranged for a secret series of meetings with the full board of directors. He proposed that they issue 650,000 shares of new capital stock, which he would buy and which would provide him with effective control of the $300 million institution. Shortly after those meetings the first stories of the plan were leaked to the local press—by bank directors who had strong reservations about a liaison with Arab interests.

Then several things happened:

—Bank directors who had previously supported the idea in private sessions began to soften their views in the wake of a public outcry from the institution's depositors.

—Khashoggi threatened to offer greatly inflated prices for existing bank stocks and to buy up a controlling interest of the bank on his own if the directors did not go along with his original proposal for a new stock issue.

—Both bank directors and community politicians charged that Khashoggi was now trying to bludgeon his way into control of the bank.

—As part of a strong public relations campaign, Khashoggi granted an interview to a San Jose *Mercury* reporter who accompanied the Saudi across the Middle East in his private jet. After returning from that fact-finding tour, the reporter wrote in the *Mercury* that Khashoggi was "a stocky Arab with twinkling eyes" and that the Saudi Arabian had "mistakenly been identified with Arab oil money."

—More bank directors publicly broke with the Khashoggi proposal.

—Khashoggi filed suit, asking the courts to force the bank directors to go through with the original proposal, which had never been voted upon.

—Then Congressman Fortney Stark—who gave Khashoggi his original entrée into the American banking circles by selling him the National Security Bank of Walnut Creek—was forced to make the details of that transaction public, said he had made a "mistake" in selling a bank to an Arab and that he was recommending legislation to prohibit such takeovers in the future.

—Khashoggi, describing himself to reporters as a spokesman for the Arab world, theatened that if the "fanatics" who were blocking his attempt to gain control of the bank did not desist, the flow of Arab oil money into the American business community would stop.

—The bank directors asked stockholders to vote on the pending stock sales proposal, thereby avoiding having to make a decision themselves. Bank officials, who declined to make the vote public, said the response showed a "strong shareholder feeling against the transaction" and announced to Khashoggi and the press that the deal was off.

—Khashoggi charged that he had been the victim of a "Zionist-inspired wave of anti-Arab hatred."

A San Jose financial official close to the controversy explained, "The intensity of the struggle behind the scenes on that [Khashoggi] proposal was extraordinary. A lot of friendships and old comfortable business relationships were ruffled there. The lure of the money and the connections that Mr. Khashoggi represented were very tempting and evoked some very strong emotions."

In 1976, largely because of the publicity generated by the Pharaon, Mahfouz and Khashoggi bank takeovers, the issue of Arabs and the American banking system became a highly politicized one. The U. S. Treasury, Commerce Department and White House, in keeping with the confidentiality protocols instituted to attract Arab investments, declined to make public any information concerning Arab activities in banking or any other area of business throughout the country. A subcommittee of the Senate Foreign Relations Committee on Multinational Corporations made an attempt to explore the extent of Arab activity within the nation's banking system. The subcommittee prepared to subpoena records of American banks to pursue the investigation but suddenly ran into opposition from several of the large New York banks as well as the governments of Saudi Arabia and Kuwait.

Both Saudi Arabia and Kuwait informed the subcommittee that they did not want the congressional investigation to continue. The two countries threatened to immediately withdraw $7 billion in short-term deposits from American banks if the subcommittee attempted to enforce the subpoenas and force the banks to turn over the records detailing the Arab holdings in those institutions.

Senator Frank Church of Idaho and Senator Clifford Case of New Jersey were in favor of forcing the issue. They argued that the Congress had a right to know how much of the country's banking system was controlled by Muslim governments. Senator Charles Percy of Illinois and Senator Stuart Symington of Missouri were in favor of ending the investigation without forcing the issue. Percy explained, "It is simply not worth the risk."

The fifth member of the five-man subcommittee, Senator Richard Clark of Iowa, remained neutral. He said he was too new to the subcommittee to take a stand on the issue. The investigation of Arab holdings in American banks halted.

The vote to close off the investigation of Arab banking activities was one of the last made by subcommittee member Symington. Later in 1976, after twenty-four years in the Senate, Symington retired. He was one of Washington's venerables, having begun his career as Secretary of the Air Force in the Truman administration and gone on to become a senator and member of both the Armed Services and Foreign Relations committees.

Immediately upon leaving the Senate, Symington went into private legal practice in the capital. He became counsel for an Arab investment consortium which was in the process of trying to purchase one of the nation's largest banking companies, the $2.4 billion Financial General Bankshares Corporation.

Arab investors have made extraordinary inroads into America's banking community during the last decade with the aid of such advisers as Symington, Connally and other former government officials previously charged with overseeing the banking industry. By 1982 Middle Eastern bankers had become a major influence at every level of the nation's banking community through massive deposits, through purchases of bank stock and through the outright purchases of banks from Florida to California. According to government and industry reports, Arab individuals and consortiums now own the First National Bank of Miami and the Caribbean National Bank of Coral Gables, Florida; the National Bank of Georgia; the Du Quoin State Bank of Du Quoin, Illinois; the Bank of the Commonwealth of Detroit, Michigan; the Great Western Bank and Trust Company of Phoenix, Arizona; the Alamosa National Bank of Alamosa, Colorado; the Western Bank, the Main Bank and the People's Bank of Houston, Texas, and the Security National Bank of Walnut Creek, California.

In addition Arab investors have bought up large blocks of stock in banks, establishing part ownership of those institutions. Suliman Olayan, for instance, is the second-largest stockholder in the Chase Manhattan Bank—only David Rockefeller holds a larger interest. Olayan and Saudi Prince Khaled bin Abdullah al Saud together own 7.6 percent of the First Chicago Corporation, also one of the largest banks in the country. Industry and government reports also indicate that Arab investors have purchased large blocks of stock in such other banks as Manufacturers Hanover Corporation and Bankers Trust Corporation of New York; Mellon National Corporation and the National Bank of Pittsburgh, Pennsylvania; the South Carolina National Bank; the Wachovia Corporation of North Carolina; the First Alabama Bancshares Corporation; the First Bank System of Minneapolis, Minnesota; the Continental Illinois Corporation of Chicago; First International Bancshares Corporation of Dallas, Texas; First New Mexico Bancshares Corporation; First Oklahoma Bancshares Corporation, and the BankAmerica Corporation of San Francisco.

And in the final years of the 1970s a new dimension of Arab banking activities in the United States began as banks of the Middle East began reaching out to establish their own operations in North America. The first to open was the UBAF Arab-American Bank in New York City. Then came the Abu Dhabi International Bank in Washington, D.C. By 1981 the Arab-African International Bank, Transarabian Investment Bank, Bank of Credit and Commerce International and the Saudi International Bank had also opened American offices. In 1982 banking authorities reported that the Arab Banking Corporation, Banque Arabe et Internationale d'Investissement and the National Commercial Bank of Saudi Arabia were preparing to open offices in the United States. Early indications are that such Middle Eastern banking operations have little difficulty attracting customers in the American market. In fact some of the nation's largest corporations have begun using institutions such as the Saudi Arabian Monetary Agency as a major source of operating capital. SAMA, for instance, has recently lent $650 million to AT&T, $300 million to IBM and $200 million to U.S. Steel.

For the first few years of the post-embargo era, banks, banking and passive investments such as government securities remained the focus of most individual and institutional Arab investors in America. But by the late 1970s they were diversifying into all levels of the economy. One area drawing large amounts of Arab interest was the domestic oil and energy industry. Operating out of Houston, Arab consortiums and government investment agencies took over or became partners in a large number of companies involved in oil, gas, coal and other energy resource enterprises.

Beyond energy projects, Middle Easterners also evidenced a growing interest in real estate and commercial development, the bulk of which holdings are not reported. But those transactions which have left a public trail indicate that in less than a decade Arab entrepreneurs have become an integral part of urban America's physical and financial landscapes. Frequently they purchased failing hotels, office complexes and shopping centers and, with massive recapitalization, turned those ventures into revenue producers. In other cases Arab consortiums—often working through their American architectural and construction firms—have erected some of the most visually striking and commercially successful business and office developments in several major American cities.

Middle Eastern groups have purchased at least twenty major office and residential complexes in Boston, as well as the nearby Holyoke Shopping Center. A consortium of Kuwaiti and Pakistani investors are reported to have purchased the Buckyarns yarn mill in New Hampshire. In Vermont, in an unusually ambitious project, Arab industrialist Saad Gabr has purchased the Space Research Corporation. Located in both Canada and Vermont, the science facility has developed a process which employs a giant, cannonlike launcher to blast communications satellites into orbit.

In Manhattan, Adnan Khashoggi purchased the forty-sixth and forty-seventh floors of the posh Olympic Tower on Fifth Avenue.

The $3 million living quarters even has its own swimming pool. Khashoggi's is only one of a wave of such purchases in a city where *Newsweek* magazine reported "the new condominium market is largely being driven by Arab cash." Suliman Olayan has taken over much of the building that formerly served as Aramco's headquarters on Park Avenue. One Broadway is the site of a $12 million building owned by Libya's government. The landmark Warner Building at 75 Rockefeller Plaza is owned by Qatari investors Abdu and Mohammed al Fayed. Not far away, in northern New Jersey, Saudi Arabian investors own the Whalite Manufacturing Company, Pyah Industries and Boonton Moulding Corporation, all plastics firms located north of Princeton. At the southern end of New Jersey, in the new gambling and entertainment hub of Atlantic City, a Saudi firm is reported to be a partner in the proposed Camelot Casino and Hotel. Dal Vera Contract and Engineering, which is owned by Saudis, is said to have offered up to $70 million in financing and construction services for the off-Boardwalk development project.

In Baltimore the double skyscrapers which house the Hilton Hotel and serve as the centerpiece of that city's much-heralded urban renewal and harbor-front development efforts are owned by a consortium headed by a member of Kuwait's royal family. The Baltimore hotel complex was only the latest such venture for the Arab group, which also has Sheratons and Marriotts in Kuwait, Saudi Arabia, Sudan and Egypt.

Nearby, in metropolitan Washington, D.C., another Arab group has taken over the Highland Towers apartment and hotel complex. Elsewhere in the capital, the Kuwait Investment Office purchased the Columbia Plaza Office on Virginia Avenue and became landlord to the U. S. General Services Administration. Across the Potomac in the fashionable Old Town section of Alexandria, Kuwaitis purchased the four-story United Way complex for $6.5 million. Beyond the shores of the Potomac, in the famed rolling hills of Virginia, the Vanguard Corporation—an Arab company headquartered in the Caribbean—purchased the sprawling $6 million Beacon Hill estate of former TV personality Arthur Godfrey as well as an adjoining cattle farm.

Down the coast, in North Carolina, the government of Kuwait has bought a 30 percent interest in the Korf Steel Company in Charlotte. Hilton Hotels in Raleigh and Greensboro are owned by an Iraqi investor. In South Carolina, Kuwait has purchased and developed Kiawah and Johns islands as major new resort centers. Kiawah, a sprawling, genteel retreat of luxurious rental villas, tennis courts, golf courses, nature trails, stately restaurants and lushly landscaped seafront gardens, has been wildly successful and a magnet for other development along the shore. In the late 1970s the government of Kuwait purchased the isolated but hauntingly beautiful Kiawah for $17.5 million; by 1981 the investment had generated more than $200 million in revenues.

In Atlanta, Georgia, Arab businessmen have also become a major, although low-key, presence. However, in the wake of the controversies involving both Bert Lance and Billy Carter during the Carter administration, Arab groups take special care to conduct business beyond the view of the press or public recordings systems. Their most visible property in downtown Atlanta is the Atlanta Hilton Hotel and the nearby Atlanta Center commercial complex, both owned by Kuwaiti interests. Other Arab firms have taken over substantial portions of Peachtree Center, the soaring, ultramodern cluster of skyscrapers which now form the centerpiece of rejuvenated Atlanta. Hanoon Investment Company—a Netherlands firm which is owned by Saudi Arabians—purchased Shakerag Farms, a 1,660-acre site outside the city for a large commercial and residential development. Another Arab consortium purchased another 565 acres of lakefront property outside the city and is known to have been negotiating for 3,000 more acres of ground in the surrounding bucolic hill country. At the 565-acre site in Henry County, the consortium cut up the parcel into eighty-four lots for large, estatelike residential development. Atlanta authorities reported that fifty of the estate sites "sold immediately" to foreign buyers planning baronial homes.

Florida has been a major center for Arab investments. In the late 1970s southern Florida business groups began imitating Houston and aggressively seeking to attract Middle Eastern investments and business ventures. L. W. Llewellyn, executive director of the Economic Development Group of the Greater Miami Chamber of Commerce, explained to reporters in 1979 that "We love Arab money as much as anybody else's." Real estate authorities in and around Dade County indicate that Arab purchases in the region have been "frenzied" but almost invisible. For one thing, realtors and sellers have been more than willing to accommodate the Arab consortiums' requests for confidentiality. For another, the heavy traffic between southern Florida and the Caribbean facilitates easy access for Arab groups seeking to make large Florida purchases from behind financial blinds in the islands. One of the most expensive residential sales —at $160 per square foot—in the area was made in Coral Gables by Mohammed Bedrawi, a Saudi businessman who bought a five-bedroom house for $1.2 million. One Biscayne Tower—a landmark steel and glass monolith in Miami—was purchased by the Jameel family of Saudi Arabia for $49 million. The Jameels have wide holdings across the country and specialize in developing business and commercial properties. Wagdi Tahlawi, the former head of the Saudi Arabian arms-purchasing mission in France, in 1980 purchased the grand old Eden Roc Hotel from Samuel Cohen in Miami Beach. Another Saudi group owns the Cone Cattle Ranch in Florida, and other Arab groups are said to have purchased substantial holdings in apartments and hotels and commercial ventures from Orlando to the Keys.

Midway across America, at the heart of downtown Chicago, construction crews in 1982 were preparing to erect a $200 million complex of offices, department stores, restaurants and condominiums for Jaymont Properties Corporation—owned by the Jameel family of Saudi Arabia. Just beyond the city limits, the Jameels are also raising a four-hundred-room hotel, the first part of a three-hundred-acre office and industrial complex. At the other end of Illinois, where the lower tip of the state stabs south into Missouri and Kentucky, is the Du Quoin State Fairgrounds, one of the world's largest, fastest and most renowned horse-racing facilities. It is now owned by Saad Jabr, an Iraqi investor. Until recently the 1,400-acre site was annual host to the Hamiltonian and is currently host to the $500,000-purse World Trotter Derby each fall. It also boasts a large amusement park and the grounds on which the farm region's annual livestock and agricultural fairs are held. Jabr is a former executive of the Iraq Petroleum Company and a consultant for several Arab banks who received his master's degree in business management from Southern Illinois University.

Beyond Illinois, west of the Mississippi, Arab groups have made similarly large and diverse investments. Texas, where the central Galleria complex of Houston and the central Plaza of the Americas complex of Dallas are owned by Arabs, has been the site of their most visible ventures. But reaching out from there they have taken up large blocks of properties and businesses throughout the region. In Colorado, Arab consortiums own the Coe, VanLoo and Jaschke Engineering Corporation of Lakewood, the Baca Grande Land Development Company of Saguache and the Farmhand Corporation, a cattle company of Greeley. Arizona became one of the first sites of major Arab interest in the early 1970s when Adnan Khashoggi scooped up the 155,000-acre Arizona-Colorado Land & Cattle Company, which he then expanded into a major oil, gas and coal exploration and development operation. Arab financial activities in the Arizona capital, Phoenix, are reported by real estate authorities to be "extensive but discreet." One of the most unusual Arizona purchases was made by a Saudi Arabian consortium that bought Switzer Mesa, a large mountain that is topped by a city-sized plateau. Located a mile south of Flagstaff, the mesa is one of the area's geographical landmarks. Phoenix and Flagstaff, like many of the major cities of Texas, Louisiana, Oklahoma, New Mexico and sixteen other states as far east as Ohio, boast La Quinta Motor Inns. La Quinta ("Country Home") is one of the fastest-growing motel chains in the nation and is owned by Saudi, Kuwaiti and United Arab Emirate interests.

In Salt Lake City, Utah, the South Arabian Investors Group of Saudi Arabia owns Deseret Plaza, the cloud-piercing cluster of red brick and glass office and bank buildings at the center of town. Adnan Khashoggi owns the Salt Lake International Center, a 740-acre industrial park and office complex not far away.

In Nevada the Landmark Hotel and Casino—one of the major establishments along Las Vegas' neon canyon—is owned by Kuwaitis.

Southern California has also experienced an inflow of Middle Eastern money. Aside from the well-publicized activities of Adnan Khashoggi throughout the lower half of the state, the region has also become the major haven for waves of Iranian businessmen who fled the Middle East in the wake of the economic disruptions caused by the fall of the Shah and the rise of the Ayatollah. Sections of Los Angeles have become, according to local realtors, "like little Teherans." Kuwaitis and Saudi Arabians are also very active in the area. Hollywood's Superior National Insurance Company, for instance, is owned by the Al Sabah family. The Al Sabahs are to Kuwait what the Al Sauds are to Saudi Arabia. Superior was formed in 1980 and specializes in providing insurance coverage to restaurants, hotels, office buildings, factories and construction contractors. Its rapid move into the lucrative California market was guided by Russell Katieb, a former official of the California Insurance Department who left to become president of the Kuwaitis' venture. Arab investors have also entered several other fields beyond banking and insurance here. Roger Tamraz, who is an agent for several Arab investment consortiums, recently spent $57 million to purchase 17 percent interest in the Kaiser Steel Corporation of Oakland. Kaiser is the ninth-largest steel firm in the country. Holstein Industries, a large construction contracting company of Costa Mesa, has been purchased by a Saudi group. And local authorities from San Francisco to San Diego indicate that various cattle ranches, downtown office complexes, residential real estate developments and agricultural technology firms throughout the area have been bought by Arab interests operating from behind corporate tangles designed to obscure the owners' identities.

In 1978 the Civil Aeronautics Board first confirmed that Arab investors were buying up stock in major American airlines. By 1982 individuals, business groups and government agencies of such nations as Kuwait, Saudi Arabia and the United Arab Emirates had amassed huge holdings in Eastern Airlines, TransWorld Airlines, United Airlines, Seaboard World Airlines, USAir and Airborne Freight Corporation. Arab investors also have large blocks of stock in corporations that design and manufacture both civilian and military aircraft such as Cessna Aircraft, General Dynamics, McDonnell Douglas and Boeing. In many cases Muslim oil nations invest in the same companies to which they are letting enormous contracts. In this manner the Arab governments obtain the industrial goods they need at home while they share in the profits made by the American company that performs the work. For instance, there are substantial Arab holdings of Litton Industries stock. Those stock purchases began in the late 1970s at the same time Litton was receiving large contracts from Saudi Arabia for the installation of airport flight-control systems throughout the country. In 1979 Litton also received a $1.6 billion contract to design and install a countrywide air defense system for Saudi Arabia and received other military and civilian orders from the Middle East. The double-ended arrangement benefits the corporation as well as the Arab investors. The company, at one end, gets new infusions of investment capital with which to expand and grow while, at the other end, it receives the orders which make that expansion profitable.

The Arab world, which is one of the largest markets in the world for industrial tools of every type, has also invested heavily in the stock of U.S. companies that manufacture and export industrial tools and machinery such as Black & Decker, Allis-Chalmers, Caterpillar Tractor Company, John Deere & Company, General Electric and Ingersoll Rand.

The Middle East has also evolved during the last decade as the largest single new market for packaged foods of all sorts, importing them by the shiploads. Arab investors have also purchased large amounts of stock in such firms as Beatrice Foods, General Mills, Nabisco, Pepsi-Cola, R.J. Reynolds, Standard Brands and the Carnation Corporation.

Arab investors have also taken up large holdings in U.S. chemical corporations such as DuPont, Rohm & Haas, and Dow; computer companies such as Hewlett-Packard, Texas Instruments, Apple, Control Data, IBM and Honeywell; department-store chains such as K-Mart, J.C. Penney and Woolworth's, and other corporations which are household words such as Eastman Kodak, Colgate-Palmolive, Procter & Gamble and Burlington Industries. In late 1981 Arab investors were reported to hold more than $46 million in the stock of the McDonald's Corporation—that ubiquitous institution that has made the hamburger a staple of daily American life.

The ultimate meaning of such vast patterns of foreign investment in the United States is not clear and has been reported by various authorities to mean several different things.

In the latter half of 1981, for instance, the subject of Arab financial activities once again surfaced as a major topic in the general American press. At that time a new round of disclosures by Middle Eastern financial experts, Wall Street authorities and U.S. government agencies confirmed that the amount of money flowing into the country from Muslim oil nations was continuing to increase at an astronomical rate. Government reports also confirmed that Presidents Ford, Carter and Reagan had aggressively sought to attract further

Arab investments and, as part of that effort, had assured Muslim governments that the details of their investments would not be publicly revealed.

Four of America's most widely read and respected periodicals—the New York *Times, Time* magazine, *Forbes* and *Newsweek*—were among those informing the public of these events. Each publication, however, handled the same material in a somewhat different manner. A comparison of the four indicates that the editors who control the public's sense of reality about Arabs have wildly divergent views on the subject.

Each publication presented the following excerpt as a factual news report:

The New York *Times:* "Many members of Congress and Federal officials are becoming increasingly fearful that the concealed acquisition of largely unknown and unidentified investments may be seriously detrimental to the American national interest, leaving the country's economy vulnerable to adverse influence by Arab interests."[1]

Time: "Less orthodox in their Islamic observance than the Saudis, the Kuwaitis also have a more relaxed and open attitude toward banking and financing. Sniffing out a deal is in their blood. . . . The Saudi Arabian Monetary Agency's (SAMA) vast holdings of dollars, German marks and Japanese yen are a worrisome wild card in money markets from New York to Tokyo. Adding to SAMA's menacing aura is its abiding secrecy."[2]

Forbes: "A year ago *Forbes* found U. S. Treasury and Wall Street officials alike rejoicing because OPEC's money men were putting ever more of their 300 billion surplus dollars into American securities. If the money changers were happy in 1980, they should be dancing today. OPEC's sheikhs have continued to pour dollars into the U.S. at an accelerating pace."[3]

Newsweek: "The flood of Middle Eastern capital into U.S. investment havens is rising steadily—and dramatically. For the most part, the latest round of OPEC investments in the United States has been welcomed by Americans. On balance, most experts think the current wave of Arab investment is good for both sides."[4]

24

ATOMIC SWORDS AND THE FUTURE OF THE WORLD

During the last decade, as they have been rising to positions of economic power in America, Arab groups have made concerted efforts to use their growing domestic political influence in connection with only two issues: the plight of the Palestinians and the hotly contested sale of U.S. military equipment to Saudi Arabia.

The F-15 vote of 1978 and the AWACS vote of 1981, which confirmed the Arab lobby's clout and provided Saudi Arabia with the components of a regional, space-age war machine, also dealt a critical blow to two of the three remaining pillars on which Israel has based its existence for three decades: exclusive hold on the domestic American political process and exclusive access to America's most advanced military technology. The F-15 and AWACS votes also ultimately brought Israel's third and last pillar of power into sharper focus: the atomic bomb.

Since its introduction of nuclear weapons into the Middle East conflict in 1973, Israel has pressed forward in bomb production as well as bomb delivery systems.[1] In the wake of the war and the oil embargo it caused, Israeli officials who had previously been circumspect about the nuclear arsenal in the Negev spoke openly about its weapons and their willingness to use them against Muslim population centers.

In 1974 Israeli Premier Yitzhak Rabin warned in a television interview that Israel's arsenal could inflict "ten times more destruction on Arab cities" than Arabs could inflict upon Israel.

Israeli President Ephraim Katzir in 1974 met with reporters of *New Scientist* and other scientific journals and confirmed that Israel's bombs were "in the twenty-kiloton range." Katzir indicated that the nuclear threat to incinerate whole sections of the Middle East was being used against the United States to ensure that Washington "doesn't desert Israel morally and diplomatically under any future pressure from Middle East oil exporting countries."

Simultaneously, at the end of 1974, the U. S. Central Intelligence Agency prepared a top-secret memorandum reporting that the Israeli Government was continuing to make a "large investment in a costly missile system designed to accommodate nuclear warheads." The Israeli Government in 1975 also requested that the United States supply it with Lance missiles, which are designed primarily as short-range nuclear delivery systems, and Pershing missiles. The Pershing is one of America's larger atomic weapons vehicles for theater warfare. It has a range of 450 miles and would allow Israel to strike the Aswan Dam with a nuclear bomb—loosing a flood that would obliterate all Egyptian civilization, which is congested in a tight band along the flood plain of the Nile River. The Pentagon balked at supplying Pershings to Israel. Israel has received Lance missiles, which have a range of seventy miles.

Israel has also been working to greatly enhance the efficiency of its enriched-uranium- and plutonium-producing capacity, the process by which the core material of atomic bombs is made. Scientific journals report that the Israeli Ministry of Defense is the leading pioneer in using new laser and chemical methods for enriching uranium isotopes. In an investigative documentary prepared in 1980 and broadcast in mid-1981, ABC-TV reported that Israel, which had thirteen bombs in 1973, had increased its arsenal to at least twenty-seven atomic bombs.

In 1976 Israel and the apartheid government of South Africa began cooperative nuclear weapons development efforts. South Africa, whose government faces the same problem with native blacks that Israel faces with native Palestinians, has been reported by various intelligence agencies to have a full-scale atomic weapons program which can provide it with the only tools capable of holding back an entire continent of Africans. The nature of the Israeli-South African atomic weapons alliance has been reported to be so extensive that it even involves a top-secret nuclear submarine construction project at Simonstown, the sprawling Indian Ocean naval base near Cape Town, South Africa.

In 1980 further details of that alliance became public when Walter Cronkite of CBS-TV reported, "CBS News has learned that Israel exploded a nuclear bomb last September in the Atlantic Ocean off the coast of South Africa. Informed sources confirmed that this was an Israeli nuclear test conducted with the help and cooperation of the South African Government."

And at the same time the Israelis have been forging ahead on atomic weapons testing and stockpiling, they have been accelerating the clandestine war aimed at thwarting the Muslim world's atomic development programs. Exclusive possession of nuclear bombs and the threat to use them against Muslim population centers and oil fields have now become Israel's last remaining levers of influence in international diplomatic circles.

In 1979, in an article on the underground activities of Israel's Mossad, *Parade* magazine reported that the nuclear programs and personnel of Muslim states had become the prime targets of the Israeli secret service and that "Mossad agents are determined to maintain Israel's nuclear superiority in the Middle East and to prevent the development in Islamic countries of any nuclear weaponry."[2]

Israeli Defense Minister Ariel Sharon has also publicly proclaimed that Israel will not permit any Muslim country "to produce or possess" atomic weapons and vowed that those which attempted to do so would be attacked.

In 1978 British officials confirmed that Israeli agents were the primary suppliers of intelligence about the front companies being used by Pakistan and Libya to obtain nuclear designs and equipment in Europe. Such disclosures resulted in publicity and government action that halted some planned equipment shipments.

That same year Iraqi nuclear personnel began to experience increasing difficulties as they traveled through Europe. Dr. Yahya Meshed was attacked by "unidentified" and unsuccessful assassins in late 1978 as he attended to business in Paris. An Egyptian, Dr.

Meshed was the Arab world's most renowned nuclear physicist. He had studied in the Soviet Union and was a specialist in nuclear reactor technology and design. After joining the Iraqi atomic programs in the early 1970s he became the chief executive overseeing the transfer of technology and parts from France to the Baghdad reactor construction site. In June 1980 he was arranging for the shipment of the first load of enriched uranium from France to Iraq when a second attempt was made on his life by "unknown assailants." The physicist was found on the floor of his hotel room, his skull crushed in by a blunt object. French police investigations established that a prostitute, Marie Claude Magal, was a key witness to events which led up to Dr. Meshed's murder. However, she, too, died when "unknown assailants" ran her down with a car in a Paris street.

Not long afterward another Iraqi nuclear scientist, Salman al Lami was attending to government business in Switzerland when he died suddenly. Authorities found that he had been poisoned by "unknown assailants."

In April 1979 several of the large, crucial parts of the French reactor being readied for shipment to Baghdad were stored in a warehouse at the port city of La Seyne-sur-Mer, just east of Marseilles. Three men arrived in a small boat, climbed three barbed-wire barriers, used keys to enter the guarded warehouse, shut off the electronic alarm systems and immediately singled out those crates containing the Iraqi nuclear parts. Seven charges of military explosives were attached to the items. The resultant explosion destroyed the equipment and delayed Iraqi's reactor construction by eighteen months. French police immediately focused their probe on an Israeli ship which had moored nearby the night before the attack. The investigators reported that the "unknown assailants" had been a commando squad of Mossad operatives.

Some months later, and with similar surgical precision, "unknown assailants" blew out the front of the Roman office building of SNIA Techint, one of the smaller companies providing various equipment and services to the Iraqi nuclear project.

In September 1980 the Baghdad reactor was nearing completion at the same time Iraq was involved in a border war with the Iranian regime of the Ayatollah Khomeini. The fighting was largely confined to the region around the Shatt-al-Arab waterway at the head of the Persian Gulf. On September 30 two Phantom jets of the sort supplied by the U.S. to both Iran and Israel attacked the reactor with rockets. South of the city the two planes also attacked a power station, killing eleven persons and injuring more than eighty. Witnesses said the two planes had Iranian markings. Iran, which was then claiming credit for attacks throughout the lower war zone, denied any of its planes had attacked the reactor site or the Baghdad power plant providing energy to that construction site. The damage done to the reactor site was minor and delayed work only three months.

In April of 1981, in an incident whose details have never been explained by Iraqi officials, a band of "unidentified men" were captured as they attempted to break into the reactor area.

In June of 1981, according to *The Sunday Times* of London, Israeli agents disguised as French nuclear technicians entered the site and planted explosives in the lower reaches of the labyrinthine structure. Shortly after that an Israeli invasion force of six F-15s and eight F-16s screamed across the reactor releasing waves of bombs. The extraordinary precision of the bombs and the manner in which they struck the facility indicated they were "smart bombs," developed by the United States for knocking out fortifications in Vietnam and supplied by the hundreds of thousands to Israel during the 1970s. The aerial bombardment destroyed the upper levels of the massive concrete construction, while the planted explosives devastated the lower levels, reducing the entire complex to rubble. Several delayed-action bombs—devices designed to lie in the rubble and explode when touched by workmen—were dropped into the debris.

Immediately after the bombing the French and Italian governments announced that they would rebuild the Iraqi facility and that the new design would incorporate heavy antiaircraft fortifications as well as underground constructions safe from bomb attacks.

While the reactor bombing did temporarily halt Iraq's potential for producing plutonium, it did not alter the country's ability to continue gathering enriched uranium—an equally potent bomb material —from around the world. Nor did the Israeli strike halt the construction of the Soviet reactor and nuclear research center being erected in Islamabad. Ironically, the same Israeli action which sought to thwart Muslim atomic development may have unwittingly provided the pivot for new levels of regional cooperation and sharing of nuclear technology by Islamic countries.

Ten days after the Israeli planes returned to base—and on the same day the United States led the United Nations in a vote condemning the Israeli invasion of Iraq—other, less-publicized fleets of airplanes were landing just outside Damascus, Syria. There entourages of military, industrial and scientific authorities arrived with government officials from eleven Arab states to open the first Arab Nuclear Conference. The four-day proceeding was aimed at establishing a regional network supporting the simultaneous development of nuclear facilities in several Muslim Middle Eastern nations. The conference was sponsored by the Organization of Arab Petroleum Exporting Countries, the agency which guided the Arab takeover of the oil fields, the Arab Organization for Mineral Resources, the agency overseeing the development of uranium prospecting and mining facilities throughout the Middle East, and the Arab Fund for Economic and Social Development, the agency providing the funds and financial guidance for many of the vast industrial projects being raised across the Middle East.

This meeting, although hardly mentioned in the Western media, triggered widespread debate throughout the Muslim press concerning the question of full-scale regional nuclear development.

The Islamic Review, the voice of the Organization of the Islamic Conference headquartered in Mecca, wrote:

"Interviews with Pakistani scientists amply demonstrate that there are no technical barriers to [building] the bomb. . . . Even so, the nuclear option is not an easy one. The Israeli raid on Iraq's nuclear reactor illustrates that setbacks will occur and the Muslim countries concerned must be prepared to bear the significant economic and political costs. . . . The Organization of the Islamic Conference could play a central role in ensuring that a coordinated nuclear strategy be developed which takes into account the vulnerability of individual countries, selects appropriate sites for the development of technology, makes suitable arrangements for a wide regional distribution of the weapons and establishes an inter-governmental supervisory and coordinating machine to ensure that no country—or group of countries—has the ability to unilaterally exercise the nuclear option."

By the end of 1981 top intelligence sources in both the United States and Asia confirmed that, forty miles east of the Afghanistan border, Pakistan construction crews were digging a large, horizontal tunnel into the Baluchistan Mountains—site for an underground atomic test. At the same time, Pakistan was negotiating with Chinese officials for the possible use of an isolated tract in the vast northwest desert provinces as a test site. In December 1981 the U. S. Central Intelligence Agency issued "Special National Intelligence Estimate 31-81" indicating that Pakistan will be able to detonate a bomb and proceed in mass-producing other bombs "within the next three years."

As Pakistan continued into the final phases of its project in 1982, *The Sunday Times* of London indicated that the Saudis agreed to provide $800 million in additional funding for the undertaking. The Saudis had also agreed to fund the rebuilding of Iraq's destroyed reactor and, through the Islamic organizations in Mecca, were leading the movement fostering broad Muslim cooperation in atomic ventures. This at the same time Arab entrepreneurs around the world were purchasing large industrial conglomerates—such as the Santa Fe International Corporation—which have the engineering capacity and experience for undertaking the most complex nuclear projects.

At the same time, Saudi Arabia had begun another, separate series of programs aimed at developing its own nuclear capabilities. In 1979 the Saudi Government established an Atomic Energy Center and began laying the administrative and technical groundwork to support an independent nuclear industry. The Saudis contracted with both French and American firms for exploration projects surveying the Arabian Peninsula's uranium deposits. By 1981 they had signed an atomic cooperation pact with England and launched the first $200 million phase of Lab Zero—the new atomic research facility and reactor complex being constructed at King Abdul-Aziz University. The Saudis also formed Science Transfer Associates—the new global enterprise which hires the European, American and Asian technical experts required to design, build and operate the complicated atomic center. The Italian firm La Società Italiana Costruzione & Montaggi has also been awarded a $95 million contract to build a nuclear reactor on the Red Sea coast. Another is to be built on the Persian Gulf.

And in another program begun in late 1979 the Saudi Defense Ministry contracted with the Defense Ministry of England for the design and construction of a kingdom-wide system of radioactivity decontamination stations and bomb shelters built to withstand the force of medium-sized nuclear bombs. While such shelters may save large numbers of Saudi royal family members, government officials and military personnel during the limited atomic war they anticipate, they will do nothing to prevent total destruction of the oil fields of the region. Oil industry experts have indicated that the nature of oil fields—and particularly the interconnected oil fields of the Persian Gulf—makes them particularly vulnerable to even the smallest atomic weapons. It has been estimated that a single atomic explosion would devastate most of the fields and leave the remaining oil unusable because of radioactivity.

This was one of the considerations—beyond basic compassion for millions of Muslim civilians—that motivated the world's extraordinary efforts in 1973 to deter Israel from using its prepared atomic weapons. A single blast, which would incinerate a city such as Cairo or Riyadh, could also destroy the entire industrialized world's oil supplies.

And so, in the 1980s, this is where the future of both the Middle East and the United States has come to pivot: here amid the oil derricks and the bomb shelters buried beneath the sands, decorated with Islamic motifs and decontamination instructions and each oriented, like mosques toward Mecca, toward that distant complex of tunnels in the Negev. There the tools of a nuclear Masada await only the final turn of a screwdriver and the orders of the leaders of an increasingly unstable island of Eurocentric civilization which for nearly four decades has strained relentlessly toward the far borders of Eretz Ysrael—that ancient biblical kingdom which conquered from the Red Sea to the Euphrates and completed its empire by enveloping Jerusalem and erecting a temple atop that city's central mount.

BIBLIOGRAPHY

This section has five parts: periodicals, government documents, special publications, books and other reference works.

PERIODICALS

Research for this project extensively employed the computerized periodical indexes of the New York Times Information Bank, the INFORM computerized information system of Philadelphia Newspapers Incorporated and the Dialog data bases of the Lockheed Corporation. More than 4,600 reports from newspapers, magazines and journals of Asia, Europe and North America were used to compile the chronologies of events in the post-World War II portions of the manuscript.

Included in the primary periodical sources were:

The New York *Times*
The Washington *Post*
The Atlanta *Constitution*
The Los Angeles *Times*
The San Jose *Mercury*
The Miami *Herald*
The Philadelphia *Inquirer*
The Philadelphia *Daily News*
The Chicago *Tribune*
The Houston *Chronicle*
The Wall Street Journal
Time
The *World Business Weekly* of the *Financial Times*
The Economist
The Middle East Economic Digest
The Middle East

8 Days
The Gulf Weekly Mirror
The Kuwait *Times*
The *Saudi Gazette*
The Jerusalem *Post*

U. S. GOVERNMENT PUBLICATIONS

Committee on Energy and Natural Resources of the U. S. Senate, report, *The Geopolitics of Oil,* November 1980.

Subcommittee on Reports, Accounting and Management of the Committee on Government Operations of the U. S. Senate, report, *Corporate Ownership and Control,* November 1975.

Subcommittee on Intergovernmental Relations and Budgeting, Management and Expenditures of the Committee of Government Operations of the U. S. Senate, report, *Disclosure of Corporate Ownership,* March 1974.

Committee on Foreign Relations of the U. S. Senate, a Staff Report, *The Proposed AWACS/F-15 Enhancement Sale to Saudi Arabia,* September 1981.

Committee on Foreign Relations of the U. S. Senate, hearings, *The Israeli Air Strike and Related Issues,* June 18, 19, 25, 1981.

Committee on Armed Services of the U. S. Senate, hearings, *Military and Technical Implications of the Proposed Sale to Saudi Arabia of Airborne Warning and Control Systems and F-15 Enhancements,* September 28, 30, 1981.

Committee on Armed Services of the U. S. Senate, report, *Military and Technical Implications of the Proposed Sale of Air Defense Enhancements to Saudi Arabia,* October 22, 1981.

Subcommittee on Energy of the Joint Economic Committee of the U. S. Congress, hearings, *Multinational Oil Companies and OPEC: Implications for U. S. Policy,* June 2, 3, 8, 1976.

Committee on Government Operations of the U. S. House of Representatives, report, *The Adequacy of the Federal Response to Foreign Investment in the United States,* August 1, 1980.

Investigations Subcommittee of the Committee on Armed Services of the U. S. House of Representatives, report, *Department of Defense Petroleum Requirements and Supplies,* June 10, 1980.

Subcommittees on International Security and Scientific Affairs on Europe and the Middle East and on International Economic Policy and Trade of the Committee on Foreign Affairs of the U. S. House of Representatives, hearings, *Israeli Attack on Iraqi Nuclear Facilities,* June 17, 25, 1981.

Subcommittee on Oversight of the Permanent Select Committee on Intelligence of the House of Representatives, report, *Intelligence on the World Energy Future,* December 1979.

Subcommittee on Government Operations of the U. S. House of Representatives, hearings, *The Operations of Federal Agencies in Monitoring, Reporting On, and Analyzing Foreign Investments in the United States:*

    Part 1, September 19, 20, 21, 1978.

    Part 2, July 16, 17, 18, 26, 1979.

    Part 3, July 30, 1979.

    Part 4, July 31, August 1, 1979.

Subcommittee on International Trade and Commerce of the Committee on International Relations of the U. S. House of Representatives, hearings, *Discriminatory Arab Pressure on U. S. Business,* March 6, 12, 13, December 11, 1975.

Special Subcommittee on Investigations of the Committee on International Relations, a report, *Oil Fields as Military Objectives: A Feasibility Study,* August 1975.

Subcommittee on the Near East and South Asia of the Committee on Foreign Affairs of the U. S. House of Representatives, hearings, *Proposed Expansion of U. S. Military Facilities in the Indian Ocean,* February 12, March 6, 12, 14, 20, 1974.

U. S. Central Intelligence Agency, report for the U. S. Atomic Energy Commission, *Prospects for Further Proliferation of Nuclear Weapons,* October 3, 1974.

U. S. Central Intelligence Agency, a report, *The Burgeoning LDC Steel Industry: More Problems for Major Steel Producers,* July 1979.

U. S. Central Intelligence Agency, *National Basic Intelligence Factbook,* July 1979.

U. S. Central Intelligence Agency, *Atlas/Issues in the Middle East,* 1973.

U. S. General Accounting Office, a report to Congress, *Airlift Operations of the Military Airlift Command During the 1973 Middle East War,* April 16, 1975.

U. S. General Accounting Office, J. Dexter Peach, Director, Energy and Minerals Division, statement text, *OPEC Financial Holdings in the United States,* July 16, 1979.

U. S. State Department Bureau of Intelligence and Research, report, *OPEC: History and Prospects of an Oligopoly,* January 21, 1976.

Federal Energy Administration, Office of International Energy Affairs, report to Congress, *Foreign Ownership, Control and Influence on Domestic Energy Sources and Supply,* December 1974.

U. S. Department of Energy, report, *An Analysis of Petroleum Company Investments in Non-Petroleum Energy Sources,* October 1979.

U. S. Department of Energy, report, *Petroleum Supply Vulnerability,* 1985 and 1990, September 1979.

U. S. Department of Energy, report, *Energy Programs/Energy Markets, an Overview,* July 1980.

White House Council on International Economic Policy and Office of Management and Budget, a joint report, *United States Government Data Collection Activities with Respect to Foreign Investment in the United States,* March 1975.

U. S. Department of the Treasury, report, *Taxation of Foreign Investment in U. S. Real Estate,* May 1979.

U. S. Department of Commerce, Chief Economist, Courtnay M. Slater, statement text, *Information and Studies Concerning OPEC Investment in the United States,* July 18, 1979.

U. S. Department of Commerce, report, *Foreign Direct Investment in the United States, 1976 Transactions—All Forms; 1974–76 Acquisitions, Mergers and Equity Increases,* December 1977.

U. S. Department of Commerce, report, *Foreign Direct Investment in the United States,* March 1979.

U. S. Department of Commerce, report to Congress, *Foreign Direct Investment in the United States:*
Vol. 1: *Report of the Secretary of Commerce to the Congress.*
Vol. 2: *Benchmark Survey, 1974.*
Vol. 3: *Industrial and Geographic Concentration.*
Vol. 4: *Energy and Natural Resources.*
Vol. 5: *Financing.*
Vol. 6: *Taxation.*
Vol. 7: *Federal and State Law.*

Vol. 8: *Land Law.*
Vol. 9: *Federal Agency Sources of Data.*
All volumes, April 1976.

U. S. Comptroller General, report, *The United States Remains Unprepared for Oil Import Disruptions,* September 29, 1981.

U. S. Department of the Army:
Area Handbook for Israel, Pam. 550–25, 1979.
Area Handbook for Saudi Arabia, Pam. 550–51, 1977.
Area Handbook for Persian Gulf States, Pam. 550–185, 1977.
Area Handbook for Iraq, Pam. 550–31, 1971.
Area Handbook for Syria, Pam. 550–47, 1971.
Area Handbook for the Hashemite Kingdom of Jordan, Pam. 550–34, 1974.
Area Handbook for Libya, Pam. 550–85, 1973.
Area Handbook for the Yemens, Pam. 550–183, 1977.
Area Handbook for Algeria, Pam. 550–44, 1979.
Area Handbook for Morocco, Pam. 550–49, 1978.
Area Handbook for Egypt, Pam. 550–43, 1976.

SPECIAL PUBLICATIONS

Congressional Quarterly Inc. *The Middle East: U. S. Policy, Israel, Oil and the Arabs* (fourth edition). Washington, D.C., 1979.

———. *The Washington Lobby* (third edition). Washington, D.C., 1979.

Economist Intelligence Unit Ltd. *Japan's Role in the 1980's.* London, 1980.

Economist Newspaper Ltd. *The World in Figures.* London, 1978.

Anti-Defamation League of B'nai B'rith. *P.L.O. and Arab Terrorism: A Decade of Violence.* New York, 1979.

Association of Arab-American University Graduates Inc. *Israel's Sacred Terrorism.* Belmont, Mass., 1980.

The Research Project on Energy and Economic Policy. *A Survey of Arab Oil Monies.* Christ Church College, 1975.

New York Times Information Service, Inc., Corporate Information Series. *Investment and Development in the Middle East, a Survey of Business Trends and Prospects.* Parsippany, N.J., 1977.

———, a Topical Report. *Investment and Development in the Middle East, Issues and Trends.* Parsippany, N.J., 1979.

New York Times Information Bank/Arno Press. *News in Print, the Middle East, Issues and Events of 1978.* New York, 1980.

————. *News in Print, the Middle East, Issues and Events of 1979.* New York, 1980.

Banker Research Unit. *Banking Structures and Sources of Finance in the Middle East* (second edition). London, Financial Times Business Publishing Ltd., 1980.

WGBH-TV, transcript. *The Islamic Bomb.* Boston, broadcast November 5, 1980.

ABC-TV, transcript. *Near Armageddon: The Spread of Nuclear Weapons in the Middle East.* New York, broadcast April 27, 1981.

International Atomic Energy Agency, report, *The Provision of Technical Assistance by the Agency with Special Reference to 1980.* Vienna, August 1981.

BOOKS

Al-Chalabi, Fadhil J. *OPEC and the International Oil Industry: A Changing Structure.* London: Oxford University Press, 1980.

Alexander, Herbert E. *Financing Politics: Money, Elections and Political Reform.* Washington, D.C.: Congressional Quarterly Press, 1980.

Allon, Yigal. *The Making of Israel's Army.* New York: University Books, 1970.

Almana, Mohammad. *Arabia Unified: A Portrait of Ibn Saud.* London: Hutchinson Benham Ltd., 1980.

Ambrose, Stephen E. *Rise to Globalism: American Foreign Policy, 1938–1980* (second edition). New York: Pelican, 1980.

Antonius, George. *The Arab Awakening.* New York: Capricorn Books, 1965.

Ball, Max W. *This Fascinating Oil Business.* New York: Bobbs-Merrill Inc., 1965.

Barrow, Simon. *The Arab Business Yearbook, 1980/81.* London: Graham and Trotman Ltd., 1980.

Barnet, Richard J. *Global Reach.* New York: Simon & Schuster, 1974.

Begin, Menachem. *White Nights.* New York: Harper & Row, 1977.

Beling, Willard A. *King Faisal and the Modernization of Saudi Arabia.* Boulder, Col.: Westview Press, 1980.

Bell, J. Bowyer. *Terror Out of Zion.* New York: St. Martin's, 1977.

Bermant, Chaim. *The Cousinhood: An Account of the English–Jewish Aristocracy.* New York: Macmillan, 1971.

————. *London's East End: Point of Arrival.* New York: Macmillan, 1975.

Bethell, Nicholas. *The Palestine Triangle.* New York: G. P. Putnam's Sons, 1979.

Dickel, Lennard. *The Deadly Element: The Story of Uranium.* New York: Stein & Day, 1979.

Bidwell, Shelford. *Brassey's Artillery of the World.* New York: Bonanza Books, 1979.

Blair, John M. *The Control of Oil.* New York: Vintage Books, 1978.

Bonds, Ray. *The Encyclopedia of Land Warfare in the 20th Century.* New York: Thomas Y. Crowell, Inc., 1977.

————. *The Soviet War Machine.* Secaucus, N.J.: Chartwell Books, revised edition, 1977.

————. *The U. S. War Machine: An Encyclopedia of American Military Equipment and Strategy.* New York: Salamander, 1978.

Bowman, Martin W. *U. S. Military Aircraft.* Secaucus, N.J.: Chartwell Books, 1979.

Bricault, Giselle C. *Major Companies of the Arab World, 1980/81.* London: Graham and Trotman Ltd., 1980.

Carver, Michael. *War Since 1945.* London: Weidenfeld and Nicholson, 1980.

Clarkson, Jesse D. *A History of Russia.* New York: Random House, 1969.

Cohen, Bernard C. *The Public's Impact on Foreign Policy.* Boston: Little, Brown, 1973.

Collier, Peter. *The Rockefellers: An American Dynasty.* New York: Signet/New American Library, 1976.

Cook, Chris. *The Atlas of Modern Warfare.* New York: G. P. Putnam's Sons, 1978.

Costigan, Giovanni. *Makers of Modern England.* New York: Macmillan, 1967.

Cottrell, Alvin J. *The Persian Gulf States: A General Survey*. Baltimore: Johns Hopkins University Press, 1980.

Crankshaw, Edward. *The Shadow of the Winter Palace: The Drift to Revolution*. New York: Penguin, 1976.

Crowe, Kenneth C. *America for Sale*. Garden City, N.Y.: Doubleday, 1978.

Dallek, Robert. *Franklin D. Roosevelt and American Foreign Policy 1932–45*. New York: Oxford University Press, 1979.

Dawdidowicz, Lucy S. *The War Against the Jews 1933–45*. New York: Bantam, 1975.

Dimbleby, Johnathan. *The Palestinians*. London: Quartet Books, 1979.

Donovan, Robert J. *Conflict and Crisis: The Presidency of Harry S. Truman*. New York: Norton, 1977.

Dornan, Dr. James E. *The U. S. War Machine: An Illustrated Encyclopedia of American Military Equipment and Strategy*. New York: Crown Publishers, 1978.

Duncan, Andrew. *Money Rush*. Garden City, N.Y.: Doubleday, 1979.

Durant, Will. *The Age of Faith*. New York: Simon & Schuster, 1950.

Dupuy, Ernest. *Encyclopedia of Military History*. New York: Harper & Row, 1977.

Engler, Robert. *The Politics of Oil*. Chicago: University of Chicago Press, 1961.

————. *The Brotherhood of Oil*. New York: Mentor/New American Library, 1977.

Ensor, Sir Robert. *England 1870–1914: The Oxford History of England*. London: Oxford University Press, 1975.

Eveland, Wilbur Crane. *Ropes of Sand*. New York: Norton, 1980.

Gervasi, Frank. *The Life and Times of Menachem Begin: Rebel to Statesman*. New York: G. P. Putnam's Sons, 1979.

Gervasi, Tom. *Arsenal of Democracy*. New York: Grove Press, 1977.

Graham, Gerald S. *A Concise History of the British Empire*. London: Thames and Hudson Ltd., 1978.

Grayzel, Solomon. *A History of the Jews*. New York: Mentor/New American Library, 1968.

Grierson, Edward. *Death of the Imperial Dream*. Garden City, N.Y.: Doubleday, 1972.

Glubb, Sir John. *A Short History of the Arab Peoples.* New York: Stein & Day, 1969.

————. *The Life and Times of Muhammad.* New York: Stein & Day, 1971.

Guellouz, Ezzedine. *Mecca: The Muslim Pilgrimage.* New York: Paddington Press Ltd., 1979.

Guillaume, Alfred. *Islam.* London: Pelican, 1977.

Gunston, Bill. *The Encyclopedia of World Air Power.* New York: Crescent Books, 1980.

————. *Rockets and Missiles: A Comprehensive Technical Directory.* New York: Crescent Books, 1979.

Haber, Eitan. *Menachem Begin, the Man and the Legend.* New York: Dell, 1978.

Hayes, J. R. *The Genius of Arab Civilization.* Cambridge: MIT Press, 1978.

Hewitt, John D. *Arab Maritime Data.* London: Benn Publications Ltd., 1979.

Hibbert, Christopher. *The Royal Victorians: King Edward VII, His Family and Friends.* New York: Lippincott, 1976.

Hoag, John D. *Islamic Architecture.* New York: Abrams, 1977.

Hodgson, Marshall G. S. *The Venture of Islam:*
Vol. 1: *The Classical Age of Islam.*
Vol. 2: *The Expansion of Islam in the Middle Periods.*
Vol. 3: *The Gunpowder Empires and Modern Times.* Chicago: University of Chicago Press, 1974.

Hogg, Ian V. *The Encyclopedia of Military Vehicles.* Englewood Cliffs, N.J.: Prentice-Hall, 1980.

Howarth, David. *The Desert King: The Life of Ibn Saud.* London: Quartet Books, 1965.

Howe, Russell Warren. *Weapons: The International Game of Arms, Money and Diplomacy.* Garden City, N.Y.: Doubleday, 1980.

Hudson, Michael C. *Arab Politics.* New Haven: Yale University Press, 1977.

Hunsberger, Warren S. *New Era in the Non-Western World.* Port Washington, N.Y.: Kennikat Press, 1971.

James, Robert Rhodes. *The British Revolution 1880–1938.* New York: Knopf, 1977.

Jansen, G. H. *Militant Islam.* London: Pan World Affairs Books, 1979.

Jenkins, Alan. *The Rich Rich.* New York: G. P. Putnam's Sons, 1978.

Johnson, Lyndon. *The Vantage Point: Perspectives of the Presidency 1963–1969.* New York: Holt, Rinehart and Winston, 1971.

Judd, Denis. *The Victorian Empire.* New York: Praeger, 1970.

Kassiha, Walid. *Revolutionary Transformation in the Arab World.* New York: St. Martin's, 1975.

Keegan, John. *World Armies.* New York: Facts on File Inc., 1979.

Kent, Marian. *Oil and Empire.* New York: Harper & Row, 1976.

Kissinger, Henry. *White House Years.* Boston: Little, Brown, 1979.

Kochan, Mariam. *The Last Days of Imperial Russia.* New York: Macmillan, 1976.

Kohn, Hans. *Nationalism and Imperialism in the Hither East.* New York: Howard Fertig, Inc., 1969.

Kosut, Hal. *Israel and the Arabs: The June 1967 War.* New York: Facts on File Inc., 1968.

Kurian, George Thomas. *Encyclopedia of the Third World,* vols. 1 and 2. New York: Facts on File Inc., 1978.

Landes, David S. *Bankers and Pashas: International Finance and Economic Imperialism in Egypt.* Boston: Harvard University Press, 1979.

Levin, Nora. *The Holocaust: The Destruction of European Jewry 1933–1945.* New York: Schocken Books, 1978.

Lewis, Bernard. *Islam and the Arab World.* New York: Knopf, 1976.

Lustick, Ian. *Arabs in the Jewish State.* Austin: University of Texas Press, 1980.

MacDonald, Robert W. *The League of Arab States.* Princeton: University of Princeton Press, 1965.

Mansfield, Peter. *The Arabs.* London: Pelican, 1978.

Massie, Robert K. *Nicholas and Alexandra.* New York: Dell, 1978.

Morris, Eric. *Weapons and Warfare of the 20th Century.* Secaucus, N.J.: Derbibooks Inc., 1975.

Morse, Arthur D. *While Six Million Died.* New York: Hart Publishing, 1968.

Morton, Frederic. *The Rothschilds.* Greenwich, Conn.: Fawcett Crest, 1961.

Mosley, Leonard. *Power Play: Oil in the Middle East.* Baltimore: Penguin, 1974.

Mostert, Noel. *Supership.* New York: Warner Books, 1978.

Nixon, Richard. *The Memoirs of Richard Nixon.* New York: Grosset & Dunlap, Inc., 1978.

O'Ballance, Edgar. *No Victor, No Vanquished.* San Rafael, Calif.: Presidio Press, 1978.

Odell, Peter R. *Oil and World Power* (fifth edition). New York: Pelican, 1979.

Ornstein, Norman J. *Interest Groups, Lobbying and Policymaking.* Washington, D.C.: Congressional Quarterly Press, 1978.

Parsons, Iain. *Encyclopedia of the World's Combat Aircraft: A Technical Directory.* New York: Chartwell Books, 1976.

Patai, Raphael. *The Arab Mind.* New York: Charles Scribner's Sons, 1976.

Philby, H. St. John. *Saudi Arabia.* New York: Arno Press, 1972.

————. *Arabia of the Wahhabis.* New York: Arno Press, 1973.

Potok, Chaim. *Wanderings: History of the Jews.* New York: Knopf, 1978.

Pringle, Peter. *The Nuclear Barons.* New York: Holt, Rinehart and Winston, 1981.

Quilici, Folco. *Children of Allah.* Secaucus, N.J.: Chartwell Books, 1978.

Rahman, Fazlur. *Islam* (second edition). Chicago: University of Chicago Press, 1966.

Rodinson, Maxime. *Muhammad.* New York: Pantheon Books, 1980.

Rogers, Michael. *The Spread of Islam.* New York: E. P. Dutton, 1976.

Roseboom, Eugene H. *A History of Presidential Elections.* New York: Collier Books, 1979.

Sachar, Howard M. *A History of Israel from the Rise of Zionism to Our Times.* New York: Knopf, 1976.

Said, Edward W. *The Question of Palestine.* New York: Times Books, 1979.

Sampson, Anthony. *The Seven Sisters.* New York: Bantam, 1976.

Sanger, Richard Harlakenden. *The Arabian Peninsula.* New York: Books for Libraries Press, 1970.

Saunders, John J. *The Muslim World on the Eve of Europe's Expansion.* Englewood Cliffs, N.J.: Prentice-Hall, 1966.

Schacht, Joseph. *The Legacy of Islam* (second edition). New York: Oxford University Press, 1979.

Schama, Simon. *Two Rothschilds and the Land of Israel.* New York: Knopf, 1978.

Shazly, Lt. General Saad El. *The Crossing of the Suez.* San Francisco: American Mideast Research, 1980.

Sheean, Vincent. *Faisal, the King and His Kingdom.* Riyadh: University of Arabia Press, 1975.

Sinai, Anne. *Israel and the Arabs: Prelude to the Jewish State.* New York: Facts on File Inc., 1972.

Slater, Robert. *Golda: The Uncrowned Queen of Israel.* Middle Village, N.Y.: Jonathan David Publishers, 1981.

Smith, Goldwin. *A History of England.* New York: Charles Scribner's Sons, 1974.

Sobel, Lester A., *Facts on File Energy Series:*
Energy Crisis, 1969–1973, Vol. 1, 1974.
Energy Crisis, 1974–1975, Vol. 2, 1975.
Energy Crisis, 1975–1977, Vol. 3, 1977.
Energy Crisis, 1977–1979, Vol. 4, 1980. New York: Facts on File Inc.

––––––. *Israel and the Arabs: The October 1973 War.* New York: Facts on File Inc., 1974.

––––––. *Palestinian Impasse: Arab Guerrillas and International Terror.* New York: Facts on File Inc., 1977.

––––––. *Peace-Making in the Middle East.* New York: Facts on File Inc., 1980.

Solberg, Carl. *Oil Power.* New York: Mentor/New American Library, 1976.

Spanier, John. *How American Foreign Policy Is Made.* New York: Praeger, 1974.

Stevenson, James Perry. *McDonnell Douglas F-15 Eagle.* Fallbrook, Calif.: Aero Publishers, 1978.

Stewart, Desmond. *Mecca.* New York: Newsweek Inc., 1980.

Stobaugh and Yergin. *Energy Future.* New York: Random House, 1979.

Stoff, Michael B. *Oil, War and American Security: The Search for a*

National Policy on Foreign Oil, 1941–47. New Haven: Yale University Press, 1980.

Stork, Joe. *Middle East Oil and the Energy Crisis.* New York: Monthly Review Press, 1975.

Times of London. *Atlas of World History.* London: Times Books Ltd., 1978.

Tugendhat, Christopher. *Oil, the Biggest Business.* New York: G. P. Putnam's Sons, 1968.

Twitchell, K. S. *Saudi Arabia with an Account of the Development of Its Natural Resources.* Princeton: University of Princeton Press, 1958.

Von Pivka, Otto. *Armies of the Middle East.* New York: Mayflower Books, 1979.

Wasserstein, Bernard. *Britain and the Jews of Europe, 1939–45.* Oxford: Clarendon Press, 1979.

Wigoder, Dr. Geoffrey, editor. *The New Standard Jewish Encyclopedia.* Garden City, N.Y.: Doubleday, 1977.

OTHER

Encyclopaedia Britannica. Chicago: Encyclopaedia Britannica Inc., 1980.

Encyclopedia Judaica. Jerusalem: Keter Publishing Ltd., 1972.

Encyclopedia of Islam. Ithaca: Cornell University Press, 1965.

Encyclopedia of Islam. London: Luzac and Company, New Edition, 1960.

The Cambridge History of Islam. London: Cambridge University Press, 1977.

NOTES

ONE
VICTORY ON THE HILL

1. A technical history of the F-15's development is provided in James Perry Stevenson, *McDonnell Douglas, F-15 Eagle* (Fallbrook, Calif.: Aero Publishers, 1978).
2. *8 Days,* August 9, 1980, p. 34.
3. Charles McC. Mathias, Jr., "Ethnic Groups and Foreign Policy," in *Foreign Affairs,* Summer 1981, p. 993.
4. Thomas A. Dine, Executive Director, American Israel Public Affairs Committee, Washington, D.C., October 6, 1981, letter, AIPAC Alert series mailing.
5. New York *Times,* September 11, 1981; p. D2, col. 1.
6. U. S. Comptroller General, *The United States Remains Unprepared for Oil Import Disruptions,* report to Congress, September 29, 1981, vols. 1 and 2.
7. New York *Times,* September 14, 1981; p. A25, col. 1.
8. Washington *Post,* October 29, 1981; p. A27, col. 1.
9. Washington *Post,* October 29, 1981; p. A4, col. 1.
10. Washington *Post,* October 30, 1981; p. A13, col. 1.
11. Washington *Post,* October 30, 1981; p. 1, col. 1.
12. Washington *Post,* October 30, 1981; p. C1, col. 1.
13. Washington *Post,* July 26, 1982; p. A3, col. 3.
14. New York *Times,* August 8, 1982; p. 1, col. 4.
15. Reagan's "Fresh Start" speech, New York *Times,* September 9, 1982; p. 1, col. 6; and *Time,* September 13, 1982, p. 10.

TWO
TOWARD NUCLEAR MASADA

1. The most detailed work documenting Israel's atomic weapons program was written in the 1970s by Israeli journalists Eli Teicher and Ami Dor-On. However, the manuscript was seized

by the Israeli Government, which prohibited its publication.
See:
  New York *Times,* February 22, 1980; p. 8, col. 4.
  New York *Times,* February 25, 1980; p. 3, col. 2.
Two other recently published books provide extensive detail of
the evolution of the Israeli nuclear weapons programs:
  Peter Pringle and James Spigelman, *The Nuclear Barons*
  (New York: Holt, Rinehart and Winston, 1981); and Rus-
  sell Warren Howe, *Weapons: The International Game of
  Arms, Money and Diplomacy* (Garden City, N.Y.: Double-
  day, 1980).
The Israeli atomic weapons projects have also been the subject
of an ABC-TV investigative report. See:
  Transcript, *Near Armageddon: The Spread of Nuclear Weap-
  ons in the Middle East,* broadcast 10 P.M., April 27, 1981
  (New York: American Broadcasting Companies, Inc.).
Substantial amounts of significant material concerning Israel's
atomic weapons can be found in the following:
  U. S. Central Intelligence Agency, *Prospects for Further
  Proliferation of Nuclear Weapons,* report to the Atomic En-
  ergy Commission, October 3, 1974, section 3.
  Time, April 12, 1976, p. 39.
  Time, May 30, 1977, p. 32.
  New York *Times,* September 19, 1971; section VI, p. 6,
  col. 5.
  New York *Times,* March 16, 1976; p. 1, col. 2.
  New York *Times,* January 15, 1980; section III, p. 2. col. 5.
  New York *Times,* May 2, 1981; p. 2, col. 3.
  New York *Times,* June 25, 1981; p. 1, col. 4.
  New York *Times,* June 28, 1981; p. 15, col. 1.
  New York *Times,* July 9, 1981; p. 6, col. 1.
  New York *Times,* July 14, 1981; p. 6, col. 1.
  World Business Weekly, June 22, 1981, p. 6.
  World Press Review, May 1980, p. 29.
  World Press Review, August 1981, p. 40.
  Facts on File Annual, 1970, p. 509.
  Facts on File Annual, 1972, p. 602.
  Facts on File Annual, 1974, p. 994.
  Facts on File Annual, 1974, p. 1040.
  Facts on File Annual, 1977, p. 416.
  Facts on File Annual, 1978, p. 61.
  The Middle East, August 1977, p. 28.
  The Middle East, June 1980, p. 8.

The Middle East, August 1981, p. 8.
8 Days, February 28, 1981, p. 4.
8 Days, May 9, 1981, p. 3.
8 Days, June 6, 1981, p. 27.

THREE

JIHAD FOR JERUSALEM

1. Lt. Gen. Saad El Shazly, *The Crossing of the Suez* (San Francisco: American Mideast Research, 1980), p. 234.
2. Richard Nixon, *The Memoirs of Richard Nixon* (New York: Grosset & Dunlap, 1978), p. 920.
3. Robert Slater, *Golda: The Uncrowned Queen of Israel* (Middle Village, N.Y.: Jonathan David Publishers, 1981), p. 241, 242.
4. *Time,* April 12, 1976, p. 39, 40.
5. Shazly, *The Crossing of the Suez,* p. 251.
6. *Time,* April 12, 1976, p. 39, 40.
7. U. S. General Accounting Office, *Airlift Operations of the Military Airlift Command During the 1973 Middle East War,* report to Congress, April 16, 1975.
8. Nixon, *The Memoirs of Richard Nixon,* p. 928.
9. Ibid., p. 941.
10. Shazly, *The Crossing of the Suez,* p. 270.
11. Ibid., p. 282.

FIVE

ROOTS OF CONFLICT: OIL, ISLAM AND ZIONISM

1. Dean Acheson, *Present at the Creation* (New York: Signet, 1969), p. 241.
2. Robert J. Donovan, *Conflict and Crisis: The Presidency of Harry S. Truman, 1945–1948* (New York: Norton, 1977), p. 330.

SEVEN

IN THE FLAMES OF AL AQSA

1. Lyndon B. Johnson, *The Vantage Point: Perspectives of the*

Presidency, 1963–1969 (New York: Holt, Rinehart and Winston, 1971), p. 296.
2. *Facts on File Annual,* 1969, p. 670.
3. See diary reprint excerpts: Livia Rokach, *Israel's Sacred Terrorism* (Belmont, Mass.: Association of Arab-American University Graduates, 1980).
4. Henry Kissinger, *The White House Years* (Boston: Little, Brown, 1979), p. 368.

EIGHT
THE UNSHEATHED SWORD

1. *Facts on File Annual,* 1974, p. 782.
2. Special Subcommittee on Investigations of the Committee on International Relations of the U. S. Congress, *Oil Fields as Military Objectives: A Feasibility Study,* government report, August 1975.

NINE
REVOLUTION AT THE UN

1. *Facts on File Annual,* 1979, p. 823.

FOURTEEN
MASTERS OF THE CHAMPS ÉLYSÉES

1. Four Islamic countries actively began seeking to develop or acquire atomic weapons in the early 1970s: Pakistan, Saudi Arabia, Libya and Iraq. Two television investigative reports have been done on the subject and provide a great deal of information:

    Transcript, *The Islamic Bomb,* broadcast November 5, 1980 (Boston: WGBH Educational Foundation, Inc.). Transcript, *Near Armageddon: The Spread of Nuclear Weapons in the Middle East,* broadcast April 27, 1981 (New York: American Broadcasting Companies, Inc.).

    Two London-based magazines that cover the Middle East have also provided comprehensive details about the ongoing nuclear weapons development activities of Islamic nations. See:
    The Middle East, August 1977, p. 28.
    The Middle East, July 1979, p. 93.

The Middle East, March 1981, p. 8.
The Middle East, August 1981, p. 9.
8 Days, June 23, 1979, p. 8.
8 Days, June 30, 1979, p. 4.
8 Days, July 7, 1979, p. 11.
8 Days, July 14, 1979, p. 3.
8 Days, August 18, 1979, p. 5.
8 Days, August 25, 1979, p. 3.
8 Days, September 15, 1979, p. 27.
8 Days, December 1, 1979, p. 37.
8 Days, December 8, 1979, p. 20.
8 Days, December 22, 1979, p. 4.
8 Days, January 12, 1980, p. 39.
8 Days, March 8, 1980, p. 46.
8 Days, March 15, 1980, p. 18.
8 Days, March 29, 1980, p. 44.
8 Days, April 19, 1980, p. 33.
8 Days, July 26, 1980, p. 3.
8 Days, August 9, 1980, p. 2.
8 Days, September 27, 1980, p. 39.
8 Days, October 25, 1980, p. 5.
8 Days, November 1, 1980, p. 20.
8 Days, November 29, 1980, p. 25.
8 Days, June 27, 1981, p. 17.
8 Days, July 11, 1981, p. 27.
8 Days, August 29, 1981, p. 56.
8 Days, September 19, 1981, p. 13.
Also see:
World Press Review, March 1980, p. 26.
World Press Review, December 1980, p. 6.
World Press Review, February 1981, p. 10.
World Press Review, August 1981, p. 40.
World Business Weekly, March 24, 1980, p. 18.
World Business Weekly, May 26, 1980, p. 19.
World Business Weekly, September 22, 1980, p. 18.
World Business Weekly, December 29, 1980, p. 38.
World Business Weekly, February 23, 1981, p. 19.
World Business Weekly, August 3, 1981, p. 19.
World Business Weekly, August 17, 1981, p. 19.
Also see:
South (London), December 1980, p. 33.
Time, August 11, 1980, p. 43.

SIXTEEN
GERMANY AND NUCLEAR JIHAD

1. See Chapter Nine reference notes on atomic weapons development in the Islamic world.

SEVENTEEN
ARABIA-UPON-THE-THAMES

1. *Arabia, the Islamic World Review,* November 11, 1981, p. 50.

EIGHTEEN
LATIN AMERICA'S NEW PARTNERS

1. "Latin America and the Middle East, a Special Report," *Middle East Economic Digest* (London), September 1981, p. 12.
2. John Keegan, "Brazil," in *World Armies* (New York: Facts on File Inc., 1979), p. 77.
3. See Chapter Nine reference notes on atomic weapons development in the Islamic world.

TWENTY
PETRO-YEN AND PALESTINIANS

1. *8 Days,* August 23, 1980, p. 58.
2. *World Business Weekly,* February 2, 1981, p. 29.
3. Washington *Post,* October 3, 1981; p. 17, col. 2.
4. New York *Times,* September 27, 1981; p. 8, col. 1.

TWENTY-ONE
COMING HOME TO HOUSTON

1. "Houston's Arab Businessmen," *8 Days,* November 28, 1981, p. 11.
2. *Voice of Islam* (Houston), July 1981, p. 11.
3. Houston *Chronicle,* February 20, 1980; p. 8, col. 2.
4. Houston *Chronicle,* August 23, 1978; section I, p. 24, col. 1.
5. Houston *Chronicle,* November 8, 1979; section II, p. 11, col. 5.
6. *Houston Business Journal,* August 17, 1981, p. 1.

7. *Boycott Law Bulletin,* published by *Middle East Monthly,* P.O. Box 73326, Houston, Texas 77090.
8. *Newsweek,* October 22, 1979, p. 49.
9. *Time,* March 24, 1980, p. 18.

TWENTY-TWO
AMERICA'S ARAB ENERGY CZARS

1. New York *Times,* July 17, 1978; p. A14, col. 1.
2. See four items:
   New Orleans *Times-Picayune,* January 2, 1978, p. 1.
   New Orleans *Times-Picayune,* January 7, 1978, p. 1.
   New Orleans *States-Item,* January 3, 1978, p. 1.
   New Orleans *States-Item,* January 7, 1978, p. 1.
3. Chicago *Tribune,* September 18, 1980; section IV, p. 8, col. 2.
4. "Arab Money Fuels the Rise of Coal Power," *8 Days,* July 11, 1981, p. 7.
5. Houston *Chronicle,* July 6, 1981; p. 2, col. 2.

TWENTY-THREE
"WE LOVE ARAB MONEY AS MUCH AS ANYBODY ELSE'S"

1. New York *Times Magazine,* September 20, 1981, p. 142.
2. *Time,* July 13, 1981, p. 46.
3. *Forbes,* October 26, 1981, p. 17.
4. *Newsweek,* October 26, 1981, p. 65.

TWENTY-FOUR
ATOMIC SWORDS AND THE FUTURE OF THE WORLD

1. See Chapter Two reference notes on atomic weapons development in Israel.
2. *Parade,* July 1, 1979, p. 20.

INDEX

A-4 attack jet planes, 42
Abalkhail, Mohammed, 11
Abbasid Muslim dynasty, 37
Abdel Aziz Bin Salman Mohamed al
  Saud, Prince, 232–33
Abu Dhabi, 151, 197, 208, 276; Fund
  for Economic Development, 111
Abu Dhabi International Bank, 276
Acheson, Dean, 71
Adabiya, Egypt, 55
Afghanistan, 37, 113, 222
Agence Kapnist, 148
Agnew, Spiro, 262
Aid programs. See Foreign aid
  programs
Airlines, U.S., Arab investments in,
  282
Al Aqsa Mosque (Jerusalem), 65–66,
  82, 86–92, 105, 117; burning of,
  82, 86–92, 94, 111; 113
Al Assad Missile City, 8, 154,
  242
Albano, Vincent, 252
Algeria, 11–12, 79, 85, 114, 117, 128,
  130, 192, 220, 224, 265; Arab
  conference in Algiers (1973), 101
Al-Ghanim, Kutaybah, 239–40
Alhegelan, Faisal, 2, 17, 23, 27,
  28–29
Alhegelan, Nouha, 27–28
Al Jihad Camel Corps, 64, 66
Alkantara Trading Company, 195
Al Sabah family, 281–82
Amar Line Maritime Company, Ltd.,
  210
Amaya, Naohira, 222
America (ship), 127–28
American Indians, 256
American Israel Public Affairs
  Committee (AIPAC), 14, 15–16,
  18–19
American Jewish Committee, 16, 23
American-Jewish lobby. See Jewish
  lobby
American Muslim movement, 244

American Telephone and Telegraph
  Co. (AT&T), 154, 277
Andréotti, Giulio, 199
Anti-Semitism, 61, 150. See also
  Boycott, Arab
Aqaba, 83–84
Arab Abela Investment Group,
  147–48
Arab-American Chamber of
  Commerce, 243, 250
Arab Bank for Economic
  Development, 111
Arab Banking Corporation, 172
Arab Bank of Credit and Commerce
  International, 183
Arab Boycott Office, 244–50
Arab Commercial Enterprises, 182
Arab Drilling and Workover
  Company, 266
Arabian Pipeline Construction Co.,
  241
Arabian Seaoil Corporation, 264
Arabian Services Corporation, 255
Arabian Singapore Corporation, 208
Arab-Israeli wars. See Middle East
  wars
Arab League, 70, 80, 130, 181;
  Council of Foreign Ministers, 92
Arab lobby, 3ff., 27ff., 250–51. See
  also specific issues, organizations
Arab-Malaysian Development Bank,
  207
Arab Maritime Petroleum Co., 129
Arab News, 243
Arab Organization for
  Industrialization, 154
Arab Organization for Land and Sea
  Transport, 130
Arab Petroleum Services Company,
  266
Arab Ship Building and Repair Yards
  Company, 130
Arab War Risk Insurance Syndicate,
  187
Arab Women's Council of
  Washington, 27

x